RTH POLE

Ocean

+8 +9 +10 +11 +12 +13

180°

160°

140°

120°

100°

80°

Kolyma

70°

Ust Nera • Artyk

Verkhoyansk • Oymyakon •

Lena

Yakutsk •

60°

Sea of Okhotsk

Vilvuy

Nyurba •

SOCIALIST REPUBLIC

Chernyshevskiy • • Mirny

Lensk •

Kirensk •

Angara

Bratsk •

Lake Baikal

Irkutsk • • Posolsk
Listvyanka • • Karymskoye
Ulan Ude
Petrovsk

Amur

50°

• Khabarovsk

PEOPLE'S REPUBLIC OF CHINA

• Nakhodka

MONGOLIA

40° Sea of Japan

JAPAN

NORTH KOREA

SOUTH KOREA

30°

To obtain their material for *Journey Across Russia:
The Soviet Union Today*, the author and photographer
traveled in all 15 constituent republics of the U.S.S.R.; and
one or both visited every city and town shown on this map.

JOURNEY ACROSS RUSSIA

The Soviet Union Today

By **Bart McDowell**

Photographed by **Dean Conger**

Prepared by the Special Publications Division
National Geographic Society, Washington, D. C.

JOURNEY ACROSS RUSSIA: THE SOVIET UNION TODAY

By BART McDOWELL, *Assistant Editor,*
  NATIONAL GEOGRAPHIC
Photographed by DEAN CONGER, *Assistant Director
  of Photography,* NATIONAL GEOGRAPHIC
Foreword by GILBERT M. GROSVENOR

Published by
THE NATIONAL GEOGRAPHIC SOCIETY
ROBERT E. DOYLE, *President*
MELVIN M. PAYNE, *Chairman of the Board*
GILBERT M. GROSVENOR, *Editor*
MELVILLE BELL GROSVENOR, *Editor Emeritus*

Prepared by
THE SPECIAL PUBLICATIONS DIVISION
ROBERT L. BREEDEN, *Editor*
PHILIP B. SILCOTT, *Senior Editor*
MERRILL WINDSOR, *Managing Editor*
LINDA McCARTER BRIDGE, *Assistant to the Editor*
SUSAN C. BURNS, SUSAN P. BYRNES, SALLIE M.
  GREENWOOD, *Research*

Consultants
EDWARD ALLWORTH, NICHOLAS V. RIASANOVSKY,
  HARRISON E. SALISBURY, THEODORE SHABAD,
  J. THOMAS SHAW

Illustrations and Design
DONALD J. CRUMP, *Picture Editor*
WILLIAM L. ALLEN, *Associate Picture Editor*
URSULA PERRIN VOSSELER, *Art Director*
SUEZ B. KEHL, *Assistant Art Director*
JANE H. BUXTON, *Illustrations Assistant*
WENDY W. CORTESI, JULIANA V. GOLDBERG, TOM
  MELHAM, H. ROBERT MORRISON, *Picture Legends*
JOHN D. GARST, JR., PETER J. BALCH, VIRGINIA L.
  BAZA, CHARLES W. BERRY, GEORGE E. COSTANTINO,
  NANCY SCHWEICKART, ALFRED ZEBARTH, *Map
  Research, Design, and Production*

Production and Printing
ROBERT W. MESSER, *Production Manager*
GEORGE V. WHITE, *Assistant Production Manager*
RAJA D. MURSHED, JUNE L. GRAHAM, CHRISTINE A.
  ROBERTS, *Production Assistants*
JOHN R. METCALFE, *Engraving and Printing*
DEBRA A. ANTONINI, ALICIA L. DIFFENDERFFER,
  ALICE K. JABLONSKY, SUZANNE J. JACOBSON, AMY E.
  METCALFE, CLEO PETROFF, DAVID V. SHOWERS,
  KATHERYN M. SLOCUM, SUZANNE VENINO, NANCY J.
  WATSON, MARILYN L. WILBUR, *Staff Assistants*
JOLENE M. BLOZIS, *Index*

OVERLEAF: ST. BASIL'S CATHEDRAL, STAR-TOPPED SAVIOUR'S TOWER,
AND THE BLOCKY PYRAMID OF THE LENIN MAUSOLEUM DOMINATE RED
SQUARE IN MOSCOW. PAGE 1: SCENE FROM A FAIRY TALE DECORATES
THE LID OF A LACQUERED PAPIER-MÂCHÉ BOX MADE IN PALEKH.
BOOKBINDING: FROM AN ICON OF ST. NICHOLAS, NOVGOROD MUSEUM.

CONTENTS

GROVE OF BIRCH TREES STARTS CHANGING TO AUTUMN GOLD IN A FOREST NEAR MOSCOW.

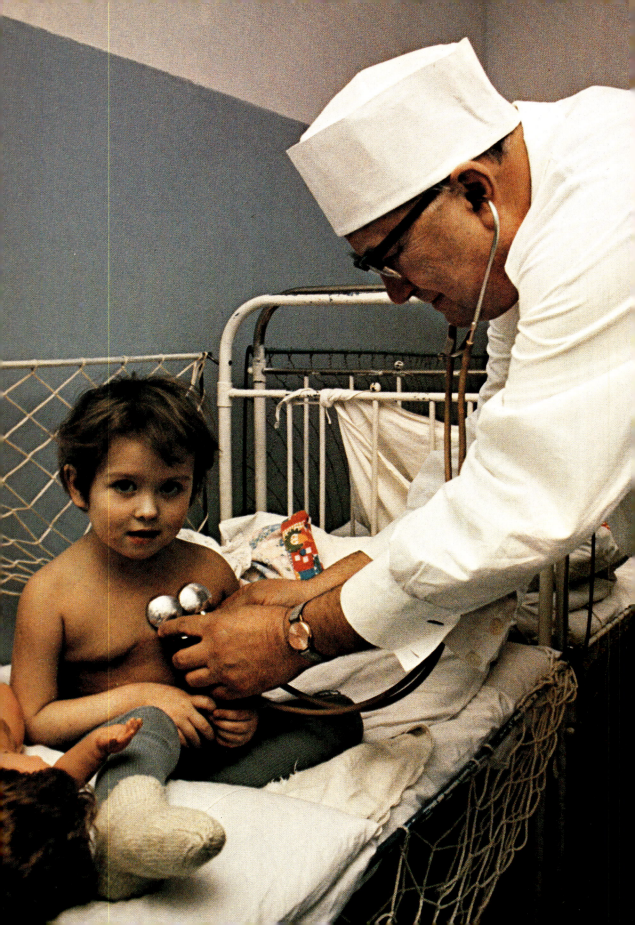

TINY FLAG STOPS TRAFFIC FOR A CLASS OF NURSERY-SCHOOL CHILDREN IN TALLINN, ESTONIA. AT LEFT, A PHYSICIAN
EXAMINES A LITTLE GIRL AFTER OPEN-HEART SURGERY AT AKADEMGORODOK, NEAR NOVOSIBIRSK IN SIBERIA.

FOREWORD

My first ride on a Russian train some years ago gave me a lesson
in geographic journalism. From the window I caught fleeting
glimpses of farm, forest, and village life. I thought of the
newspapers I regularly read—the formidable daily briefing on
diplomatic and political news of the Soviet Union—and I was
shocked that I could have read so much and still feel so woefully
ignorant about this vast land's rural landscape and the
simple yet vigorous life-styles of its people. Surely such graphic
details as I was observing help to shape the large events.
Wasn't there a need, then, for a book different from and supple-
mental to the rows of volumes on Soviet government and economics
already lining our library shelves? A book that would focus,
through firsthand reporting heavily illustrated with color

photography, on the people
and their heritage; that would
not emphasize the large
cities but instead would
roam through the 15 Soviet
republics — in all their
rich ethnic, historical,
and geographical variety?

It was not a simple under-
taking. There began two years
of negotiations with the
Novosti Press Agency, discussions of conditions under
which a National Geographic
writer-photographer team
would be permitted to visit
places of interest
throughout the Soviet Union —
including many that are
normally off-limits to
the Western press.

Now, as a result of those
negotiations, we have
achieved our goal: to produce
a book that gives readers
a chance to supplement
existing literature with
photographs and facts
from places long inaccessible
to Westerners. Within our
editorial limitations we
have tried to show you the

BRONZE HORSE AND RIDER MARK THE ENTRANCE TO
A NEW HOUSING AREA IN VILNIUS, LITHUANIA.

varied people of this amazing land — people who will help determine the future of the world as surely as will we who live in the West.

The political and ideological differences between the United States and the Soviet Union are as wide as global geography; we do not pretend that this book encompasses those enormous subjects. We leave the politics and ideology to others. Instead, we emphasize the physical geography, the cultural legacies, the diversity of peoples which other publications rarely portray.

Working in the Soviet Union demands special skills. Journalists are required to

EARLY-MORNING SUNBATHERS COMPETE FOR SPACE ON A CROWDED YALTA BEACH; BELOW, A GIRL'S RED CHEEKS ATTEST TO THE STRONG SOUTHERN SUN.

follow predetermined itineraries, accompanied by a Soviet interpreter-guide. For Western correspondents, these restrictions of movement and access contribute experiences both frustrating and harrowing. One result is that this volume is

WILD FLOWER BRIGHTENS THE WORK AREA OF A METAL-LATHE OPERATOR IN LENINGRAD.

incomplete, and we do not delude ourselves that it will be entirely fulfilling; we know that certain disquieting realities of Soviet life are beyond its purview. Two of our ablest, most experienced staff men undertook this

NEVA RIVER TOUR BOAT APPROACHES THE WINTER PALACE IN LENINGRAD. AT RIGHT, TWO GIRLS
ADMIRE THE REMBRANDT PAINTING "DANAE" IN THE PALACE'S FAMED HERMITAGE COLLECTION.

demanding project: Assistant Director of Photography Dean
Conger, who has endured the exhilaration of 26 trips to
the Soviet Union during the last 16 years, recording on film an epic
unmatched by any other Western photographer; and
Assistant Editor Bart McDowell, whose manuscripts for
earlier National Geographic books and articles have enjoyed
immense popularity. In his writing, Texan McDowell uses quotation
marks like barbed wire. The work of these two deserves not
just passing attention but careful study. Together, Conger and
McDowell have produced a book of personalized geography
useful not only for readers planning a trip to the U.S.S.R., but also
for those simply seeking a broader background on that
vitally important country.

GILBERT M. GROSVENOR

1

INTRODUCTION: THE EPIC LAND

Bulb-shaped domes crowning the Cathedral of the Nativity of the Virgin rise high above nursery-school pupils at play in Suzdal, a town 120 miles northeast of Moscow. The church, erected more than 700 years ago and rebuilt many times through the centuries, now serves as a museum of Russia's past—as does much of Suzdal, living reminder of a rich historical heritage.

LET ME WARN YOU with words a thousand years old. I found them in Soviet Central Asia where they begin the epic poem *Manas*, as sung by generations of bards in Kirgizia:

> *...Half of this is truth;*
> *Half of this is probably not truth....*
> *Don't hold it against us if we add something*
> *Or miss something.*
> *We're telling you the way we heard it....*

Like old Kirgiz bards, photographer Dean Conger and I borrow epic words for an epic land. We here offer our incomplete views of the largest country on earth, the Union of Soviet Socialist Republics.

We have repeatedly traveled the 11 time zones of its length, east and west—a length equaling nearly 2½ trips between New York and San Francisco. We've crisscrossed its width, north and south, from the Baltic to the Black Sea and the Caspian, and from the Arctic Ocean to the Sea of Japan. Under the easiest conditions, the U.S.S.R. would challenge the journalist and geographer with immensity: one-sixth of the inhabited land of our planet, 256 million people speaking more than a hundred languages, each with its own opportunities for misquotation.

But the U.S.S.R. is more than a geographic challenge. "It is a riddle wrapped in a mystery inside an enigma," in Winston Churchill's famous words. We have not solved that riddle, but we've tried to diminish the mystery for readers who can ask questions for themselves.

We were the first writer-photographer team from the Western press allowed to travel so widely in the 15 constituent republics of the Soviet Union. For each of the 50-odd cities and towns we visited, we had separate, specific visas from Soviet authorities, just as the United States requires journalists of the U.S.S.R. to obtain permission before traveling.

To get this unprecedented access to Soviet geography, we signed a contract with the Novosti Press Agency, or APN, "an information agency of Soviet public organizations," as defined by its charter, "to promote international understanding, confidence and friendship." A Soviet interpreter-guide from APN accompanied us on all our journeys, arranged all our formal interviews, and assisted us almost continuously.

To ensure "accuracy and fairness," our contract provided that the National Geographic Society would submit both manuscript and pictures to APN for review before publication. We further agreed "to find a mutually satisfactory solution for every difference," as our contract phrased it. "Not a single controversial point shall be left unsettled." The book you hold in your hand is our attempt to fulfill those terms.

You may be surprised at the frankness of some comments included here. Naturally, Novosti does not share all our opinions or viewpoints; the inclusion of such material shows how far Novosti cooperation differed from censorship.

Our goal is to give some notion about the people who live and work in the Soviet Union—something of their history and customs, the atmosphere of their city streets and rural landscapes, the climates of their varied regions: a book of personalized geography. Not politics, not diplomacy, not polemics. Not the whole truth.

"All geography is political," said one Novosti agent. I disagreed, and asked him how the elevation of a mountain could be political. But he was right and I was wrong—to wit, the second highest point in the U.S.S.R., Lenin Peak, elevation 23,405 feet, located in the Pamirs near China; and its companion Communism Peak, at 24,590 feet the tallest mountain, formerly named Stalin Peak.

"And the tallest mountain in North America?" asked the Novosti agent. *"Mount McKinley!"* I concede his point. Politics will sometimes intrude. Even so, we have tried to avoid obvious political contention.

In Volgograd we met a photographer eager to show Dean pictures he had taken on a recent trip to the U.S.A. In his collection he had some photos of an old woman foraging in a garbage can in San Francisco—authentic, unposed pictures, the sort many American journalists commonly publish. But in this book, you'll find no garbage-can foraging. In the spirit of our contract, we don't picture everything we saw nor repeat all we heard. If our view seems shadowless, remember that we only claim to show fragments, and generally the favorable fragments.

Thus we come to value judgments—and to the individual prejudices and viewpoints of photographer and author. Please allow for any inadvertent slant or coloration. I am a bourgeois capitalist of the middle-income bracket, an Episcopalian, a Texan by birth, an individualist, and a political conservative. Photographer Dean Conger comes from Wyoming; he is a Unitarian, and considers himself a political liberal. We argue a good deal. Though we traveled a hard 30,000 miles together within the U.S.S.R. as close as skin grafts, neither of us got angry nor convinced the other. Our arguments probably accomplished no more than to embarrass some of our Soviet hosts who had never before heard such irreverent American discussions.

A sophisticated friend at Novosti once took wry note of my conservative viewpoints and told me this story: "It seems a woman from Britain came here and went on a tour of the Moscow Zoo. But when she

Photographer Dean Conger pauses on the slopes of Cheget Mountain in the Caucasus between sessions of the 1976 International Geographical Congress. In the background rise the distinctive twin peaks of Mount Elbrus.

passed the exhibit with a camel, the British woman stopped and exclaimed, 'Ah, you poor horse! What have those Communists done to your back?' "

So watch out for my horses and camels.

Another question was access to the people. "They won't show you how we live," a retired librarian told me. I had met her on a tour far from her native Moscow. "I don't mean workers: They'll show you workers' apartments—but not those of intellectuals like me." That pleasant little ex-librarian underestimated the hospitality of her countrymen and perhaps my own curiosity. I was invited to many a private apartment in the U.S.S.R.—all kinds, with and without my chaperon, from the cheerfully untidy studios of nonunion, unsanctioned artists and the modest rooms of old pensioners to the smart digs in new high-rise apartments. But such access to people was usually confined to the larger cities where we stayed long enough to make informal friendships.

During his 26 tours of duty in the U.S.S.R.—some lasting many months at a time—Dean has collected friends throughout the country; and over the years, he has watched youngsters grow up and form families of their own. On half a dozen long journeys from 1974 to 1976, I have felt the same kind of friendly continuity. Among families of all kinds, we have joined in the celebration of weddings and births, the observance of funerals, the recognition of changing seasons and holidays, and all the rites for welcoming guests and bidding them goodbye. We have tasted the symbolic Russian bread and salt. And with such ritual feasts: steaming boiled potatoes and sausages, mounds of caviar and plump forest mushrooms—a whole landscape of calories—with neat shots of vodka and Armenian cognac, and fragrant, foggy glasses of Georgian tea from the samovar. Meals sumptuously seasoned by open friendliness.

Young people I found especially curious about Western ways—and far more open in their conversation than I had expected. "They're a lot more relaxed with Westerners now," Dean observed. His Soviet experiences date from the days when the body of Stalin still lay in a place of honor inside Lenin's tomb. Much has changed since then. For example, I once assured an outspoken young artist I would not quote him by name. "But I don't care," he shrugged. "Use my name if you like: I am bored with fear."

I don't mean to imply that Communists have become less conscientious. I am well aware of the vigilance of this, "the most organized force of our time," as Communists call the only political party in the Soviet Union.

"The Party has . . . organized a system of people's control," writes Vasily Ashanin in *Leninist Party Principles and Norms of Party Life*. "There are groups of people's inspectors at every enterprise, collective and state farm, and state institution, and inspection posts at lower units —workshops, production sections, etc. The so-called people's inspectors, and there are about ten million of them, are workers, engineers, technicians, employees elected at general meetings. The people's inspection groups see to it that Party and state policy is correctly implemented by offices and enterprises concerned."

All along our way, local authorities and Party workers assisted and closely watched over our schedule and itinerary. The Deputy Minister

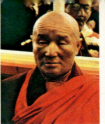

BURYATIA, R.S.F.S.R.

LENINGRAD, R.S.F.S.R.

SUKHUMI, GEORGIA

BAKU, AZERBAIJAN

DUSHANBE, TAJIKISTAN

VILNIUS, LITHUANIA

ALMA ATA, KAZAKHSTAN

TALLINN, ESTONIA

URGENCH, UZBEKISTAN

KISHINEV, MOLDAVIA

KIEV, UKRAINE

ASHKHABAD, TURKMENISTAN

RIGA, LATVIA

FRUNZE, KIRGIZIA

ROSTOV, R.S.F.S.R.

YAKUTIA, R.S.F.S.R.

TASHKENT, UZBEKISTAN

THE MANY FACES OF THE SOVIET UNION

BUKHARA, UZBEKISTAN

AKADEMGORODOK (SCIENCE CITY), R.S.F.S.R.

Varied ethnic roots of the U.S.S.R. yield a montage of strikingly different physical features, costumes, and traditions. The faces pictured here reflect photographer Dean Conger's travels through a land so huge it embraces large parts of both Europe and Asia, and more than a hundred ethno-linguistic groups: people as diverse as a Tajik shepherdess, a Buryat Buddhist monk, a Russian scientist, a Moldavian student. Captions identify each photograph geographically but not ethnically; increasing mobility has contributed to the changing mosaic of Soviet society. The black-hatted farmer photographed in Uzbekistan may be a transplanted Turkmen, and the bearded Armenian artist lives in Moscow.

On the following pages, an ethnic "spectrum" sorts the Soviet people into families of similar heritage and related languages. Brackets indicate the percentage of the U.S.S.R. population each such family represents (based on the 1970 census total of 242 million).

ALTAY TERRITORY, R.S.F.S.R.

TALLINN, ESTONIA

MINSK, BELORUSSIA

KHABAROVSK, R.S.F.S.R.

MOSCOW, R.S.F.S.R.

ALTAY TERRITORY, R.S.F.S.R.

KHANTY-MANSI DISTRICT, R.S.F.S.R. (RIGHT)

—later Minister—of Foreign Affairs for the Lithuanian Soviet Socialist Republic, Vytautas Zenkevicius, for example, welcomed us to Vilnius and remarked, "Naturally, we shall show you the best we have, just as you would do for us in the U.S.A."

Often we had too much attention. I thoroughly sympathized with a Russian fisherman I met in Murmansk. Over his fourth vodka, he proposed a toast to the relaxation of tensions between the U.S.A. and U.S.S.R. "And there has been much room for improvement," he said with some bitterness. "I have fished off your coast on Georges Bank, and the U. S. Coast Guard helicopters used to hover over us every minute. Terrible! To be *watched* all the time!"

Although I realized that the aircraft primarily were policing United States coastal fishing waters, I tried to explain that the Coast Guard might simply have been suspicious: His fishing trawler could have been sent on a mission of espionage or attack. Conversely, some Soviet citizens might have suspected me of the same dark purposes in their country. They felt safer keeping an eye on me.

Soviet and American citizens have their well-observed differences: history, language, ideology, and their separate pantheons of heroes. But my friend Igor Zaseda in Kiev had another observation. Igor was a swimmer, journalist, and Olympic sportswriter. "Around Olympic Village in Mexico City," he told me, "the people I liked at once were the Americans. Why not? Yours is a big country with a variety of peoples—like the Soviet Union."

He has a point. Even humor and pranks there have an expansive, familiar ring. "This really happened with some Aeroflot employees," said interpreter-guide Boris Lunkov. "They found a friend drunk—passed out—on a bench in Moscow's Pushkin Square. So they took him onto an airplane. And when the drunk woke up next day, he was in Pushkin Square, all right—but it was the Pushkin Square in Tbilisi, in Georgia, a thousand miles distant."

Away from big cities, I found Russians a lot like people in the western United States—hearty, quick to speak, unreserved in gesture and hospitality. So I should record another prejudice: I find Russians enormously appealing. I like Georgians, too, and Estonians, but for different qualities. Estonians are certainly neater, and Georgians more musical. But I have a particular rapport with Russians.

At Moscow State University, a professor told me an old saying of the geographers: "If you want to know a new town, you have to taste the ice cream at the railroad station, go to church to hear the music, and then visit the market."

Well, in most towns, I found the ice cream and the deep-voiced a cappella church music better than in the U.S.A. But I am an enthusiastic admirer—and sampler—of many other things in the U.S.S.R.

I like the way parents take their children to concerts and, during intermission, escort them up front to look at the instruments in the orchestra pit. I like the pure elegance of the Bolshoi Ballet, of course, and even more, its ballet school where lean-lined youngsters live in a secular cloister dedicated to a classic art.

I like both Russian bread and circuses—the bread for its sour fragrance and dark, vitamin-rich vitality, the most delicious bread I've

ETHNO-LINGUISTIC GROUP
(Percentage

Relative sizes of the color blocks are somewhat modified; the numerical differences among the groups are so great that precise proportions cannot be shown at this scale.

74.62%

13.38%

2.55%

1.77%

1.69%

1.17%

.95%

.19%

.08%

.02%

.01%

.01%

3.56%

SLAVIC BELORUSSIAN BULGARIAN CZECH POLISH RUSSIAN SLOVAK UKRAINIAN

TURKIC ALTAY AZERBAIJANIAN BALKAR BASHKIR CHUVASH CRIMEAN-TATAR DOLGAN GAGAUZ KARACHAY KARAIM KARAKALPAK KAZAKH KHAKASS KIRGIZ KUMYK NOGHAY SHOR TATAR TOFA TURKI TURKMEN TUVAN UYGHUR UZBEK YAKUT

CAUCASUS ABAZ ABKHAZ ADYGEI AGUL AVAR CHECHEN CIRCASSIAN DARGIN GEORGIAN INGUSH KABARDIN LAK LEZGIN OSSET RUTUL TABASARAN TSAKHUR UDI

FINNIC ESTONIAN FINNISH IZHOR KARELIAN KOMI KOMI-PERMIAK MARI MORDVIN SAAM(LAPP) UDMURT VEPS

BALTIC LATVIAN LITHUANIAN

ROMANCE FRENCH MOLDAVIAN ROMANIAN

IRANIAN AFGHAN BALUCHI KURD PERSIAN TAJIK TAT

MONGOLIAN BURYAT KALMYK KHALKHA-MONGOL

UGRIC HUNGARIAN KHANTY MANSI

TUNGUS-MANCHU EVEN EVENK NANAY NEGIDAL OROCH UDEGEY ULCH

SAMOYED NENETS NGANASAN SELKUP

PALEO-SIBERIAN CHUKCHI ITELMEN KET KORYAK NIVKH YUKAGHIR

OTHERS ALBANIAN ALEUTIAN ARMENIAN ASSYRIAN DUNGAN ESKIMO GERMAN GREEK GYPSY INDIAN-PAKISTAN JEWISH KOREAN ETC.

eaten, bar none, in the 46 countries where I have worked. And the state circus, with more than a hundred companies and 13,000 employees, stands easily greater than the Greatest Show on Earth.

I like the aeronautical purity of the small Yakovlev-40 jet airplane with its stylish takeoffs and landings. I like the cold summertime soup called *okroshka*. And Caspian caviar. And birch trees brightening forests. I like Russian fairy tales told by grandmothers with crinkling, expressive eyes. I like as many Russian writers as the characters who populate their books. I like the bright, white crackle of Siberia in February, and old cottage windows framed in wooden jigsaw doilies. I like icons as incense for the eye. And the sassy style of the Kiev soccer team named Dynamo. And more, and more.

My list of enthusiasms does not include Soviet beer, nor salads, nor the custom of having handsome youngsters march around monuments in a goose step. And more. But for all these highly personal reactions, you should make allowance.

Traveling through Russia, I often recalled a fable told about a court favorite of Empress Catherine the Great. According to legend, when Catherine toured her southern domains, her prince built artificial villages like theatrical sets along her route. In such a deceptive way he impressed Catherine with his success as a colonizer. But the trouble with that colorful tale is that it is probably false. So traveling through the modern Soviet Union, a Westerner should remember that false story—and sometimes mistrust even his own mistrust.

Catherine the Great leads us to another caution. Writing about her first five years of power and the bureaucratic inefficiency of her empire, Catherine had this to say:

"In the provinces the decrees of the Senate were implemented so negligently that the saying 'wait for the third decree' became a virtual proverb since no one acted on the first or second."

Modern Party spokesmen make similar laments. ("Communists do not consider that the noble ideals for which they are fighting automatically safeguard the Party against the danger of bureaucratization.") Cartoons in the humor magazine *Krokodil* poke harsh fun at the bureaucrat. A recent cover shows a brace of buck-passing executives deflecting a lightning-bolt labeled *vygovor*, "rebuke"; the bolt zigzags down the line and finally hits the charwoman.

Russians have a formidable word (*perestrakhovshchik*) that means "reinsurer," one who covers all bets—or, as a friend once defined it for me: "one who is afraid to permit much, but whose position requires him to do so."

Sometimes Dean and I found ourselves in the nervous hands of a *perestrakhovshchik*—and waiting impatiently for the third decree.

More often we followed other venerable traditions of old Russia. One of these was the quest of the Holy Wanderers, who left their homes and roamed the earth in search of truth. Some even feigned a sort of madness, to make people scorn them, and were called Holy Fools.

We, too, wandered widely and often asked foolish questions; but our shelter and travel conditions usually surpassed an ascetic's. Our wisdom and comfort increased, however, in places usually closed to Western travelers—for example, the remote northern town of Mirny in Yakutia. We went there in dark February to learn how miners scoop diamonds from the permafrost. In the vibrating heat waves of summer, we traveled across sand dunes of the Kara Kum to a desert research station with the highest recorded temperatures in the U.S.S.R. (around 120° F.). Staff rangers there were riding camels.

At an Abkhazian village of the Georgian Republic, we feasted with a woman calculated by researchers to be at least 133 years old. In wine and vodka, our antique hostess proposed numerous toasts to world amity, and drank us under the table.

We have lived some weeks' worth of time on Soviet trains—the crack limiteds of the Trans-Siberian Railroad as well as local milk trains nearer Moscow. We have traveled a respectable share of the 138,000 kilometers of Soviet track. We've ridden riverboats, fishing vessels, and hydrofoils. We've used motorcars and buses, and—excessively—the Soviet's state-owned and only airline, Aeroflot. ("I'm Natasha, Fly Me," read a headline about the world's largest airline in the *Wall Street Journal*.) We have ridden scores of the 1,500-odd airplanes flown by Aeroflot. (That estimate is Western; no official figure is available.) Perhaps we know the segregated foreigners' waiting rooms at the Tashkent and Irkutsk airports as intimately as any Westerners.

Throughout most of these travels, two Novosti-assigned Russian companions aided and informed us. I have already mentioned Boris Lunkov, a studious linguist in his forties. Boris comes originally from Siberia. His father was killed in the Great Patriotic War, as World War II is called in the U.S.S.R., and Boris was reared by his musician mother. "She was a good atheist and revolutionary, and I learned much from her," Boris recalled. "I grew up a nearsighted, bookish boy in a Siberian garrison town. And I could not wait to go to school in Moscow." He graduated highly proficient in the English language and Marxist philosophy. In the Novosti publishing house he generally edited and translated political tracts. Boris wore suits of conservative cut and color; his manner was unobtrusive and his vigilance great. He seemed more at home in cities than in the country, and he wore his dark suit and his urban formality into the fertilized fields of collective farms.

Boris read widely, not just Marxist essays but also Russian classics, and a surprisingly broad range of both British and American fiction in English. "I have more time to read," Boris explained, "since I am divorced." Later we met his shining-eyed teenage daughter, Olga—but not his girl friend. An attentive suitor, Boris had told us a bit about his romance with a woman who earned a salary larger than his own.

"Perhaps I am old-fashioned," confessed Boris, a grin on his broad Slavic face, "but I do not help her with the cooking or housework. She doesn't expect it."

Our other principal companion, Gennady Sokolov, represented the younger generation; he was a handsome, modishly dressed chap in his mid-twenties. Gena knew all the rock groups, East and West; he wore carefully pressed American blue jeans, turtlenecks, and fashionably long hair. But his political background was just as pure as Boris's.

"My mother was a poor girl, and while young she struggled against the *kulaks*," Gena told us. He seemed even prouder of his mother's class struggles than of the subway stations in Kiev that his engineer father had designed.

"When her father died, my mother was only 14. She wrote a letter to

Vostok rocket like those that thrust the first cosmonauts aloft stands near a Tupolev-134 aircraft at the Cosmos Pavilion, an aerospace museum. It and 77 neighboring pavilions comprise Moscow's 175-acre National Economic Achievements Exhibition, displaying Soviet accomplishments in virtually every field from atomic energy to zinc mining.

Nadezhda Krupskaya, the widow of Lenin, and asked for help. Krupskaya personally answered the letter, and helped my mother get a part-time job in a Moscow textile factory and a chance to attend night school and finish her education. Then she worked for a while on a collective farm, and there she had to fight kulaks. You know who the kulaks were? Well, the word *kulak* means fist, and the kulaks were the better-off peasants. It was not easy to subdue them; they resisted the Revolution fiercely and selfishly. Several times they tried to kill my mother.''

A bright girl, Gena's mother also proved a leader in Communist Party activities. During World War II, she was sent to Tehran to work in liaison with the U. S. lend-lease mission.

I met Madame Sokolova one day at a rally in Red Square. I found her to be a handsome, round-faced woman of great charm, with a chestful of clanking medals in honor of her faithful service.

Coming from such a patriotic background, Gena was always highly motivated. His grades were excellent, and he was accepted as a journalism student at the Moscow State Institute of International Relations, which trains functionaries for the Soviet Ministries of Foreign Affairs and Foreign Trade and similar sensitive agencies. His petite brunette wife, Natasha, was a scholar of English literature. Both Gena and Natasha had long been officers in the Young Communist League.

Gena never actually tried to convert me to his political philosophy, but he let no opportunity pass to score a point. When I complained once about the high cost of laundry in a Yalta hotel, Gena was quick to note, "That's the private sector—the chambermaid did your laundry as a kind of capitalist." At least Gena smiled when he wielded his socialist rapier.

In general, both Boris and Gena practiced ideological coexistence with Dean and me. We agreed that we'd never agree about some things, and moved on to other subjects like personalized geography.

It's a land of wide ironies. People aside, the single most exciting fact about Soviet geography is its monotony. The word itself belongs to historian V. O. Klyuchevsky, as he described the vast expanse of his Russian homeland: "Monotony is the chief characteristic of her surface: one form of relief dominates almost her whole extent. . . . In its . . . structure this steppe is exactly like the steppes of Central Asia, of which, geographically, it constitutes a direct and uninterrupted prolongation. Temperate in all things, western Europe does not know such exhausting summer droughts and such terrible winter snowstorms as are common on this steppe plain. . . ."

The continental terms seem muddled. Is it Europe or Asia? And that riddle remains unanswered and unanswerable: No one can say for sure where Europe ends and Asia begins.

"The Georgians are to blame," laughs the leading geographer of the U.S.S.R., Academician I. P. Gerasimov. "Georgians insist they're Europeans." So Soviet scholars leave the continental line undrawn in the area of the Caucasus Mountains.

But what about the Urals? When I met the Soviet cosmonaut Valery F. Bykovsky, I asked him what the Urals looked like from space. After all, in 1963 Bykovsky had repeatedly flown over those mountains during his record 81 earth orbits.

My question quite puzzled him. "It's been so long," he smiled. "I'll have to stop and think. . . ." He scratched his head. "You know, the Urals are *not all that big.*"

Right. No Ural summit exceeds 6,300 feet, and the range's mean elevation is only about 1,600 feet. The Urals' old Russian name *Kamenny Poyas,* or Stony Girdle, did not even appear on Western maps until the 16th century. Historian Arnold Toynbee used to scoff at this "unconvincing line" that is "no more noticeable . . . than the Chiltern Hills . . . not strongly enough pronounced even to serve as a boundary between one local province of the Russian Empire and another."

So I need feel no personal guilt: I have twice flown directly over the Urals and missed seeing them entirely.

Scholars have tried to cleave Europe and Asia in other ways. The Roman historian Tacitus, in the first century, used anthropology as his criterion. Tacitus asked himself whether the old Slavs were Asians or Europeans, and chose the latter because "they have fixed abodes, and carry shields, and delight to use their feet and to run fast. . . ."

"Once we tried to draw the continental boundary by considering linguistic differences between Asia and Europe," reported geography Professor E. M. Murzaev. "But we failed. Look at the Finno-Ugric groups! We are even now discussing this question. Time will solve the problem. In history, of course, the accepted border of Europe has steadily moved farther east."

Biologists would certainly move the line dramatically eastward— by some 1,200 miles to the Yenisey River, which separates two different environments of plant and animal life. "Siberian taiga extends from the right bank of the river," wrote geographer N. A. Gvozdetsky, one of the explorers of the area, "—dense forests of huge spruce, silver fir, pine and larch, with impassable undergrowth of young spruce and silver fir. And extending from the left bank of the Yenisey, directly opposite these wild, dense and trackless forest masses, were areas of cheerful forest-steppe. The contrast was amazing!"

Dean Conger, who suffers from hay fever, has even suggested a kind of allergy test for continents: He has commonly found ragweed in Asia, but never in Europe. (Georgians will be saddened to hear that Dean sneezed energetically all through their republic.)

Cartographers stand in mumbling disarray: Should the continental boundary ride the crest or embrace the foothills of mountains? And what do we mean by Siberia and the Far East? Lacking consensus, we strive here for convenience: In this book, *Siberia* means all the Russian Soviet Federated Socialist Republic east of the crest of the Urals, including those regions east and northeast of Lake Baikal known as Transbaikal and the Soviet Far East. *Russia* here means all the Russian Federated Republic of the U.S.S.R., or—in a historic context—the Russian Empire; the word *Russian* refers to the language or to the ethnic group—also called Great Russian—as a recognized nationality.

Whatever the boundaries drawn by men, nature has striated the Soviet map with great, slow, but powerful rivers that fall gently and meander toward the seas both north and south. "Don't think of the U.S.S.R. as dry land at all," a poetic American geographer once told me. "Think of it as an ocean. All 8,650,000 square miles of it."

"He has a good point," concedes Moscow State University's Vladislav Grigorievich Marchukov, assistant to the dean of the Geography

Faculty. "We have many rivers, lakes, and canals—and like an ocean, we are constantly in dynamic processes of development.

"You Americans say your industry was created by rail. We can say that river transport played a major part in the development of our areas, especially in pre-revolutionary Russia. Rivers carried nearly one-fourth of our freight before the Revolution—and still carry about 5 percent."

The oceanic metaphor bears a closer look: The Soviet Union possesses 25 percent of the world's fresh water. Alone, Siberia's Lake Baikal—astonishingly, more than a mile deep—contains a fifth of all the world's supply.

Because of their northerly latitude, the eastward rotation of the planet, and the pull of inertia, Russian rivers have carved high, cliffy western banks while their waters lie low on their eastern shores.

The Lena is longer than the Mississippi, and the Yenisey has almost the Mississippi's volume of water. The Ob and Amur lag not far behind in their flow. And the Volga, personified as the Mother of Russia, has gathered perhaps even more folklore than America's Old Man River.

Throughout Siberia, boats ply rivers only in the summer; winter turns artery into bone. On the frozen surface, transportation is far easier. Trucks drive along the part-time pavement of the rivers and on the *zimniki*, as Siberians call their icy winter roads, a system far more reliable than the same quagmire routes during the brief summertime. Also more exhilarating: I've ridden with speed-loving drivers who scorned snow tires, the better to show their virtuosity.

Today technological ambitions involve the great Siberian rivers. Engineers are seriously proposing that perhaps 15 percent of the waters from the Ob, Yenisey, and Irtysh be deflected south and used in dry Soviet Central Asia. Irrigation projects have seriously reduced river flow into the salty Caspian and Aral seas. In particular, the Aral seems endangered: It has recently fallen by three feet a year. The Caspian has also mysteriously fallen for half a century, but has somewhat stabilized. ("At least we added more land to our republic," an Azerbaijanian remarked as we stood on the widened Caspian seashore.)

The Ob-Caspian Canal—some 3,000 kilometers long—would bring springtime floodwaters from western Siberia south, through the valleys of other rivers like the Turgay, to the irrigation systems of the Amu Darya—the ancient river that Alexander the Great knew as the Oxus. Millions of desert acres could be made to bloom.

The whole wide country brims with contradictions. Every Westerner, for example, has heard of the old Siberian salt mines. And yet, though Soviet citizens relish the chance to tell foreigners about tsarist oppression, the topic of salt mines draws a blank. Siberian prisoners mined gold under especially brutal conditions. But Siberian salt mines? Prisoners apparently never mined a grain.

The Baltic Sea is also short of salt. Along the Estonian coast, for example, some Baltic waters are only slightly brackish, so that livestock drink and thrive on this seawater. By contrast, dry Kazakhstan is pocked with white-rimmed salty swamps in its broad deserts.

Deserts, in fact, comprise about one-tenth of the U.S.S.R., not counting tundra and taiga—northern regions of limited rainfall. In the Far North east of the Yenisey, a sparsely populated area exists with an annual precipitation of only six inches. But the hard-frozen underlayer of earth — the permafrost — retains near the surface almost all of this meager moisture, permitting trees to thrive. So in its taiga, Siberia boasts a green, forested desert as another geographic paradox.

The lowlands between the Urals and the Yenisey — some 900,000 square miles — may well comprise the largest area of level ground on earth. And west of the stubby little Urals, the black-earthed Russian steppes stretch on again — for all their famous droughts, incredibly fertile. Within this largely flat mass of land, we find geographic superlatives not even inventoried. The U.S.S.R. now claims to pump more crude oil than any other country (over ten million barrels a day); her coal reserves look even better. And gold and iron. . . . No wonder that outsiders have long coveted that level ocean of rich soil.

Everyone recalls the noisy, galloping invaders: Genghis Khan and his Mongol warriors . . . Tamerlane's crashing cavalry generations later. But this geography has also invited quieter invasions. Norse merchants and piratical Vikings plied the great riverways, moving from Scandinavia to Byzantium upon the Western Dvina and the Dnieper. For early Europe, this route was simply a northern extension of the camel caravans carrying spices and fabrics from the East.

Invaders and importers have brought a cargo of irony to this land. Some of the most intensely Russian symbols often contain an alien surprise. Like vodka. The strong national drink came from the West in the 16th century. Earlier Russians drank wine, mead, and mild, beery kvas.

The most famous icon of old Russia, the Virgin of Vladimir, inspired the faithful for seven centuries. Soldiers bore it into battle to work miraculous victories against foreign foes. Tsar Ivan the Terrible carried it against the Tatars on his siege of Kazan. Nicholas II invoked the same icon when he declared war on the Kaiser's Germany. Yet the Virgin of Vladimir was not Russian at all; the icon was a Byzantine import, painted in the 12th century in old Constantinople.

By the same exotic token, the founding genius of Russian literature, Alexander Pushkin, boasted an Ethiopian great-grandfather. And Lenin, the Soviet Union's founding revolutionary, counted both Germans and Tatars among his forebears.

The historian Klyuchevsky summed up a thousand years when he called Russia "a country which colonizes itself." And, in the ways of the 20th century, restless human tides continue to flow.

"We now have a reindeer herder from northern Yakutia," a doctor told me in an Estonian sanitarium. "It is his first trip to Europe, and he feels bad. His pulse rate has even increased." The doctor pointed to a brown-skinned man sitting on a bench; he looked like an Eskimo — square-faced, strongly Oriental. This Yakut reindeer herder was recovering from a full spectrum of change: jet-lag factors, food, climate, continent, culture, language, nationality. The whole changing population of the U.S.S.R. now faces a similar quickening of pulse.

Between 1959 and 1970, the portion of ethnic Great Russians living in the Russian Federated Republic *declined* by 2.3 percentage points. The figure reflects the Russian farmer moving to the virgin lands of Kazakhstan and the engineer transferring from Siberia to the Ukraine, as well as a rare Uzbek coming westward to work in a Volga factory.

And birthrates figure into the equation of nationalities. Soviet

Europeans have the lowest rates—in 1974, 15.1 per thousand for Estonia, 15.6 for Great Russia. Soviet Central Asians have by far the highest rates: in 1974, again, 34.2 for Uzbekistan, and 37 for Tajikistan. So the Great Russians, now numbering only about 53 percent of the total Soviet population, look at the future with the quizzical feelings of some American WASPS.

"The most distinguishing feature of socialist nations is their growing social homogeneity...," says Dr. Suren Kaltakchyan, expressing the Communist view. "Culture which is national in form and socialist in content speeds up ... development ... and drawing together of nations."

The term "drawing together" *(sblizhenie)* gets a lot of use. After all, much of the ethnic variety of the tsarist empire is historically recent. The Crimea was not added to the Russian Empire until 1783, and Caucasia not until the 19th century. Exotic Tashkent fell to the tsar's imperial army in 1865—the first large town in Islamic Central Asia annexed by old Russia.

"And today," says poet Robert Rozhdestvensky, "you can eat Near Eastern *shashlyk* in the Far North. It is fast becoming our national food."

Costumes, languages, songs, folklore get strong official encouragement. Soviet citizens carry an internal passport for identification. Along with the bearer's picture, vital statistics, and social category (worker, peasant, or "people's intelligentsia"), his nationality is listed: "Russian," "Tatar," "Jew," "Uzbek," whatever. "Under the tsars," a Novosti agent told me, "we had passports that said only 'Russian' and 'non-Russian.' Now everyone can announce his nationality." The child of a mixed marriage can choose either nationality when he comes of age.

Once in Tbilisi I asked a Georgian artist which foreign countries had most influenced Georgian art. He thought and then replied, "Two: France and Russia."

But for all the strength of other cultures, one group remains "the first among equals," as many note. In the Far Eastern river city of Khabarovsk, Dr. Iosif Yefimovich Trop, a Jewish microbiologist, talked to me about the rearing of his two children. "The Russian culture is very rich," said Dr. Trop. "It conquers every person. So though Jewish, we are Russian in spirit."

I attended a wedding in Alma Ata, only about 175 miles from China, and as the young Kazakh bride and groom signed the marriage book, the registrar observed that "the family is the basic cell of the state." A recording of the Kremlin chimes then sounded through the hall—"the heart of the country," the registrar added. Each republic has its own variations of the marriage ceremony, but the Kremlin chimes ring for all.

With Orbita satellite television, and Moscow radio programs broadcast everywhere, tastes and attitudes grow more standardized. Even circus clowns note the difference. "Audiences are more sophisticated," remarks the famous septuagenarian clown Karandash. "The country is changing its face, and the people are changing, too. In the 1930's, they laughed at primitive things. The old circus was addressed to illiterates. But now even children know about science. They have atomic toys!"

An old Slavic proverb warns us: "Read for a century, study for a century—and you'll die a fool." So let us ignore libraries for a while and look at old Russian history through the windows of three living, changing cities: Kiev, Moscow, and Leningrad.

Most venerated and perhaps the oldest icon in Russia, the Virgin of Vladimir, by an unknown artist, gave comfort to the faithful in Constantinople at least eight centuries ago. It traveled to Kiev, later to the town of Vladimir, and in 1395 to Moscow, then anticipating an attack by Tamerlane. Unexpectedly, the Turkic-Mongol conqueror turned back— and the icon gained credit for the city's salvation.

IMPERIAL LEGACY

Tsarist treasures such as the diamond-and-ruby-encrusted pendant at left, worn by Catherine the Great, now sparkle as museum pieces within Moscow's Kremlin. A tour guide (below) lectures in the Armory, repository for regal mementos of the past: jeweled crowns and thrones, royal armor, rich embroideries, and a collection of gems that includes the 189-carat Orlov diamond. Nowhere in the Kremlin does opulence shine more brightly than in St. George's Hall (right)—built to celebrate Napoleon's retreat from Moscow, named for the tsarist military Order of St. George, and currently used for the most important diplomatic receptions. Each chandelier blazes with the light of 500 bulbs; the elaborate parquet floors display 20 varieties of wood.

LARGEST AIRLINE IN THE WORLD

One hundred million passengers—a third of the world's airline travelers—each year climb aboard the planes of state-owned Aeroflot, the Soviet Union's only air carrier. Some still fly the TU-104 (in the distance, below), Aeroflot's first jet, introduced in 1956 and now mostly replaced. But having faster planes—including the supersonic TU-144, still under test—doesn't speed up the reception at customs, where arriving international visitors fill out detailed currency forms (below, left), a procedure they must repeat when leaving the country. Flights

within the U.S.S.R. often rely on the sturdy, short-range YAK-40 (bottom, left). In addition to carrying a heavy traffic of passengers and freight, Aeroflot provides a wide range of other aviation services, operating helicopters and single-engine planes for crop dusting, fire fighting, aerial ambulance service, delivering machinery to mines and factories, even dropping off supplies for reindeer herders of the Far North (bottom, right) and calling at remote spots recently served only by dogsled or camel caravan.

THE TRANS-SIBERIAN

Children peer from a car on the Trans-Siberian Railroad through portholes melted in the frost on the inside of

the window. At this stop the outdoor temperature hit -40° F. The panel identifies the terminals of the line—Moscow and Vladivostok—in the Russian Cyrillic alphabet.

SOVIET BIRTHDAY: NOVEMBER 7

Eyes right! "Ravnenie napravo!" shouts an officer, and rows of faces snap as one toward the reviewing stand. Crisp commands mark every November 7 in Leningrad's Palace Square, when Soviet soldiers march by in a 45-minute parade followed by a procession of workers and other groups that lasts for hours. The marchers commemorate the day in 1917 (October 25 on the old Julian calendar) when the Bolsheviks gained control of the city, then called Petrograd, and overthrew the provisional regime that eight months earlier had deposed Nicholas II, Russia's last tsar. The November 7 celebration, much more than just a show of military strength, marks a major holiday of feasts, champagne, and vodka—a day when balloons and paper roses buoy the joyful moods of army cadets and a friend.

GRANARY OF THE U.S.S.R.

Combines harvest a golden expanse of wheat at Comintern State Farm near Kharkov, in the Ukraine. Famed for rich black earth, the Ukrainian steppes supply much of the nation's produce—such as the truckload of cucumbers picked by the women at right. Agriculture engages about 28 million men and women—roughly a fourth of the Soviet Union's labor force—on state and collective farms. (Salaried government employees man a state farm; worker-partners run a collective farm, a sort of cooperative, and each shares in the profits.) But unpredictable rainfall patterns plague Soviet growers. Though 1973 brought a record grain crop of 222.5 million tons, drought slashed production in 1975, requiring Moscow to import wheat from the United States, Canada, and Australia.

GROWING CITIES:
BARNAUL AND KISHINEV

As a streetcar rolls past a new apartment building in Barnaul, in the Altay Territory of the Russian Federated Republic, two nonpaying passengers ride along. The Soviet housing-construction industry often erects large buildings by precasting concrete wall and floor units, then hoisting them into place with cranes. At right, residential towers rise in a row in Kishinev, Moldavia. A deputy editor and a pressman (top, right) check over a copy of Altayskaya Pravda fresh off the conveyor at its printing plant in Barnaul.

UNDAUNTED AT 70° BELOW

At home in the fierce Arctic winds, "reindeer people" of north-eastern Siberia routinely endure -70° F. temperatures as they follow their roaming herds, often riding selected animals (far right). The breathing of the reindeer causes much of the frozen fog floating above the herd. Siberia harbors some two million

reindeer, nearly 80 percent of the world's total. For centuries the
semiwild creatures have provided Yakuts, Evenks, and other northern nomads with transportation, milk, meat, and clothing. Today,
collective farms and new feedlots promise more efficient tending of
reindeer—and an end to the herders' wanderings.

RIVER HIGHWAYS

Summer cruise on the Irtysh River lures vacationers to Siberia. Such diesel-powered craft as the Alyabiev (above) offer inexpensive excursions—some as long as a month—as well as commuter service between river ports. Near here the Irtysh joins the Ob River; together they make up one of the world's longest river systems. The thousands of navigable streams in the Soviet Union, linked by other inland waterways, carry 150 million passengers and 500 million tons of

freight each year. Most of the rivers freeze over in winter,
sometimes serving then as temporary roadways; in much of
Siberia, ice may limit boat transportation to a three-month
season. At left, a father and son while away the three-hour
Dnieper River trip between Kiev and Kanev aboard a hydrofoil.
Gradually replacing many slower vessels, hydrofoils travel
Russia's main waterways at speeds up to 60 miles an hour.

LAND OF COTTON

Shaped by laborers, a mountain of cotton grows on a collective farm in Soviet Central Asia. The Tajik Soviet Socialist Republic produces the finest long-fiber cotton in the Soviet Union and the highest-yield cotton in the world. This arid region, watered by more than 10,000 miles of irrigation canals, produces some 650,000 tons of cotton annually. Harvesting relies both on pickers (left) and mechanical methods (far left); workers then spread the bolls to dry (below, right) before collecting and packing them in storage piles where they remain until they can be ginned and baled. Tajik farms also yield grains, fruits, silk, and oil-producing plants.

Cloudswept crags of the Caucasus mountain range, which extends from the Black Sea to

the Caspian, tower above climbers on their way down from Mount Elbrus (out of picture).

2

KIEV, MOSCOW, LENINGRAD

Resplendent cross-vaults anchored by a central pillar form the ceiling of the throne room in the Kremlin's Hall of Facets. The building, completed in 1491, takes its name from diamond-patterned stonework in the facade. The hall's restored 16th-century frescoes depict biblical, historical, and allegorical subjects.

ONE WINTER DAY in Siberia I met a man fishing through the ice of the Amur River. He had caught five fish, more than any of his companions. What was his secret?

"No secret," he said through chapped and stiffened lips. *"No secret —only endurance."*

He had instantly summarized both the geography and history of his homeland.

Unlike its geography, the history of Russia and the Soviet Union has been neither monotonous nor level. On the steppes, man had no place to hide. Armies substituted for mountains. Survival depended less on protective terrain than on courage, cunning, and cruelty—and at other times generosity, forgiveness, and the capacity to suffer. Always Russian history, like Amur ice-fishing, has required endurance.

In tsarist days, people quoted the proverb, "Moscow is the heart of Russia, St. Petersburg its head; but Kiev, its mother." Though times and names have changed, those three cities still provide an outline of the national history.

A visitor's first view of Kiev shows him why. I arrived at sunset. On the way in from the airport, our car crossed Paton Bridge (inaccurately described as "the world's first completely welded bridge"). Beneath us, barges heavy with Donets Basin coal rippled a red reflection on the surface of the Dnieper; beyond and above, gold domes bulged out from forested hills. Our view encompassed the very origins of old Russia, for the Dnieper created Kiev, and Kiev the nation.

Details of the rich Kievan past are still emerging. For example: "We were digging tunnels to extend our metro system in 1972," reported Dr. Pyotr Petrovich Tolochko of the Institute of Archeology. "And near the river in the Podol neighborhood, eight meters below the surface, the excavators found some wood. I examined their discovery—and immediately asked them to stop digging! They had struck a tenth-century log house. It even had an oak fence around it.

"Since then, we have worked closely with the metro engineers. Without them we couldn't work at such a depth. We have found whole layers of preserved buildings, for old Podol had been flooded—the lower areas were covered with sand."

The origins of the Kievan Rus state remain as murky as Podol's floodwaters. Even the word *Rus* provokes scholarly quarrels. Was the name Slavic or Scandinavian? Or was the principality named for the River Ros, near Kanev?

"A state is not born as a single event," said Dr. F. E. Los of Kiev's History Institute. "But during the eighth and ninth centuries, as the settlements here began to unite, the Russian land was being born."

By the time sand and silt covered the log cabins of Podol, an extraordinary and forceful man ruled Kiev, "courteous Prince Vladimir.... Fair Sun Prince" with "white hands and ... yellow curls," as minstrels fancily described him in their songs of heraldry, the old *byliny*. Vladimir's court was sumptuous and at his "great honorable feast... many princes, boyars [nobles], and mighty Russian heroes ... sat eating bread and salt, carving the white swan, and quaffing sweet mead and green wine." A single cup of wine "drained at one draught" weighed "a pood and a half," or some 55 pounds, according to one song.

Love of the cup figures strongly in the story of Prince Vladimir's most famous decision. According to chroniclers, the prince sent emissaries abroad to study various religions. Islam was firmly rejected because—tradition has it—Muslims were not permitted wine and "drinking is the joy of the Russians." The emissaries "beheld no glory" in the Latin rites of Western Christians. But ceremonies of the Byzantine Greeks inspired awe: "... we knew not whether we were in heaven or on earth.... Their service is fairer than the ceremonies of other nations. For we cannot forget that beauty."

Today the result of Vladimir's research is commemorated by a statue overlooking the Dnieper: Vladimir himself holds aloft a cross, for he accepted Orthodox Christianity and forcibly baptized his subjects. In 990 the prince pulled down the idols of the pagan gods Perun and Volos that he himself had erected on the hill beside his castle, and thenceforth turned his back on a life that one chronicler called "insatiable in vice." The once-vicious prince is known today as St. Vladimir, "equal to the apostles."

His new church required educated men for the priesthood, so Vladimir established schools for "the children of the best families," comparable to Charlemagne's palace schools. The written language was Old Church Slavonic, and the alphabet was one formalized by two brothers from Macedonia, the missionaries Cyril and Methodius. In time the alphabet—adapted largely from Greek—came to be called Cyrillic after the more scholarly brother. Old Church Slavonic through the next half-dozen centuries remained the basic language of both liturgy and literature. The Cyrillic alphabet, edited and purged through the centuries, endures today with 32 characters.

Vladimir's son, Yaroslav the Wise, gave Kiev its richest architectural legacy, and every modern visitor to Kiev can feel himself to be

Yaroslav's heir. Here stands the Cathedral of St. Sophia, "a great and holy house of God . . . adorned . . . with every beauty," one of the most monumental religious structures in all the Slavic lands and the burial place of Yaroslav. Built in the 11th century as a Kievan Rus adaptation of the Byzantine style—but with 13 cupolas symbolizing Jesus and the Apostles—St. Sophia set a pattern for other churches in northern cities like Novgorod and Vladimir.

Thus Kiev spread the Christian faith. "Conversion was apparently more important than colonization in unifying the region," writes historian James Billington. The new religion, imported and imposed by force, was soon just as forcefully propagated.

Modern Kiev follows another official ideology, of course; and another unofficial ambience pervades this capital city of the Ukraine. Kiev has an easier, lighter feel than the great northern cities of the U.S.S.R. Greenery helps. "When people come for the first time," boasted native son Igor Zaseda, "they see the forest and ask, 'Where is the city?' for buildings are hidden by trees. We have 20 square meters of green for each of our two million citizens."

Even the lines of large, faceless apartment buildings are softened by vines that spill from balconies, a cataract of green. Study a Kiev hillside and you are conscious of textures: tall poplars jutting up, locusts with rough bark and soft leaves, willows supple and bending, and—most of all—chestnuts with ripening burr-shaped fruit and foliage splayed out like fingers of a hand.

To me, it is reassuring that the history of old Russia began in the warmer, wider, brighter, deciduous regions near Kiev—away from the gloom of northern forests and brief winter days. Kiev broods and dozes less.

"When we dance the *hopak,* we touch the ceiling," said my Ukrainian friend Igor. "And our borscht here—you can stand a spoon in it. Of course, Ukrainian borscht is bad for lovemaking." I asked why. "No—no secret ingredients! It's just that a man can eat two kilos of it, and then he goes to sleep." Ukrainian men are famous as lovers, "but we probably do no more than Italians," said Igor. "The climate is warm. And we appreciate beauty."

Appreciatively, Igor showed us what he had in mind on the city's riverside beaches. Few large inland cities can claim so many accessible beaches. Along the Dnieper and the shores of its islands, Kiev citizens sun themselves luxuriantly—half a million at a time on a hot summer Sunday. We rode the subway to the Hydropark Station, in the thick of the weekenders. Little bikinis were very big there. Perhaps a hundred chess players had gathered below the parapets of one bridge. All of them wore bathing trunks, though a few old fellows also affected hats or caps. Some had placed special alarm clocks beside their chessboards "for blitz games," Igor noted, "with all moves confined to five minutes. It sharpens their responses." Others played against the calendar, scarcely blinking as they pondered each move. The tableau—of bare skin, seriousness, and players about as mobile as their chessmen—suggested the whimsy of some allegorical sculptor. But bare-chested chess somehow catches the spirit of Kiev, a city with its own civilized concerns.

Street names here seem less strident than in other Soviet cities. The

Ukrainian poet Taras Shevchenko rates a longer boulevard than the nearby parallel named for Lenin. And the main thoroughfare, the Kreshchatik, retains a name of long ago and an atmosphere as well-rooted as the trees and flowers growing along its ample width. Kiev is a city of memory.

Not all the memories are gentle. As recorded in the poetic chronicle that inspired the Borodin opera *Prince Igor*, "The grass bends in sorrow. ... Victory of the princes over the infidels is gone, for now brother said to brother: 'This is mine.' ... And on all sides the infidels were victoriously invading the Russian land." The grudge lives on against those medieval people that Westerners call Mongols and Soviet citizens call Tatars—not to be confused with either the Mongolians or the Islamic Tatars of today. (I follow here the terminology of my hosts.) A pretty, dark-eyed Ukrainian girl remarked bitterly, "The Tatars took everything —and gave our land only foul speech and a disrespect for women." A Kiev history professor drew a long sigh and quoted the ultimate writ: "Karl Marx said the Tatar yoke dried the soul of the Russian people."

Whatever the metaphoric mix, Kiev still recalls with dread the year 1240. It was then that horsemen in the service of a grandson of Genghis Khan overran their city. "People in the Church of the Tithe defended the building heroically," said the History Institute's Dr. Los. "They used all kinds of weapons—even molten tar and fire. But they couldn't resist long. There were perhaps a thousand of them, and all died."

A papal envoy, Friar John of Plano Carpini, passed through Kiev in 1246 on his way to Mongolia and wrote, "... we found lying in the field countless heads and bones of dead people; for this city ... has been reduced to nothing: barely two hundred houses stand ... and ... people are held in the harshest slavery."

Times were as harsh as the Oriental overlords. We need not rely on prejudiced Slavs. The Chinese had long watched their neighbors, nomads with a strange language and raw habits. As one Chinese observer wrote, "... they are preoccupied exclusively with their flocks, they roam and they possess neither towns, nor walls, neither writing, nor books.... From childhood they practice riding and shooting arrows ... and thus they acquire courage necessary for pillage and war.... They respect only the bravest; old age and feebleness are held in contempt."

The Mongols in just two generations swept to the Arctic Ocean and the China Sea, and to the Danube River and the Persian Gulf. The warriors who occupied the western portion of the empire were called the Golden Horde—named not for the color of their skin but for the golden tent of their leader, Batu Khan—and they established their capital on the Volga River at Sarai. When a Russian prince left for that dread place, he customarily drew up his will lest he not return alive.

As the Golden Curtain descended, progress temporarily stopped on the Russian steppes. Contact with the rest of Europe—the trading of goods and ideas, the exchange of travelers—was at first entirely cut off. While Western craftsmen built the flying buttresses of their stone cathedrals, the Slavs chopped logs. No Gothic churches, no Age of Chivalry.

In Pushkin's phrase, the Tatars—unlike those ruthless conquerors of other lands, the Moors—dispensed "neither algebra nor Aristotle." They levied a crude head tax and counted their profits. Even today, the Russian language uses Mongol-Tatar words for *customhouse, money,*

Four faces of the Slavic god Svantovit fend off evil from all directions. Prince Vladimir ordered such idols destroyed in 990 when he converted the people of his Kievan Rus state to Orthodox Christianity. Vladimir ruled from Kiev, today's Ukrainian capital, where this replica stands in a park.

treasury, and *profit.* And Tatar troops swiftly drowned every Slav uprising in blood. Tatar rule was absolute, if generally distant, and the glory of old Kiev was all but forgotten.

But Kiev had made a lasting mark. One amber afternoon in late summer, as chestnuts ripened along the Kiev esplanade, I visited Pecherskaya Lavra, or Monastery of the Caves, and the small, Byzantine church of Berestovo. Within that squat, rounded 12th-century building rests a black, 20th-century sarcophagus for Yury Dolgoruky, Prince of Suzdal, briefly Grand Duke of Kiev and founder — in 1147 on the muddy bank of the Moskva River — of a village called Moscow.

The date 1147 is partly spurious. A settlement — perhaps as a country estate — existed before that time, but a chronicle cites 1147 as the year Yury Dolgoruky entertained a friend with "a mighty dinner" on what is now called Kremlin Hill. And since feasting punctuates all great human events in Russia — births, weddings, deaths, arrivals, and departures — it seems fitting that a dinner marks the founding of Moscow.

Yury's Moscow today is a city of power and platitudes. Billboards exhort the public not to acquire but to act ("KEEP HIGHER THE BANNER OF PROLETARIAN INTERNATIONALISM"). Sidewalks bulk with crowds, and everyone seems to carry a string bag, called a "just-in-case," for the impromptu, windfall purchase.

Seasons change Moscow's moods. Autumn's clouded light forebodes, but winter stimulates: spirits, tempo, and even appearance, for snow cleanses the overwhelming urban gray. "Our traffic never stops," an engineer of street maintenance, B. D. Klimovitsky, told me expansively. "Our 22,000 employees stand by night and day. They move 29 million cubic meters of snow in an average year." That's probably a record for any city in the world. Yet, winter has its price: 7,845 Muscovites died during a recent January, versus 5,464 in June. ("We have an explosion of business in winter," said M. V. Popkov, director of the city funeral trust.)

Spring, sometimes called the *rasputitsa* or mud season, starts haltingly with International Women's Day in March; men celebrate the day by buying flowers for their wives and vodka for themselves. Soon the crab apples bloom in the small park facing the Bolshoi Theater. Young lovers hold hands beside the fountain, and older overweight pedestrians rest their feet. Gorky Park along the river fills up on Sundays; children happily join their working parents for weekend treats: puppet shows, songfests, often a boat ride. Gypsies amuse visitors with furtive, illegal fortune-telling.

May Day brings the famous demonstration in Red Square, but also a rare moment of downtown ease: Some streets are roped off at night for strollers with guitars and ice cream snacks. At such relaxed intervals, with soft light and new grass, Moscow actually seems romantic.

By midsummer the city falls into a hot torpor. The population sweatily evacuates apartments for beachside sanitariums and Young Pioneer camps — usually separate outings for husband, wife, and children. "We produce 40 percent less bread in summer," a baker in a residential area told me. The bread-eaters return by September 1 — the first day of school for every Soviet youngster — and the autumn season starts another year.

Moscow spreads far and wide. Five airports sit on its outskirts, as does Zvezdny Gorodok, or Star City, the grassy campuslike space training center. Skyscraping Moscow State University takes a lofty view of the snaking Moskva River and the whole center city; nearby, workers prepare for the 1980 Moscow Olympics.

The Bolshoi Theater offers special Moscow insights. Its circle of red plush and gilt embraces history—Richard Wagner setting a new vogue for Russian conductors by facing the orchestra instead of the audience, Kalinin announcing the death of Lenin to the Congress of Soviets in 1924—and today, the memorable ballet artistry of Maya Plisetskaya, reigning queen of the dance.

I met Plisetskaya backstage one evening in a prim, stuffy little parlor. The sprightly dancer had just completed a performance of *Swan Lake* and was still wearing the white tutu and tiara of Odette. Our talk turned to her native Moscow and the way its audiences respond. "Moscow is more like New York than Leningrad!" said Plisetskaya. "In Leningrad they admire colder things. Leningrad responds like London. In New York and Moscow, audiences like emotional things."

Perhaps the most emotional spot in Moscow is that touristic cliché, Red Square: St. Basil's Cathedral, the Kremlin, Lenin's tomb—and on the opposite side the GUM department store. A pedestal-like structure draws visitors' attention—and a few shudders—the Lobnoye Mesto, a place where officials once proclaimed new laws and read the sentences for crimes.

Soon or late, most visitors on Red Square recall *War and Peace* and the burning of the city in 1812. To a French witness, Moscow "looked like a volcano with many craters." Three-fourths of the old city was destroyed. And Napoleon himself, barely escaping with his life, exclaimed, "To burn one's own cities! . . . A demon inspires these people!"

Others have thought the inspiration holy, and after every catastrophe Muscovites have been inspired to rebuild. They have had ample practice. After the first Mongol-Tatar sweep, the river nourished Moscow as it grew. While the patient Slavs paid Tatars tribute, they watched their old enemies, waited, and learned to beat the Tatars at their own hard game. In 1380 Grand Prince Dimitry defeated the Tatar masters on

Drawn by multiple teams of two or three horses each, this great sleigh carried Elizabeth, daughter of Peter the Great, through the snow-covered streets of St. Petersburg in winter. Now it rests among other imperial vehicles in one hall of the Kremlin's Armory museum, a treasure house of historic regalia.

the battlefield at Kulikovo on the upper Don, winning from the river his own surname, Donskoy, and from the Tatars the knowledge that Slavs need not always lose. True, Tatars burned Moscow just two years later—and again in 1409. But ashes always seem to fertilize that soil. Later came Ivan III, "the great gatherer of the Russian land," as the historian Karamzin called him. Moscow's domain now stretched from the Gulf of Finland almost to the Urals. Ivan III was a builder in other ways. His walls and towers for the Kremlin still command Moscow's greatest view. And construction of the Cathedral of the Archangel Michael began in the last months of his life.

Ivan's son Basil III, who finished the work, found other causes. His sense of religious and secular grandeur fed upon an idea promulgated by a monk named Filofey of Pskov, who wrote the Grand Prince these words: "The first Rome fell because of . . . heresy, the second Rome, Constantinople, was captured and pillaged by the infidel Turks, but a new third Rome has sprung up in thy sovereign kingdom. . . . Two Romes have fallen, but the Third Rome, Moscow, will stand, a fourth is not to be." Moscow: repository of truth—the attitude would not quickly vanish in the Orthodox Church.

The Third Rome spread its power under Basil's heir, just three years old when he became Grand Prince and 17 when he was crowned and took the title tsar. Ivan IV believed himself the descendant of Augustus Caesar, and *tsar* meant Caesar. History has given Ivan another title— *Grozny*, the Terrible.

The red Kremlin walls remind a visitor just how terrifying Ivan was: As a precocious boy he dropped small animals from the wall to watch them die. "And when he came to his fifteenth year, he began to harm people," wrote his enemy Prince Kurbsky. "Incline your ears. . . ," urges Kurbsky. "A young tsar brought up fatherless in evil passions and self-will, and most excessively vicious. . . ."

In a rage, the tsar even killed his own son and heir (his subsequent anguish is captured in Ilya Repin's painting in the Tretyakov Gallery). Yet Ivan considered himself, as he wrote, "the humble scepter-bearer" who had "grown up and ascended the throne by the bidding of God." Often he dressed like a monk, and his cruel *(Continued on page 64)*

Moonrise over the Dnieper River recalls Nikolai Gogol's description: "... the earth is all bathed in a silvery light.... Heavenly night! Enchanting night!" From the west bank where early Slavs built fortified

Kiev, a bronze St. Vladimir looks across Trukhanov Island toward the suburb of Darnitsa. Tradition says Vladimir ordered the baptism of the entire population of Kiev in the river near this spot.

KIEV PROMENADES

Ice cream vendors gossip on Kiev's main boulevard, the Kreshchatik; Cyrillic letters spell out the Ukrainian term for their product. Rebuilt after World War II, the broad avenue—the "Champs-Elysees of Kiev"—attracts shoppers, strollers, and tourists to its tree-lined promenades. At left, a local couple's informal dress reflects an international trend in clothing styles. Below, Kiev University's facade, once painted red as a rebuke to students involved in anti-tsarist rioting shortly before the Revolution, has retained its bright hue in honor of those who died in the clash with police. The school, like all others in the Soviet Union, provides state-supported, tuition-free education.

MUSEUM OF ST. SOPHIA

Fading sunlight ushers late-afternoon visitors from the Cathedral of St. Sophia—or Holy Wisdom—in Kiev. Its 11th-century architects patterned the building after the Byzantine masterpiece of the same name in Constantinople. Crowding into the central nave (below), a tour group admires frescoes and icons that decorate the walls and altar screen. A splendid mosaic, the Praying Virgin (right), commands the semi-dome of the apse against a background of shimmering gold. Once the central church of the Russian Orthodox communion, St. Sophia today serves only as a museum.

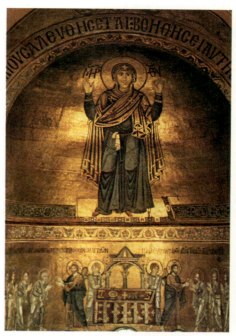

excesses were intersticed with brooding remorse. When a fire ravaged Moscow in 1547, Ivan blamed his own sinful life, and repented publicly in Red Square. There, just beyond the Kremlin wall, Ivan commemorated his conquest of Kazan and Astrakhan, the last great Tatar cities on the Volga, with a building of extraordinary design: the asymmetrical, multiple-domed, fancifully painted cathedral known as St. Basil's. The fact that St. Basil himself survived is a comment on Ivan's strange and inconsistent restraint. The story was told by bearded Father Alexey, a teacher at the Russian Orthodox seminary in Zagorsk:

"You know about the Holy Wanderers in our church?" he asked me. "In centuries past, the Holy Wanderers refused all good things—marriage, food, drink—but also normal clothing and shelter. They were sometimes called Holy Fools.

"St. Basil was such a man. In winter he went naked. And he told absolute, pure truth. Even to Ivan the Terrible, whom he blamed for unjust acts. And Ivan did not punish him, for Ivan knew St. Basil was God's voice and the people's conscience."

Not every critic fared so gently. Kurbsky writes of one feast, when a guest angered Ivan: "The tsar straightway blazed up . . . and with his own hand transfixed him with a spear. . . . And thus did he cover the floor of the room with blood. . . ." In Novgorod alone, Ivan's executioners killed perhaps 60,000 people during a single persecution that started abruptly and stopped with little explanation.

Ivan shared his century with the Borgias in Italy and the Inquisitors in Spain, so his whole historic context was cruel. And not all Ivan's madness lacked method. He brilliantly consolidated tsarist power; his conquest of Kazan and Astrakhan ended Russian tributes to the Tatars; and he moved Russian dominion eastward. No less important, Ivan conquered the Russian imagination: historians, statesmen, poets. Sergei Eisenstein's film *Ivan the Terrible* shows the idealized but formidable figure one might expect to be portrayed in the 1940's, for Ivan was a hero of Joseph Stalin. Sergei Prokofiev's music for that film has recently been choreographed by the Bolshoi Ballet: Ivan struggles against villainous nobles, and brings social unity and glory to the Russian realm. I

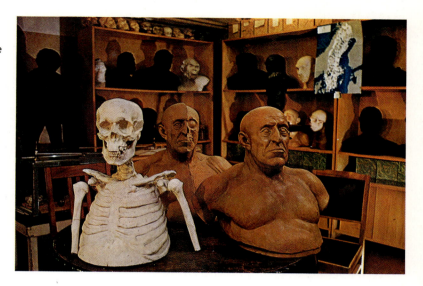

In three stages, a model of Ivan the Terrible takes shape at the Institute of Ethnology in Moscow. A plaster cast taken from the 16th-century ruler's exhumed skeleton provided the basis for the reconstruction. The late Mikhail Gerasimov, Soviet anthropologist and sculptor, created many such busts for museums, working in this basement laboratory.

once asked a Leningrad journalist which tsars he most respected. "Peter the Great," he said, "and Ivan IV."

The controversial Boris Godunov soon came to the throne. Pushkin's play and Musorgsky's opera have made Godunov into a kind of Slavic Macbeth, the murderer of young Prince Dimitry. One of the opening scenes of the play takes place outside Novodevichy Monastery —once far from the city, but today across the river from the Kiev Railway Station. Bulging gold domes and a notched wall resemble a smaller Kremlin. Here Godunov at first coyly refuses the Cap of Monomakh, that fur-trimmed crown of Russia: "He shrinks . . . with lowering brow, like some sly toper at the proffered cup." But Boris Godunov yields and rules as tsar for seven guilty years, until his death. In the opera's final scene, one of the wanderers called Holy Fools sings Godunov's epitaph: "All will be sorrow. . . . O you poor hungry Russian folk, weep—weep!"

Weep they did during the Time of Troubles, a 15-year period of social convulsion. Nobles warred; Poles and Swedes invaded; pretenders rose up, at least three of them claiming to be the murdered Prince Dimitry (the most successful False Dimitry met an explosive end when his ashes were fired from a cannon over Red Square in the direction of Poland). From this disorder came Tsar Michael, first ruler from the family Romanov.

One cloudy day I visited the royal apartment where Tsar Michael brought up his son Alexis. "The furniture here was burned in 1812," apologetically remarked Antuanetta Dmitrievna Melnikova, chief scientific researcher for this Kremlin palace.

With its ornate wall painting freshly restored, the royal apartment probably looks very much as it did when the Romanovs lived here: Windows are small and northern light stingy, walls richly but darkly painted. Surprisingly, ceilings are oppressively low, and rooms seem cramped.

"When I show a general or a deputy these rooms," said Mrs. Melnikova, "he usually remarks, 'I wouldn't want to live here! Give me a good apartment.' Yes, in a way, it *is* dark in here. Of course, there were once fewer buildings nearby."

But only meager light for reading, I thought. No wonder that a prince named Peter, growing up here in the 17th century, yearned and then declared, as Pushkin quotes him: "Nature has ordained that we shall break a window through to Europe." His were the last Romanov children brought up in the isolation of this land-locked Moscow gloom, for Peter the Great warred with Sweden to win his window. He called it St. Petersburg.

When we visited Peter's city, I was surprised to find the old name still in use. We were lodged in the elegant, vintage Astoria Hotel; and the *dezhurnaya*—or key-keeper—on my floor presented me with a quarter-pound brass key bearing a one-headed eagle and Roman letters in high relief: "Hotel Astoria—St. Petersbourg." It was like getting a key to the city from Peter himself.

During this century, of course, the city's name has turned with history's wheel. An anecdote is told by lighthearted Leningraders about a confused, nostalgic old man filling out forms: *Where were you born?* "St. Petersburg." *Where educated?* "Petrograd." *Where do you now live?* "Leningrad." *Where do you want to live?* "St. Petersburg."

But to all but the old, Lenin's name and presence seemed far closer to us during our autumn visit: We were observing the anniversary of the Great October Revolution when Lenin's Bolsheviks overthrew the Kerensky regime here in 1917. Lenin's portrait stood five stories high, facing the reviewing stand at the Winter Palace. Rain glossed the streets, and fog blurred streetlights, for daylight dies early here in autumn. The setting was festive but formal; like other Soviet cities, Leningrad impresses more than it charms. It's a low, wide city, as flat as an ocean horizon, lanced by mast-like spires. Canals and rivers score it. (Intourist tends the records: "100 islands, 66 rivers and canals, 600 bridges.") Buildings, institutional and shipshape, stand at attention like sailors awaiting a captain's inspection. If Leningrad looks like a city designed by a shipwright, it is. The shipwright was 6-foot-8-inch Tsar Peter I, who learned his marine trade on the docks of Holland and England, incognito, in the years 1697 and 1698. It was part of Peter's great effort to catch up from two and a half centuries of Tatar domination. "When Peter the Great was confronted with the more advanced countries of the West, and feverishly went about building factories . . . to supply his army . . . it was a peculiar attempt to jump out of the framework of backwardness." So wrote Joseph Stalin, who faced similar conditions himself.

Peter's design for his island-capital, begun here in 1703, underlies the city's form today. And the statue of Peter—astride a rearing horse, balanced, imperious, chin outthrust—commands the modern city as he did all Russia. The one most famous statue in the U.S.S.R., it was raised here by Catherine the Great; and, in turn, Pushkin commemorated this commemoration with his poem *The Bronze Horseman*. Part of the verse is a love song to the city:

I love thee, masterpiece of Peter . . . graceful and severe. Neva's
Mighty stream, her granite banks, stiff lace of iron fences. . . .
I love thy cruel winters, the frost and moveless air . . .
The girls with faces brighter than roses,
The balls with all their glitter, stir, and chatter . . .
With fizz of foaming goblets and azure flame of punch.

The glitter has changed since Pushkin's day, but goblets and girls still flame bright at holiday parties. Damp and cold from the autumn weather at the military parade, Dean and I were invited to warm up at the apartments of some Novosti journalist colleagues. At Rudy's and Katya's, we feasted on roast duck, home-pickled mushrooms, steaming boiled potatoes—an unlimited board, since Russians rarely drink without eating. For drink we had both variety and volume: cognac, wine, champagne, and vodka (the strong domestic brand Ekstra, which we learned to call brand X).

We faced the same festivity across town, at Valentin's basement apartment. "It's temporary," Valentin apologized, "because it's old and ground-level. Soon we shall be assigned a new place." Still, he and his wife, Irina, had decorated it attractively with posters. And their neighborhood was distinguished. "You noticed the house on the corner?" Irina asked. "That was Dostoevsky's. Yes, and he described it as the home of Raskolnikov in *Crime and Punishment.*"

When we left, I looked for the Dostoevsky house, and later found this passage with Raskolnikov's irritable view: He "looked with hatred at his room . . . a tiny cupboard of a room about six paces in length . . . dusty yellow paper peeling off the walls. . . ." The house is now a museum, though companion buildings are still inhabited by young couples like Valentin and Irina, awaiting new high-rise apartments.

But that's a wonder of this baroque and classical city: History lives here in layers. When former U. S. Ambassador George F. Kennan revisited Leningrad recently, he noticed "a real and significant change"; the city "is rediscovering its own past . . . like a person who has suffered years of amnesia . . . and now begins gradually to recover his memory."

For visitors, memories surge strongly in the suburban town of Pushkin. Once a village of royal palaces (the old name Tsarskoye Selo meant Tsar's Village), the historic buildings were laid waste by the war. Now brigades of superbly trained artisans are repairing, restoring—and rediscovering the elegance of old palaces and their gardens.

"It takes ten years to become a master," a woodworker told me in the Great Hall of Catherine Palace. He was performing cosmetic surgery on a cherub, a wood graft, carving limewood with a copy of an 18th-century tool. Next to him a woman was smoothing the gold leaf with agate. Thanks to the nervousness of Catherine the Great, the artisans can go easy on exteriors: Approaching the palace one sunny day, legend says, the empress mistook the brilliant gold leaf for a fire. Thereafter, Catherine avoided such shocks by having the outdoor gold leaf painted dark.

The roof of the handsome building took a German bomb in 1941; rain, snow, and fire finished the demolition. But with photographs, architectural plans, and even a few fragments of the painted ceiling, the Great Hall is being faithfully reconstructed. Slowly: The neighboring palace in Pavlovsk, built for Catherine's son Paul, needed a quarter century to restore.

The Leningrad area's restoration work may well be the world's most ambitious. "We have 825 historic and architectural monuments in the Leningrad area," explained V. A. Suslov, a scientist at the Hermitage who serves as president of the Voluntary Society for Historic Monument Preservation here. "This life is busy and tense, and a person needs to examine static things—art objects, monuments. Our visitors at the Hermitage—four million a year—are mainly *(Continued on page 78)*

MOSCOW: RED SQUARE

Solemn tread muffled by new snow, a state funeral procession (left)
approaches Red Square. In the 17th century the Russian word for the
square meant "beautiful" as well as "red," and had no political
significance. Above, Soviet citizens wait patiently in line to enter the
Lenin Mausoleum. In a photograph taken shortly after his death in
January 1924, Lenin lies in state; his widow appears just beyond.
Today, guards move visitors steadily through the vault, allowing each
a brief view—but no photographs—of the glass-encased hero.

MAJESTIC METRO

Rush-hour crowds (right) hurry past travelers who have paused to take their bearings in a Moscow Metro subway station. Mosaics and relief carvings decorate the vaulted ceiling of Komsomolskaya Station, named for the Young Communist League; marble covers floors and interior walls and columns. Vandals rarely mar the surfaces; offenders face a stiff fine. Although less than half the size of New York City's rapid transit system, the smooth-running Moscow subway carries more passengers—about five million a day. Escalators carry riders to and from lower-level trains. Lighted from behind, stained-glass panels (left) brighten the central hall of another station.

STUDY, PRACTICE, DISCIPLINE

*Tomorrow's cultural heroes, students of the Moscow Academic Ballet
School demonstrate disciplined grace. Their teacher, Sofya Golov-
kina, danced with the Bolshoi Ballet as a leading ballerina for 27
years; now she directs the school that trains dancers for the Bolshoi
and other companies. In leotards and ballet slippers, young girls go
through exercises at the bar. After eight years of intensive study and
grueling practice, they may rise to stardom in one of the major
Soviet ballet theaters. Introduced by Tsar Alexis in 1673, ballet has
maintained its position as a principal symbol of Russian culture.*

BORIS GODUNOV

Crowned on the Bolshoi Theater stage, Tsar Boris Godunov appears at the cathedral doors during a performance of Modest Musorgsky's opera. Written by the Russian composer in 1869, the opera draws on Pushkin's poetic interpretation of Muscovite history. Elaborate costumes and sets characterize most Bolshoi productions. Home of both the opera and ballet companies, the theater (above) hums with conversation before curtain time. Crystal chandeliers, carved balconies, and the red-draped "Tsar's Box"—still reserved for dignitaries—preserve some of the splendor of imperial Russia for today's audiences.

MOSCOW BY NIGHT

New buildings change the skyline of an old city. Planners began in the 1960's to encourage high-rise construction. Now the view from the top of the Intourist Hotel takes in a row of 25-story skyscrapers along Kalinin Avenue, between two "wedding-cake Gothic" structures built in the 1950's. In a large bakery, a night-shift worker removes rolls from an oven. Not far away at the popular restaurant Slavyansky Bazaar, a newly married couple observe their one-month "anniversary." At right, rocket-sled passengers confirm the universal appeal of dizzying, high-speed rides at Gorky Park, one of the city's most popular "parks of culture and rest."

young people. This generation is more cultured, thanks to education. All cultural enterprises feel the pressure—for books, concerts, museums. Culture purifies a personality!''

Later Gena and I attended the opening night of a new opera about Peter I, written by young Andrei Petrov (who also composed music for the 1975 film *The Blue Bird*). The singer playing the title role spent much of his time on the stage of the Kirov Opera and Ballet Theater stripped to the waist, climbing splintery stairs and hefting anchors too heavy for his men: Peter I, honorary member of the proletariat.

A revolutionary tinge colors other local heroes. Like Pushkin, exiled for a time from this city that he so loved. As long as the tsars ruled, a full 80 years after his death, some of Pushkin's poems were officially banned in Russia—but still circulated in handwritten form, as collectors showed us, for clandestine publication is an old tradition. Pushkin's house remains on display, and the place where he died of dueling wounds. Yet his poems better memorialize the dashing writer: ''I have erected to myself a monument not made with hands.''

And so with Fyodor Dostoevsky, who called St. Petersburg ''the most abstract and contrived city on the entire earthly sphere.'' ''Yet this city was the main hero of his works,'' said Professor Boris Ivanovich Bursov. The gentle, kindly Dostoevsky biographer, in fact, took us to visit the grave of the great novelist, but first we detoured through the city, exploring it as Dostoevsky-land: ''There—the red building—is the Engineer's Castle where he studied five years.'' While he was there, Dostoevsky's father, a retired physician, was murdered by his own serfs. ''And near your hotel is the house where he was arrested in 1849.'' With other intellectuals, Dostoevsky had called for an end to tsarist oppression. The whole group was imprisoned in the Peter and Paul Fortress, tried, convicted, and sentenced to die. On the Semyonovsky parade grounds, the group ''stood on the scaffold and listened to our death-sentences,'' the novelist later recalled. But the tsar commuted the sentence: At age 28 Dostoevsky went into Siberian exile at hard labor; for four years he wore leg irons. Dostoevsky's gloom and pessimism, I felt, had experiential roots.

''Pessimism?'' The gentle Professor Bursov seemed hurt. ''I see Christian optimism! He was the greatest believer of the 19th century and maybe in all history. Of course, his belief also hesitated. He stood for means, not ends. He never proclaimed a cult of suffering. He merely felt people should not *fear* suffering.''

He lies buried at the Alexander Nevsky Monastery. ''Dostoevsky's funeral drew such a crowd here that his widow was barely able to get in,'' said the professor, who knew the setting well. ''All Russian music is buried here.'' We made our way past the graves of Borodin (a guitar on his headstone), Glinka and his sister, Tchaikovsky (a covey of angels), Rimsky-Korsakov beside Musorgsky. Now, among birch trees, we approached the Dostoevsky plot.

''His widow died in Yalta and was buried there in 1918; but she had requested burial beside her husband. So in 1968 the Dostoevsky grandson—a friend of mine—finally brought the widow's remains back here. He asked me to help—well, yes, you could say I was her pallbearer.'' But the professor paused; he looked troubled. ''I have never felt certain we should have done it. Tolstoy wanted to be buried alone and said so. I am

Leningrad's main street, Nevsky Prospekt leads through the commercial heart of the city to the golden-spired Admiralty building in the distance. Colorful street decorations signal the approach of November 7, anniversary of the 1917 Revolution.

not sure Dostoevsky wanted his widow here." He sighed, shaking his head in sad confusion. Mourners, I noticed, had brought flowers for many of these graves. Not Dostoevsky's. But the professor's moral dilemma—his honest, gentle concern with rightness—seemed here the appropriate bouquet.

Leningrad's historic sites have their ironies. The pre-Revolution U. S. Embassy now serves as an official palace for marriages. But much of the city's more recent history endures in the memory of living participants. The 900-day siege of Leningrad in World War II, for example. In September of 1941 the city was surrounded by German troops, and the siege was not lifted until January 1944. A truck driver who supplied the defenders in winter by driving across frozen Lake Ladoga, on the famed Road of Life, recalls the thin ice early in winter: "We drove with the door open, ready to jump. . . . We lost some trucks."

In the Hermitage, which he now directs, Boris Borisovich Piotrovsky worked as a fireman: "I walked through these halls in complete darkness. You recall the Malachite Room where Kerensky's ministers were arrested by the Bolsheviks. . . . The windows were blown out, for the Winter Palace and Hermitage took 14 shells and two bombs. Whenever a bomb landed nearby, the air pressure caused the museum doors to open. Ghostly."

"I was in the hospital with shrapnel in my chest when the blockade began," recalled S. I. Shamray, then a Red Army captain. "My doctor told me, so I left my bed to go fight." Fight he did, winning seven decorations. "It is painful to recall those years—huge cars full of dead soldiers and civilians. Common graves. The city was bombarded all the time. And so little food. I captured a German soldier, a veteran of the French campaign. He told me, 'It is not like France.'"

Olga Iosifovna Rybakova recalls: "My husband had an airplane pass for two persons when he was evacuated with his factory late in 1941. We decided he should take his mother out. I would remain to care for my own mother and our baby daughter. I was young, full of hope, and I worked in civil defense—watching for firebombs on rooftops. Yes, just like the composer Dmitri Shostakovich.

"With winter, all pipes froze and we had no water. And no electricity, nor even candles. We left our flat and moved down into a little basement room—two families. The others were old, so I got food for them, too. And water from the river. It was not easy to keep a baby clean. Once, in the second year, I had been to the milk kitchen for the baby's ration, and a cannonade began. Shells were falling everywhere; I waited in doorways, but I worried about my child. So I returned across a bridge; shells were falling in the river, yet only one hit the bridge.

"Once a friend came from the front, so I put on boots and all my wraps and we went to a concert. And another time, we visited a friend of my mother, a pianist. He and his wife were living in the music theater —they lived in a box. He played for us, even with cold hands.

"My mother fell dreadfully ill, but survived. Our old nurse died, but there were no funerals. We wrapped her in some old coverings. . . .

"Then, on February 7, 1943, after the blockade was partially broken, the first train arrived. We kissed each other in the streets and said, 'Now we'll live.'"

They, like Leningrad, did live. Such courageous endurance, at a cost of a million or more dead, won Leningrad the designation Hero City.

But living memories can still plumb other layers of history. "I was at the Finland Station when Lenin arrived on April 3, 1917," recalled 88-year-old Fyodor Zakharovich Yevseev. (He had not revised his dates, for the old-style calendar of tsarist Russia was then still in use—making all 20th-century dates 13 days askew from the Western calendar.) "Yes, I had read all the revolutionary papers and I had fought in the streets in 1905." He laughed, eyes bright.

"But that evening at Finland Station—we had red flags. Flowers, music! And workers and sailors rushed to meet Lenin. People carried him on their shoulders."

Times were turbulent, and Bolshevik fortunes fluctuated. Soon the man born Vladimir Ilyich Ulyanov, famous by the revolutionary name Lenin, chose another alias, Ivanov, and went into hiding. "Not because he was afraid," explained my friend, Novosti editor A. V. Karpov. "But he was ordered to hide by the Party Central Committee because his life was in danger."

He looked for an apartment house with a rear exit, but he settled for a third-floor walk-up with a drainpipe outside the dining-room window —he could climb down that. It belonged to Margarita Vasilievna Fofanova, an agriculture specialist and trusted revolutionary.

"Lenin asked me to take a hammer downstairs to make a hole in the wooden fence. 'If necessary, I'll escape that way,' he told me." So reported Lenin's landlady when I met her in Leningrad. She was 91, lucid and sturdy, with eyes that were expressive, quick, sometimes suspicious, always Russian.

"He had shaved his beard, and wore a wig even when he walked from his bedroom to the dining room, but his wig was not well fitted, a cheap one he had bought at the barber's. Once when he was out to attend a meeting, the wind blew it off. So next day he brought it to me and said, 'It fell into the mud. Could you please wash it with hot water?'

"One night I returned home and found him singing. He was very happy. The song? Oh, a sort of wedding song: 'We were not married in church, fate married us'—or something like that. He took me by the shoulder and gaily showed me an article he had written. I persuaded him to eat. . . ."

Lenin inspected Fofanova's flat on September 23—as she said, using the old calendar; he stayed there until the night he carried out the Bolshevik Revolution, late on October 24.

"He was always a man of great exactness," his old friend recalled. "Punctual always."

Early even. On the night of October 24, Fofanova was taken by surprise. Charged with his security, she had exacted a promise from Lenin that he would not leave for Bolshevik headquarters in the Smolny Institute until she returned at 11 p.m. "He looked me in the eye and promised. But when I got back, I found the rooms dark. I checked to see whether he had worn his galoshes—he often did not and his shoes were dirty. But this night he had worn his galoshes. Then I saw the note lying on his plate."

Every good Communist can quote Lenin's note to Fofanova: "I have gone to the place where you did not want me to go. —Goodbye."

"He didn't sign it *Ivanov*. He left as Lenin," said Fofanova.

He had written the Central Committee that they must seize power promptly: "History will not forgive revolutionaries for procrastinating when they can be victorious. . . ." History was not given that chance. By next day, Petrograd was Bolshevik, at a cost of less than a dozen lives.

"But many historical paintings are wrong," Fofanova noted. "Although he lost his wig at Smolny Institute, he was still clean-shaven that night. He had shaved with a long razor at my apartment. The night of the revolution he was untidy and asked the photographer not to take his picture. No picture was taken until his beard was longer again. A pity we don't have a picture of him then."

Fofanova rode the train with Lenin, his wife, Nadezhda Krupskaya, and other leaders of the Bolshevik government when, with foreign invasion and civil war, the capital was moved to the less vulnerable location of Moscow.

As both friend and agriculture specialist, Fofanova often visited Lenin in the Kremlin. "His office was very small, a door to the corridor on his right side. . . . A small dining room."

We visited that same Kremlin office one morning. It was scarcely larger than Fofanova's old Petrograd flat. Behind Lenin's desk, a door led to a room with a telephone switchboard. This was his link to the civil war battlefields and to the rest of his country.

In this unimposing office Lenin wrote his decrees, inspired visitors, and took time for the incredible minutiae of creating a Communist nation. This was the command post of a man uninterested in pomp, enormously interested in proletarian power. Here by night and day Lenin spent himself, and at 8:15 p.m. on December 12, 1922, after his last appointment—with Dzerzhinsky, civil war hero and head of the Cheka, or secret police—he left his office for the last time. A few days later a cerebral stroke felled the charismatic leader, removing his hand from active control of the state.

I looked out the window of Lenin's office. It faces old Kremlin buildings and grounds, an interior view two centuries distant from Peter's western window.

LENINGRAD BALLET

Leningrad's Kirov Ballet dances to the first movement of the
Seventh Symphony by Dmitri Shostakovich. Writing the music

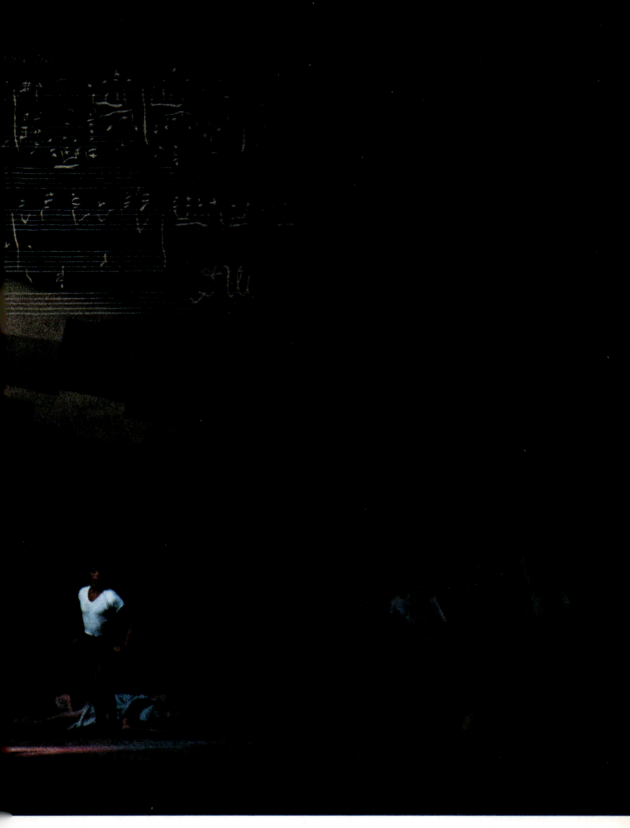

in 1941 during the siege of Leningrad, the composer attempted to portray the desperate struggle against the Germans. A portion of the original score appears above, projected onto the backdrop.

SALUTE TO THE REVOLUTION

Surface-to-air missiles roll through Leningrad's Palace Square during the annual November 7 military parade. The fast-paced review, open only to invited guests—diplomats, journalists, officials, workers' representatives, and their families—salutes the 1917 Bolshevik uprising that changed the course of history. Beyond the Alexander Column, commemorating Russia's defeat of Napoleon in 1812, stands the former headquarters of the General Staff. The celebration continues after dark: Fireworks burst high above a Soviet Navy frigate anchored in the Neva River and decorated with strings of bright bulbs. In the background glow the lights of Peter and Paul Fortress and its slender church spire.

MEMORIES OF DOSTOEVSKY

Portrait of Fyodor Dostoevsky hangs in the small Leningrad house —now a museum—where he spent his last years. Its exhibits recall various periods in the writer's life; leg irons resemble those he wore in a Siberian labor camp. Condemned to death in 1849 as a liberal dissenter, young Dostoevsky received a reprieve at the last moment. Ten years later, after exile and military service, he resumed a career plagued by debt and failing health—and produced such powerful novels as Crime and Punishment *and* The Brothers Karamazov. *Dostoevsky's biographer, Professor Boris Ivanovich Bursov, discusses the novelist's work with author Bart McDowell.*

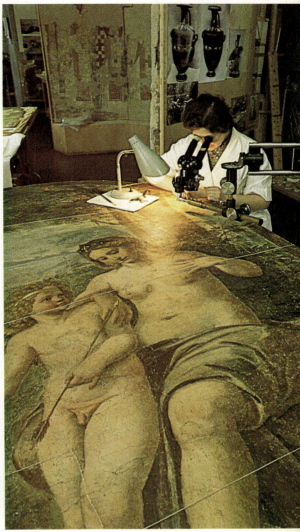

ART OF THE HERMITAGE

Leningrad's imperial palace and three other buildings comprise the State Hermitage Museum. At left, visitors wander through a gallery on the first floor of the Winter Palace. Preparing to restore a deteriorated painting, an expert (above) examines its surface under a microscope. Catherine the Great began the imperial acquisition of art treasures in 1764. After the Revolution, the new government seized the tsar's private collection; subsequent purchases, gifts, archeological finds, and expropriations have swelled the number of art objects in the Hermitage to nearly three million.

MIDSUMMER TWILIGHT

*"White nights" of late June bring out the young people of
Leningrad for a week of festivities. At this northern latitude
the midsummer sun dips only briefly below the horizon,
bathing the sky with a dusky glow. Immortalized by Pushkin's poem The Bronze Horseman, a statue of Peter the
Great overlooks his majestic city. Midnight strollers (right)
share a quiet moment on the Neva River embankment.
Another couple takes to the water, rowing on one of
Leningrad's many canals. Gathering around a guitarist,
a group of students celebrates graduation night.*

A DAY
IN THE COUNTRY

Weary from sightseeing, Soviet tourists ride the train back to Leningrad from neighboring Pushkin. Formerly called Tsarskoye Selo, "Tsar's Village," the town contained several royal summer homes. Meticulous craftsmanship has restored many of the buildings after heavy war damage. In Catherine Palace, named in honor of Peter's wife Catherine I, a master carver finishes a baroque door frame. Two miles away, experts have also restored Pavlovsk Palace —including the Italian Hall (right, above)—designed by Scottish architect Charles Cameron in the late 18th century.

Dozens of splashing fountains embellish the Great Palace and gardens at Petrodvorets, near

Leningrad—built by Peter the Great as a Russian Versailles, and still undergoing restoration.

3

THE RUSSIAN CHARACTER

TO SHOW OUR HOSTS what kind of report we were doing, Dean Conger and I often handed Russians copies of the NATIONAL GEOGRAPHIC, especially the issue of March 1966, with an article on Moscow. As they leafed through the pages, one picture usually stopped them, a photograph Dean had taken of an old woman selling beets in a Moscow market. The reader would smile with surprised recognition—even affection—and often show the picture to a friend. Time and again people used the same words—"Mother Russia!"

You see her picture on the opposite page. For many Russians, she represents a face from the family album. Study her features and expression closely: strong, patient, enduring. Capable, perhaps, of a sturdy benediction or a merciless memory.

She reminds me of Maxim Gorky's grandmother, his *babushka*, as he described her: "She was a fat, round woman with a large head, enormous eyes and a funny, puffy nose.... The way she spoke was warm, cheerful, rhythmical.... she seemed almost to sing her words and this made them take root firmly in my memory, like flowers.... When she smiled, the pupils of her dark cherry-colored eyes opened wide, blazing with a light that was too welcoming for words.... In spite of the many wrinkles...her whole face suddenly became young and radiant again.... Although she had a bad stoop ... she moved with a surprising ease and agility, like a large cat.... After a pinch of snuff she would begin her wonderful stories about good robbers, saints, and all kinds of wild animals and evil spirits.... Her wide-open eyes would stare into mine as if she were pouring strength straight into my heart...."

As in Gorky's day, respect for the old—even obedience to them—endures in the Russian family. The Soviet sociologist Kharchev surveyed some young Leningrad couples and found that 80 percent asked

Vegetable vendor weighs beets at a stall in one of Moscow's produce markets. Although Soviet agricultural families work on collective or state farms, they may sell products they raise on private plots. Such babushkas, *or grandmother figures, as this woman continue to play a key role in Russian family life.*

their parents' consent before marrying. No one knows how many babushkas still contribute their child-tending talents to a three-generation household—a third to half of all Soviet families, one sociologist estimates. For although the Soviet Union claims "the world record for the absolute volume of housing construction" (2,276,000 flats in the year 1973), crowding remains an enormous domestic concern. "The government considers that one of its main tasks is to step up housing construction," writes the social commentator N. Rimashevskaya. Whatever the reasons for doubling up, the babushkas guard old traditions.

Like the swaddling of babies.

I first became conscious of swaddling one winter afternoon in Khabarovsk. I needed to mail some books to friends in Moscow, so I went to the post office where clerks help shippers package their bundles in wooden crates and bundles of cloth. While the clerk wrapped my books, I noticed a young couple a few feet away. Their snugly tied bundle lay on the table without an address label. Startlingly, the bundle made a cooing sound. The young woman tossed back a corner of blanket, and looking out was the face of a warm and apparently happy baby.

Among Western observers, swaddling has elicited a whole literature of speculation. The practice in Russia differs from swaddling in other northern countries in several details: Russians are usually wrapped more thoroughly and for a longer time. From birth many Russian infants are "bandaged," as babushkas put it, with long strips of fabric that hold the legs straight and the arms next to the body. The child is immobile as a log. At mealtime—most Russian mothers breast-feed—the baby is unbandaged and kept warm with a loose shawl. The child also is unswaddled for changing and baths. Custom kept a baby wrapped in this fashion for about nine months in the old days; now, most infants are swaddled for five to six months, Soviet pediatricians estimate.

Swaddling is not encouraged by the pediatricians, but the practice is nonetheless widespread. Scholars who agree with Sigmund Freud that such early experiences strongly influence personality thus think that swaddling is psychologically significant. Dr. Geoffrey Gorer, for example, felt that swaddling caused discomfort and anger, and that "this rage was projected and produced guilt or fear. . . ." From such conjecture swaddling has been related to the expressiveness of Russian eyes (the only feature unrestrained), "the apparent enjoyment of unpleasant emotions," and "the exhilaration of rapid movement."

But Sigmund Freud is not considered a true prophet in the land of Lenin. "It is improper to say that political reasons are responsible for Freud's rejection here," explained Professor Andrei V. Snezhnevsky, a member of the Academy of Medical Sciences and director of the Institute of Psychiatry. "Logic has brought us to genetic studies. A new approach to the study of genetic factors in schizophrenia is examination of the brains of embryos carried by schizophrenic mothers. My opinion is that in the U.S.S.R., psychiatry is more closely integrated with general medicine. Here Pavlov's theories of conditioned reflexes have had a greater influence."

Other psychotherapists in the Soviet Union seem still farther from Freud than Academician Snezhnevsky. V. Y. Tkachenko, in the Crimean resort of Yalta, experiments with music, playing waltzes for cardiac patients to reestablish heart rhythms, and treats insomnia with perfumes (oil of lavender "takes away headaches and heartaches and you'll sleep well"). "Freud?" asks Tkachenko. "Much of Freud is rubbish. I don't recognize his ideas on war or some of his sexual interpretation of dreams. Still, it is necessary to collect information about a patient's childhood. I do it with all patients. A talk of 30 to 40 minutes at first; then 10 treatments over a 20-day period. We teach neurotic patients how to relax with recorded music during 45-minute séances."

Whatever their psychological theories, the application works to keep Russians behaving like Russians. In all the nursery centers and schools I visited, I rarely encountered a badly behaved Russian young-ster. I must agree with Western sociologists who have found them "a good deal less spontaneous and less unruly" than U. S. youngsters. (Spontaneity is not regarded as a virtue. Lenin found it necessary to warn against the "disease" he called "subservience to spontaneity.")

How do Russian parents do it? They are helped, of course, by the attention and discipline emphasized at inexpensive day-care centers and tuition-free schools. Although rent for an apartment may run only eight rubles—$10.60—a month, an office manager's 180-ruble monthly salary (for example) would be insufficient, even counting "social main-tenance" allowances, to support a large family unless the wife also worked, and took her childbirth leave with pay. ("Money is not the only reason," a friend remarked. "My wife has a high education and enjoys working. She would divorce me if I told her she had to stay home.") In any event, in 1974 one third of the preschool children—and one half in the cities and towns—attended a nursery school or a kindergarten.

Mothers lavish affection on youngsters. And though I have seen Russian parents and children in all kinds of stressful situations—shop-ping, traveling on planes and trains, waiting in lines at various clinics and offices, riding the metro and trolleybuses, and doing chores at home—I have only one time seen a mother spank or slap a child. But solicitude and patience do not mean indulgence.

Says a Soviet manual on child-training, "... a child must be *obedient* toward ... adults. ... this is the first thing the child must be taught. ... By becoming accustomed to obey from early childhood, to react to the demands of adults as something compulsory, the child will begin suc-cessfully to fulfill later demands made of him in family and school."

Candlelight enhances the pensive look of a young woman at a party in Leningrad. Foreigners often comment on the expres-siveness of Russian eyes. Some psychiatrists link this trait with swaddling of infants: The children first explore their world only with their eyes.

The visitor gets some historic perspective on Russian family life on a tree-shaded side street in Moscow. Here stands the two-story town house where Leo Tolstoy spent many of his winters. While living here, the bearded genius liked to work with his hands—fetching water in barrels, felling trees, making shoes—in the midst of a large household: a long-suffering wife and their nine surviving children, two or three ser-vants, and a French governess. At the long dining room table, his eldest son sat at the foot and his wife at the head; the strongly opinionated novelist himself sat at mid-table, beside his youngest child. And at the desk in another room, he wrote in his scribbled hand a priceless legacy of literature.

The opening words from his novel *Anna Karenina* haunt this house: "Happy families are all alike; every unhappy family is unhappy in its own way." Here among the master's personal belongings, a visitor real-izes that Tolstoy's own family resembled no other. And, in both size and life-style, Tolstoy's family was unlike Russian families of today.

Sociologists may well wonder how the future will be shaped by the smaller urban Russian family. I once asked a young scholar whether she thought today's only children would grow up more individualistic. Unfortunately, she misunderstood my meaning. To her the word meant "egotistical," and denigrated collectivism—so she took political umbrage at my inquiry.

I have no doubt at all that family life is enormously easier today in the U.S.S.R. than during the first years after World War II when 25 million people were homeless. "Twenty-two people used the same bathroom in our Moscow flat," a young man told me. Recalled another: "When I responded to an advertisement for an apartment, the woman asked whether I was married. I said yes, and she told me, 'Then you can arrange a divorce and marry my niece, who has the apartment in her name. After you are registered here, you divorce my niece and remarry your wife.' "

Since those days, housing construction—11 million flats built during the years 1971 through 1975 alone—has ended such difficulties for great numbers of families. But for all their urbanization, Russians remain curiously close to the earth. City folk still abandon their paved environment for mushroom hunting on a Sunday, or to visit their *dachas* —country places with gardens and fruit trees, often as simple as campsites. "A true dacha must be made of wood," explained a successful dramatist who stays much of the year in a two-story stone house in the country. "Yes, I have a Moscow place, but it smells like a coffin," he said. "If no one lives in a place, the house dies."

As he poured glasses of vodka for his friends, the dramatist mused about his country and countrymen: "Russia . . . an enormous land and very cold! And not that big a population. People can grow lonely in a big country—they feel sad. To be Russian is to suffer. But these are tortures you would not replace by fortune or happiness. . . ."

Hearing such words, Gena grew angry. "I feel insulted as a Russian! All that suffering!" he scoffed. "The man was only drunk." And later he handed me a 19th-century verse by Count Alexey Tolstoy. "This explains the Russian character much better," said Gena:

> If you love—then love without reason:
> If you threaten—don't threaten in play . . .
> If you storm—to full fury give way . . .
> If you punish—let punishment tell . . .
> If you feast—then, be sure you feast well!

Novosti friend Mark Borisovich Krupkin also shook his head over the notion of suffering Russians, and gave me a passage from Dostoevsky: ". . . human response is stronger in the Russian people than in any other people, and is what is best and noblest in them."

I do not quarrel with Dostoevsky; on the contrary, I shall recall forever the largeness of his heart, his compassion—and his suffering.

We sensed more of old Russia's sadness one day at the Kuzminki Cemetery, one of the 18 cemeteries serving Moscow. We had gone there to learn about the funeral trust, but our discussion was interrupted by the music of a three-piece brass band playing a dirge.

Slowly, the funeral party advanced. In the lead were men in dark suits carrying the coffin lid; next came pallbearers with the open coffin,

Clumps of milk mush-rooms yield a generous harvest for a young Siberian near Bratsk. With the arrival of the mush-room season in late summer, many urban families head for the countryside in search of edible varieties—helping satisfy a love for the out-doors and providing delicacies for pickling and eating all year round.

the dead man's face ashen in the sunlight. Behind walked the family, widow and daughter weeping openly, cheeks shining wet with tears. Last came the band, playing now the processional from *Aida.*

"A ceremony was held at the dead man's office," Gena told me. "Now they will have eulogies at graveside." Beside many of the graves I noticed small tables on which relatives had placed food. "An Easter gift," said Gena, "to share with the family. Some also bring grain for the birds —and a fir tree for the New Year."

A bright birch tree had been planted beside almost every plot. I recalled the ancient legend of the birch as the Tree of the World; the shaman climbed it in his ascent to Heaven. I wondered about other old customs, like the *strava,* or funeral banquet.

"We still have something similar," said Gena. "I remember when my father died—it's a custom called *pominki,* a table served after the funeral for relatives and close friends in the home—never in a restaurant. And since most people lack space to invite everyone at once, a second serving is made next day, and perhaps a third day. We always serve a dish of rice with raisins. We serve no sweets, no pastries, no champagne or sweet wines. Only vodka, dry wine, and cognac—yes, of course, served with foods. Everyone wears somber clothes, black neckties. It is a long party. People recall old times, the kindnesses of the dead person. . . . The custom is repeated 40 days after the death, again three months later, and at the first anniversary of the death."

Our procession had led us to an open grave, where a gravedigger in plaid shirt was finishing his work: noisily, with the scrape of spade on sandy earth. He stopped and climbed out, as eulogists spoke in front of the open coffin. Now men brought forward the coffin lid, and the widow cried out, sobbing a farewell. Friends supported her. With a noisy hammer, the wooden lid was nailed down. The mourners flinched with each blow. At last men slowly lowered the coffin into the grave; and as they did, the musicians began to play the refrain of the Soviet national anthem: *Sing to our Motherland, glory undying. . . .*

From birth to death, Russians live in a kind of community involvement. Lyudmila N. Terentieva, assistant director of the Institute of Ethnology of the Academy of Sciences, studied funeral customs among Latvian peasants who historically occupied dispersed settlements, and among whom relationships were so reserved that they attended funerals only by invitation. "Not so with Russians!" she said. "In Russian villages, where communal traditions were more stable, everyone attends."

The same intensely collective spirit pervades every Russian institution. At the theater, an enthusiastic audience claps in rhythmic cadence, all in unison. "Children learn our code early," says a young Moscow woman named Albina. "It's 'all for one and one for all.'" Plans for projects take a great deal of advance conferring; only in Japan have I noticed so much tribal communication.

"Neighbors always know each other," said Terentieva. "Old friends try to meet every year or so. Reunions are important to us."

Every person is his brother's keeper. "Old women are always warning me to wear a hat—that I'll catch cold," a visiting scholar remarked. And once when Dean fell ill, half the hotel staff came to his room with remedies, soup, and clucking concern. As one foreign businessman observed, "This country may be the world's largest encounter group."

The corporate nature of worship is important in the Russian Ortho-dox Church. (Patriarch Pimen estimates 50 million believers.) Attend a crowded service and you hear whole choirs engaged in responses or rich song. And in the Russian Baptist churches, congregations sing their hymns fervently, universally, and with spontaneous harmony—the best group singing I've heard outside of Polynesia.

"When people are united with a certain outlook," remarked Arch-bishop Vladimir of Dmitrov, rector of the theological seminary and academy at Zagorsk, "and when that uniting idea is strong, people must depict their belief in books and architecture and paintings. . . . Our church has to serve not only God but also the people. Our church has al-ways been with the people—in good times and bad. We collaborate with unbelievers and all people of goodwill."

Intourist guides explain everywhere in identical phrases: "Only old people go to church." Those guides, doubtless doubters, have surely not verified their cliché. In most places—Leningrad being the only ex-ception I recall—I found young families and even children among the Orthodox worshipers. Most of the Moscow intellectuals I met attended church regularly, though some said they merely went to hear the music. "I cannot hear church music without tears," a Russian journalist told me. "It is song that speaks to all our hearts."

In fairness, I often met atheists just as dedicated as the churchgoers. After all, Lenin wrote, "We must combat religion—that is the rudi-ment of *all* materialism. . . . The fight against religion must not be confined to abstract ideological preaching. . . ."

"We educate the people in a materialistic, scientific way," said deputy manager Y. I. Shurygin at the Museum of the History of Religion and Atheism in Leningrad. "Today we pay more attention to the *feel-ings* of believers. People may profess religion in times of hardship— grief, sickness, loneliness. People can feel overwhelmed. In our country, people in these situations receive help from public organizations, which take care *not to leave such people alone.*

"Also we are not indifferent to education in the schools: A teacher provides a base of materialistic world outlook. We try to develop new secular customs and rituals. New ceremonies, from a baby's registration to a civil wedding, are widespread in the life of the Soviet people."

Vasily Y. Leshchenko, the scientific secretary of the museum, gave an example of individual effort in a village near Leningrad. "A librarian worked for years with the children of Baptists, proposing books for them to read, interesting them step by step in science. When they fin-ished school, they joined the Komsomol youth organization! Of course, we also have scientific-atheistic programs on television and radio. We do not call them *anti*-religious—we no longer use that term."

Thus belief and zeal sometimes collide with Russian tribal unity.

"Did you like the physician with the thin wife?" a friend asked me after a party one evening. I said that I supposed so. "I didn't like him!" my friend insisted. "Did you like him, Tanya? See: Tanya did not like him either."

"Did you have some reason to dislike him?" I asked.

"Reason? Oh, no," laughed my friend. "We Russians like to like people, and to *dislike* people, and to tell each other about it."

It works something like touch football, and it has gone that way for centuries; sometimes the game turns harsh. Gorky was once asked which side had been the crueler during the civil war, the Reds or the Whites. "Both, equally," he replied, "because there were Russians on both sides." He went on, "I think that just as the English have a special gift for humor so do the Russians have one for cruelty."

One of the bitterest schisms in Russian intellectual history was the longstanding quarrel between the Slavophiles and those of Western orientation. Each time I pass Moscow's Pushkin Square and see the poet's statue, I am reminded of the account of its dedication—at another spot—in June of 1880. A memorable eulogy at that time by Dostoevsky praised Pushkin for portraying and reconciling two essentially Russian types: the wanderer alienated from his own land and the loyal idealist devoted to duty. Thus Pushkin had pointed to a higher Russian mission, as Dostoevsky saw it:

"In fact, what has Peter's reform meant to us? . . . Indeed . . . in a friendly manner, with full love, we admitted into our soul the genius of foreign nations . . . instinctively managing . . . to excuse and reconcile differences. . . . Yes, the Russian's destiny is incontestably all-European and universal. To become a genuine and all-around Russian means, perhaps . . . to become brother of all men. . . . To a genuine Russian, Europe and the destiny of the great Aryan race are as dear as Russia herself. . . . For what else has Russia been doing in her policies, during these two centuries, than serving Europe much more than herself? . . . future Russians . . . will comprehend that to become a genuine Russian means to seek finally to reconcile all European controversies . . . in our all-humanitarian and all-unifying Russian soul. . . ."

In a letter to his wife, Dostoevsky described the reaction to his speech: ". . . the whole hall was in hysterics . . . people in the audience . . . wept, sobbed, embraced each other and swore . . . to love their fellows instead of hating them."

Perhaps because of this old Russian sense of mission and duty, some Russians feel that they have not measured up to their high ideals; so they often express a heavy feeling of guilt. "We are a lazy people," said Gena. "And I am a *very* lazy Russian." He really meant it, although he is one of the hardest-working journalist-interpreters I know.

"Pushkin said we were idle and incurious," one friend complained. "And Catherine the Great called Moscow 'the seat of sloth.' "

So perhaps it's a fear of laziness that causes citizens to avoid the word *fun:* On vacation they go to sanitariums and rest houses (not *resorts*). A sign near volleyball courts reads, "ZONE OF ACTIVE REST."

"We struggle with illusion, not reality," said a young musician—slowly and carefully, for he was in his cups. "And we are exhausted by the struggle. We also grow bored. You have heard of Russian roulette? Idle aristocrats really played it in the 19th century. The nation won when they lost."

If old class resentments linger, so does deference.

A Washington friend of mine who happens to be a prince of old Russia always mentions his royal title on visits to Moscow, and reports he gets all sorts of extra favors. "Pure snobbism," he calls it.

But this respect for rank and status is often balanced by a healthy irreverence. A general may joke about his bemedaled chest by calling it

Gathering in memory of those who died in World War II, decorated veterans celebrate May 9 as Victory Day with a reunion in Red Square.

an "iconostasis"—like the wall of icons in church. Cosmonauts at Star City refer to their luxurious Turkish bath as "our chamber of high humidity." And bureaucracy—as everywhere else—comes in for ribbing: "It's hard to fire an incompetent office worker, but if you can write his fitness report with glowing praise, he is transferred to a better job somewhere else. The danger is that in five years he returns as your boss."

That wariness is characteristic. "How was your trip?" a Moscow woman asked me on my return from far afield. "Surely they didn't trust an American like you! Russians have always been suspicious!"

I once asked a young plainclothes policeman how he would describe the Russian character. I had not requested the interview; but it was May Day, and he had shown up to sit with Dean and me in our Intourist Hotel room. It commanded a view of Red Square and the Lenin Mausoleum, and leaders of the U.S.S.R. would be within artillery range of our window. So the policeman, a clean-cut young man with very cool blue eyes, sat with us—self-consciously, in his dark suit. I noticed a bulge in his pocket, pointed to it, and jokingly said that I wouldn't quarrel with him.

He laughed, said, "No gun!" and produced from his bulging pocket some heavy-rimmed spectacles. His name was Vitaly; he was a native Muscovite, and he and his wife had a four-year-old son. What kind of stories did he read to the boy? "None. That's my wife's job." We sipped North Vietnamese pineapple juice, but Vitaly wholesomely declined a cigarette. And what qualities did he feel were typically Russian?

He pondered. "Kindness," he said. "And we are open people. We say, 'What is in your heart is on your face.' And we are international." Did he like ballet? "No, not all Russians like ballet." Who was his favorite author? Vitaly answered instantly, "The poet Mayakovsky."

I had never read the poetry of this talented revolutionary, but on Vitaly's emphatic recommendation I sampled it: ". . . we . . . shall wash the world like a bursting cloud. . . . Our great god is Speed! Our heart a bellowing drum!" Mayakovsky wrote a poetic biography of Lenin and a famous lyric poem titled "My Soviet Passport." But he was no mere pamphleteer. He called himself "the thirteenth apostle." Once he wrote, "I feel that 'I' am too small for my self. Somebody keeps wanting to break out of me." These were the lines Boris Pasternak first recalled when he learned of Mayakovsky's suicide in 1930. Intellectuals did the poet homage, and Stalin was quoted in *Pravda:* "Indifference to his memory and his works is a crime." Soon minesweepers, trawlers, and tanks took the name Mayakovsky. His statue looms large in Moscow near the metro's Mayakovsky Station; and many people read his works.

And what other writers help explain Russian attitudes? "Perhaps a group of 19th-century poets," suggested Tatyana L. Postremova, scientific secretary of the Lenin Library in Moscow. "Tyutchev, Fet, Nikitin—they wrote with a gentle signature. Russians know how *not* to dramatize a situation." I returned to books, and found these gentle lines by Fyodor Tyutchev:

> Tears of my people, O tears of my people! . . .
> Falling unseen, in secret, unknown,
> Endlessly falling, welling from sorrow,
> Falling like rains of the autumn in darkness,
> Soundless and drear, in the darkness of night.

Four years old: In proud and unmistakable sign language comes the answer to photographer Dean Conger's question on the playground of a nursery school in Murmansk. Russian children regularly play outdoors in temperatures far below zero.

And other writers? The prima ballerina Maya Plisetskaya needed no time to consider: "Read Gogol—by all means Gogol! When he was writing *Dead Souls,* Gogol read the manuscript to Pushkin, who at first laughed and laughed—and then grew thoughtful, and came close to tears. That's Gogol."

On Plisetskaya's advice I reread *Dead Souls* and especially the famous passage about the troika, that wonderful three-horse conveyance. Wrote Gogol: ". . . what Russian does not love to drive fast? Which of us does not at times yearn to give his horses their head, and to let them go, and to cry, 'To the devil with the world!'? At such moments a great force seems to uplift one as on wings; and one flies, and everything else flies, but contrariwise. . . .

"Ah, *troika, troika,* swift as a bird. . . . Only among a hardy race of folk can you have come to birth—only in a land which, though poor and rough, lies spread over half the world. . . . Away like the wind go the horses . . . and a pedestrian, with a cry of astonishment, halts to watch the vehicle as it flies, flies, flies on its way until it becomes lost on the ultimate horizon—a speck amid a cloud of dust!

"And you, Russia of mine—are not you also speeding like a *troika* which nought can overtake? Is not the road smoking beneath your wheels, and the bridges thundering as you cross them, and everything being left in the rear, and the spectators, struck with the portent, halting to wonder whether you be not a thunderbolt launched from heaven? . . . What is the unknown force which lies within your mysterious steeds? Surely the winds themselves must abide in their manes, . . . and hooves which barely touch the earth as they gallop, fly forward on a mission of God? Whither, then, are you speeding, O Russia of mine? Whither? Answer me! But no answer comes—only the weird sound of your collar-bells. Rent into a thousand shreds, the air roars past you, for you are overtaking the whole world, and shall one day force all nations, all empires to stand aside, to give you way!"

I was reminded of Gogol's troika in the Volga River city of Togliatti when I met a young motorcycle buff named Anatoly Mikhailovich Onishchuk. "Yes, I founded a small motor club here," Onishchuk told me. "We organize cross-country races. A friend from Central Asia once told me, 'If you want to test yourself, go to Central Asia on your motorcycle.' So my wife and I did just that. You see, two years ago a friend went on a motorcycle rally to Siberia, but he died in a swimming accident at Lake Baikal. So I repeated that trip as a memorial to him. We visited the plants he visited, saw the same places—10,000 kilometers in 30 days of holiday.

"In Central Asia we drove through desert sandstorms—we had to use our headlights even by day! And what experiences, driving parallel to railroad tracks and trains. We could see the faces of passengers. Smiling. And on the highway in the sun it was 50° centigrade! Hot wind! We passed many cemeteries—they always bury people where they are born. And near the Aral Sea, we saw camels. Many! Through Asia it was all a kind of fairy tale."

A sentimental journey on a sublimated troika . . . or Marx and the art of motorcycle maintenance. Whatever the impression, I sensed young Onishchuk's zest for speed and space—and a zeal to overtake others—throughout his Russian Federated Republic.

PLEASURE TIME

*Favorite Russian pastimes: dancing, eating, drinking, enjoying a
steam bath, or—for the hardy—bobbing in an icy pond or river.
Glimpsed through the café window of a Leningrad hotel (right,
above), members of a wedding party rock and roll to lively music.
A Leningrad couple at home in an apartment (above) share a relaxed
evening of records, vodka, and a light supper. At right, a resident of
Murmansk relishes his daily dip in a swimming hole chopped in the
ice. Near the other end of the temperature scale, a patron of Leningrad's public baths whisks his body with birch branches; glowing
stones in the furnace give off hissing clouds of steam when splashed
with cold water. Following a ritualistic cycle, bathers go from warm
shower to steam room to cold pool—then start over again.*

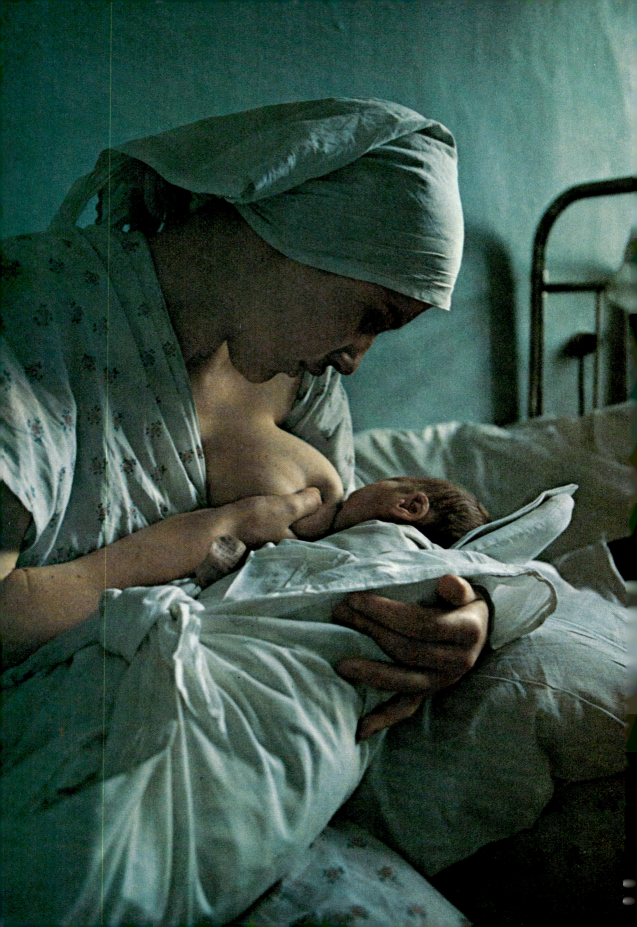

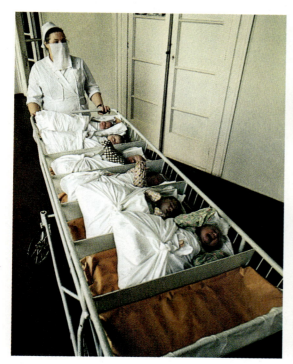

NEW SOVIET CITIZENS

*Cradled in his mother's arms (left), a baby born in a Moscow hospital
starts to nurse. At feeding time a special cart (above) delivers the
infants—wrapped and tagged—to their mothers. Soviet maternity
wards observe strict rules of hygiene and allow no visitors—not even
the fathers. To encourage large families, the government guarantees
liberal leave policies for working women and offers the financial
incentive of child allowances. A warmly bundled baby in Irkutsk
(above, right) closes its eyes against the glare of sun on snow. Even
in mild weather, many infants spend a considerable amount of time
immobilized by swaddling bandages. Mothers who follow this
practice say it protects their offspring and keeps them out of trouble.*

A FINAL TRIBUTE

Funeral procession winds solemnly through a Moscow cemetery, escorting the open coffin of a railway design engineer. Birch trees line the avenue. Marching behind, a three-piece band plays classical and patriotic music chosen by the family. At the grave site, weeping relatives take a last look at the body before attendants nail the lid on the coffin; friends and co-workers gather round to lend sympathy and support. A state funeral trust manages burials and cremations; the family may also arrange for a religious service

if desired. The funeral trust offers a wide choice of markers: artificial flowers, specially-processed ceramic photographs of the deceased, literary or musical motifs, and the red star that tops all military graves as well as many others.

SERVICE TO THE STATE

Mustering in recruits, uniformed army and navy officers line up their groups for farewell ceremonies in Ivanovo. The town salutes her departing servicemen with band music and speeches. After basic training, most draftees complete two years in the army or three in the navy. The Communist Party maintains tight control over the armed forces; many Soviet leaders once served as political

commissars attached to military units. At the Mamayev Hill war
memorial in Volgograd (far left), officer candidates from an aviation
school affirm their allegiance to the state. Stepping forward from the
ranks, each student first reads aloud and then signs the military oath.
The Mamayev memorial marks the crucial World War II Stalingrad
battleground where—in February 1943, after a five-month struggle—
the Soviet Army drove back the invading German forces.

THE CIRCUS

*"As basic to Russia as bread," says author Bart McDowell of
circuses, which draw enthusiastic crowds. Of the Soviet Union's
more than 75 companies, most—like this Moscow troupe—feature
at least one trained bear. Russians regard the circus as an art
form; the government-run School of Circus and Variety Arts trains
aerialists (right). Students enter as young as 11, and receive a
secondary-school education along with instruction in their circus
specialties. Most Soviet troupes confine themselves to one-ring shows
that enable audiences to sit close to the action and watch—and
share—emotions on the faces of the performers.*

EASTER:
A FULL CATHEDRAL

Early on Easter morning, the long midnight service draws to a close in Moscow's Yelokhovsky Cathedral as the priest gives the silver cross to each worshiper to kiss. Only those with passes gain admittance to the crowded cathedral at Easter. Many others wait outside to listen and to pray. Despite official efforts to discourage religious adherence, the Russian Orthodox Church continues to gain new followers —especially among the young.

4

HEARTLAND: THE RUSSIAN FEDERATION

Assembly-line workers add and adjust parts on slowly advancing engine blocks at the Togliatti auto plant, the Soviet Union's largest. Women fill about half the 111,000 jobs here. Other new factories continue to rise throughout the expanse of the Russian Soviet Federated Socialist Republic.

THE RUSSIAN SOVIET FEDERATED SOCIALIST REPUBLIC is a true geographic hyperbole—"the first among equals," as our Novosti colleagues style it—since among the 15 constituent republics of the U.S.S.R., the Russian Federation ranks first in area, population, and riches. "Its shores are washed by 12 seas. Its territory . . . is nearly twice that of the United States. . . . The Republic occupies three fourths of the territory of the Soviet Union. . . ." The R.S.F.S.R., stretching all the way east to the Bering Strait, is simply too big to take in a single look; so in this chapter we shall consider only the old European part—and only those sample spots we were able to see.

Samples, though incomplete, can be valid, for nations may be judged by the shrines they keep. Just as Gettysburg and Yellowstone comment on American values, so Novgorod, Borodino, Ulyanovsk— and a number of other disparate places—say something about the people of the Russian Federated Republic.

Novgorod is a good starting point. As soon as the Nazi armies were driven away in 1944, citizens began to rebuild and restore the city, one of Russia's oldest and most beautiful architectural treasures.

"Everywhere there was rubble and barbed wire—everything was damaged," said G. M. Shtender, chief of restoration. "People were living in many of the churches here—one man even lived in a cemetery vault. As people began to rebuild, some stonemasons looked at one fragile old church—the walls were ready to fall any moment, and mines and shells were everywhere—and the men refused to work in such danger. Then an old woman volunteered. 'I've already had a long life,' she said. 'I'll be the first to work there.' "

I asked to meet that old woman, and soon shook the bony hand of Lubov Mitrofanovna Shulyak. She is both archeologist and architect.

★Moscow

RUSSIAN SOVIET FEDERATED SOCIALIST REPUBLIC

"I'm proud of the year of my birth," she said. "It was 1896. Work makes people feel young.

"Yes, the story is true. It was the Church of St. Nicholas in Lipno. But four or five men later worked with me in the church. And we invited the bomb squad to take away the mines. I spent about a year working there. Only once did I feel any danger—some stones fell, but only grazed my neck. Since I had survived the Leningrad blockade, I was accustomed to risk. Besides, work prevents a thunderstorm of bad mood."

Mrs. Shulyak's face—long, intelligent, open—reminded me of the old Novgorod icons, bright and penetrating with their simplicity. The personalities of Novgorod, whether contemporary citizens or those that stare from frescoed walls, reveal warmth and humanistic respect, quite without self-concern or awe.

And that is the independent spirit of old Novgorod, a prosperous commercial city never destroyed by the Golden Horde and long ruled by a democratic assembly called the *veche*. The river folk here enjoyed a republic similar to that of Venice, developing their arts and defending their freedom. They had royalty but knew how to restrain them. An old Novgorod proverb said, "If the prince is bad, into the mud with him."

Citizens were fortunate to have many mudless princes. One was Alexander Nevsky, who rallied Novgorod to repel a German invasion. Upon the ice of Lake Peipus (or Chudskoye Ozero, as Russians call it) on a thawing April day in 1242, Prince Alexander Nevsky beat the Teutonic Knights. Eventually he became a saint of the Orthodox Church, and he still enjoys secular canonization as a patriot. Admirers of classic cinema recall the 1938 Eisenstein film when German knights splashed from the breaking ice floes in full armor and sank like anchors.

As a mercantile city on the Volkhov River, Novgorod prospered richly for centuries. The city's official name was styled Lord Novgorod the

Extending from the Baltic to the Bering Sea and from the icy Arctic to the rugged border of Mongolia, the R.S.F.S.R. encompasses three fourths of the Soviet Union's land, more than half of its people, and most of its raw materials. This chapter deals with the Russian Federated Republic's European portion, shown in the lighter shade on the map above. (Maps with greater detail appear on the endpapers.)

Great, and its motto served as a challenge: "Who can stand against God and Great Novgorod?" Ivan III answered that question in 1478 by revoking its charter.

Yet today this singular city with its low river profile and glittering domes preserves in stone and pigment the fierce, free spirit of its old greatness. The Cathedral of St. Sophia, inspired by the one at Kiev, dates from 1045, "and we have—let's see—seven churches of the 12th century," remarks architect Shtender, counting carefully. "And, too—even rarer for Russia—we have some buildings of the 13th century, after the Tatars invaded."

Shtender came here from Kiev at age 26, planning to stay only a few weeks. In middle age he remains, still making discoveries like the ones he showed us, 12th-century frescoes in the Church of the Nativity of Our Lady. Near the ceiling, pigeons flew about and the restorers clambered on ladders. "Two years ago we uncovered these faces." They were the "holy doctors" staring—ascetic and large-eyed—from their bright haloes. Some seemed only the ghosts of paintings worked in phantom colors, for they had been eclipsed by plaster for unmeasured time; now they were resurrected with a message sent eight centuries ago.

"We have money enough—700,000 rubles [$927,500] a year," Shtender said. "Our shortage is technicians." We could see why in the restoration workshop of A. P. Grekov; there acres of plaster fragments are being reassembled into their original designs. Under bright lights and in an odor of glue, Grekov, his wife, and three other restorers fit the tiny pieces together.

"One church near the front lines of battle gave us 500 boxes of mosaic fragments," said the restorer, "with 600 to 1,500 pieces in each box. We were able to restore 120 square meters of its mosaics."

His wife beamed. "You get so interested, you're eager to finish the job. You know, nervous people even come here to cure themselves."

In the Novgorod Museum, other kinds of fragments tell stories of early river settlers, for Novgorod boasts a library of birch-bark records dug out of the mud here since 1951. Many are accounts from old land and business transactions, but even bills can speak personally across the generations. An 11th-century girl named Zhirovita asks a man named Stoyan, "How could you take my cross and not send me money nine years ago? If you send me 4½ grivnas, I'd sing to your glory . . . so be so kind as to send them to me." Account past due.

A 14th-century woman writes: "Hello, Felix, this is Fevronya, with tears. My son beat me and sent me out of the house. May I come to your town or will you come to me?"

A peasant to his lord: "Please come to your land . . . we are slowly dying. Our seeds were frozen and we need more seed."

"So far, we have found 542 birch letters," said architect Shtender. "While excavating recently for a simple house, workmen found a birch ledger with wedding records of the 12th or 13th century. So we changed plans and built a new wedding palace there."

That's the sort of romantic flair one might expect of Novgorod. How different history might have been had all Russian lands been gathered by the veche of Great Novgorod.

Instead, settlements farther south shaped old Russia; and the visitor can see some of them yet, very much as they once looked.

Old Russia lived close to the earth. And today Vladimir—for all its textile mills and more than a quarter of a million people—still seems rural. When we saw it one spring day, cherry trees were shedding a blizzard of bloom onto the unhurried River Klyazma. Vladimir's 12th-century churches with helmet-like domes remind the visitor that this was once the repository for the most famous icon of old Russia, the Virgin of Vladimir—now located in Moscow's Tretyakov Gallery.

But beyond the factory smog and hurried commuters, among gentle green hills and fragrant grasses, the neighborhood of Vladimir still seems young. Out from a village called Bogolyubovo ("love of God"), the waters of the River Nerl reflect the Church of the Intercession of the Virgin, a magnificent piece of Russian architecture—famous as a place of holiness and vision. And in surrounding hayfields alive with meadowlarks and buzzing insects, bikers pedal along the paths, and youngsters whoop and swim in froggy ponds. Old rural Russia . . . not always so self-consciously sad.

Yet ancient battles here are still recalled, pagans resisting Christian arms, princes vying for power. As Russian naturalist and journalist Vladimir Soloukhin has written, "The Russian earth here drank in streams of Russian blood—only Russian, no other."

Down the road lies Suzdal, once a destination of religious pilgrims. Suzdal today is designated a "museum city," thanks to the labors of patriarchal Alexey D. Varganov, a theoretically retired architect and antiquarian. Varganov's affection for Suzdal—and his nagging persistence —launched a 30-million-ruble restoration project for the town.

"He's a lovely old man," said the young woman showing us about Suzdal. "We call him the Knight of Suzdal—but today he's confined to bed. He overexerted himself for our 950th anniversary last summer." Perhaps it was fitting that antiquarian Varganov and his antique town were both under repair. His handiwork is awesome. From one bucolic vantage, I scanned the Suzdal skyline: In the middle distance, dogs were chasing magpies, while boys lay sprawled on the grass to watch a dairy herd. Above and behind this active panorama, along the horizon, I counted 43 domes and spires.

We stopped at a newly built inn for a meal of sturgeon and old mead. "Only about 10,000 people live here now," our guide told us. "But tourism is growing. Tsars used to send their divorced wives to live in convents here. Now we have a tourist hotel in an old convent. I don't like it. No, I'm not a believer, but it seems wrong. Tourists cause fuss, and it's now so peaceful."

We found a busier sort of peace at Palekh, long famous as an artisans' village, and off the usual tourist route. Palekh bustles. Some 240 painters work here, 68 of them certified masters. We watched them turn papier-mâché boxes into lacquer-work art objects with stylized figures from legends, songs, and fairy tales.

"Once Palekh artists painted icons—some 10,000 a year. Perhaps a third of our artists still come from old icon-painting families," said Vladimir L. Bornotov, head of the Palekh Museum. "But the Revolution made icons unnecessary. So our artists retrained themselves. They average 160 rubles a month."

Dean photographed artists at work—"art brigades," five to a room. Their materials sounded like enchanted tales of the Russian forest: egg

Heroine of Novgorod, architect Lubov Mitrofanovna Shulyak savors highlights of a long and active life. A survivor of the siege of Leningrad, she alone began to restore the bombed-out Church of St. Nicholas near Novgorod, despite the peril of unexploded shells and weakened walls—inspiring fellow citizens to help rebuild the church and to save other art and architecture of the historic city

yolk for tempera applied with squirrel-hair brushes ("the softest of all") set into duck quills. For dusting, each artist used a duck's wing, and for burnishing gold leaf, the tooth of a wolf. But, we wondered, aren't wolves protected as an endangered species here?

"Well, sometimes we use a dog's tooth," one man explained. "My friend tried a cow's tooth—too soft! And sometimes we get a fox tooth, though it is smaller. And"—he smiled—"we still have hunters." If wolves are protected, so is a traditional art.

Next door to Palekh, the larger city of Ivanovo memorializes another kind of tradition. "Our community is comparatively young," the mayor, L. M. Kruglov, told us. "We celebrated our centennial only in 1971. But Ivanovo had a general strike in 1905, and we organized the first true soviet—the workers' council that originated the government term. In the Bolshevik Revolution, our workers and peasants took power without a shot." The peaceful methods seemed important to the mayor. So did the town's progress, as he and members of his city soviet ticked them off: textile mills that "dress nine million men a year," and deposits in savings banks increasing to 59 million rubles—a 59 percent growth in four years. But in the same period, private automobiles had increased 74 percent—"and the number will double in five years!" lamented T. A. Glibin, the commissioner of health. "We're against that!"

"A third of our investment goes into housing construction," said the mayor. "And we still lack space. Some people are uncomfortable. It's a major problem. And we want not only higher buildings but also *better looking* buildings."

A gas pipeline arrived in Ivanovo in 1962, so coal smoke was now diminishing. As in most larger Soviet cities, Ivanovo's water is heated centrally and piped throughout the town. "Some citizens still complain in peak-use hours that they lack enough hot water," sighed Kruglov. "So we're building more plants for heating."

After World War II, Ivanovo faced a far more serious problem: "Our textile plants at that point employed mostly women," said the mayor, "and the city population was unbalanced. Women were lonely and unhappy. So the Soviet government opened machine shops here to bring men. Now our demographic balance is fine—fifty-fifty."

Not every official in the U.S.S.R. speaks so candidly about problems, nor seems to solve them so well. For that entirely open reason, Mayor Kruglov inspires confidence that Ivanovo's future will match its peaceful past.

Peace is a different concern at the battlefield of Borodino—about 125 kilometers west of Moscow and 12 from the town of Mozhaysk. "It was not a battle. It was a prolonged massacre. . . ," wrote Leo Tolstoy in *War and Peace.*

Hereabouts, rural Russia retains a timeless atmosphere; wagons move on rubber tires drawn by horses with high romanesque collars.

A dignified, middle-aged lieutenant, V. I. Berendeyev, showed us around. The terrain seems undistinguished—lightly rolling lands, not even as steep as a Grant Wood landscape.

"Now this hill is the one where Pierre Bezukhov helped the artillery," said the lieutenant; he confirmed my own impression that the fictitious Pierre is today nearer to reality than Napoleon. What of the lieutenant himself? "In the Great Patriotic War, I was but a staff sergeant —near Leningrad, not here. But I often talk to veterans of this battle. It took the Germans four days to cross this old battlefield. Both armies— Napoleon's and Hitler's—had trouble on the high banks of the river over there. Napoleon's army reached Moscow in a week, but Hitler's tanks needed a week to take Mozhaysk."

As the lieutenant described historic maneuvers, all the wars, the centuries, the enemies made for me a kind of multiple exposure. For as a visitor views this grassy ground ("more forest then, of course, and French guns stood where those birches grow"), he feels the pull of time's great riptides. Should we view these gentle hills as Napoleon and Kutuzov saw them in 1812 when 100,000 of their men fell? Or better look through Tolstoy's eyes when he came in September of 1867? (In a letter to his wife, he complained of bad food, yet felt stimulated—even exhilarated—at the setting.) Should we listen to the battle in the music of Tchaikovsky's overture and Prokofiev's opera, or turn forward the clock and calendar to 1941 when Hitler's legions traversed the same earth, a poetic irony with thousands of prosaic casualties? Borodino lies submerged in art and history.

There is even the recent past. "Just two days ago," said Lieutenant Berendeyev, "a veteran came here and told me a story. 'The doctor made me go to the hospital during the battle,' he said, 'and my temperature went up. I ran away to fight in the battle—and my temperature returned to normal.' "

That battle was in 1941. The one Tolstoy described took a different turn. It "began with a cannonade from several hundreds of guns on both sides. Then, when the whole plain was covered with smoke, on the French side the two divisions . . . advanced. . . . Napoleon could not see what was passing there, especially as the smoke, mingling with the fog, completely hid the whole of that part of the plain. . . .

"Upon . . . misleading reports Napoleon based his instructions, which had mostly been carried out before he made them, or else were never, and could never, be carried out at all. . . .

"Over the whole plain through which Napoleon rode, men and horses, singly and in heaps, were lying in pools of blood. Such a fearful spectacle, so great a mass of killed in so small a space, had never been seen by Napoleon nor any of his generals. The roar of the cannon that had not ceased for ten hours, exhausted the ear and gave a peculiar character to the spectacle (like music accompanying living pictures)."

And here Tolstoy turns to that great one-eyed old Russian general, Kutuzov, who "had learned . . . that one man cannot guide hundreds of thousands of men struggling with death; that the fate of battles is not decided by the orders . . . but by that intangible force called the spirit of the army. . . ."

True for Borodino—any of its battles—or for Stalingrad, where for months during 1942 and 1943 the future of the world balanced on the tip of a bayonet.

That city today has a different name—Volgograd—to honor a river mightier than any man, the Mother Volga. But during World War II, as Stalingrad, the city goaded Hitler to divert men from his southern quest of oil fields, and the name itself inspired Joseph Stalin and the people he led to make any sacrifice to hold it.

"My mother was here just after the battle," Gena told me, as we drove in from the airport late one night. "She was on her way from the south to bury her own mother, near Smolensk. Stalingrad still had a terrible stench—cadavers everywhere."

No wonder. The city had held out as an embattled beachhead, the only Soviet bastion on the west side of the wide Volga here. Cut off and blockaded in late August 1942, Stalingrad defenders fought on alone until November 19, when Zhukov's forces launched a massive surprise counteroffensive, cracked the German line, and encircled the Nazi invaders. In February the Russians even captured the proud Field Marshal Paulus as a prisoner of war, along with 91,000 other invaders. Dead and wounded totaled perhaps two million here. In simple fact, Hitler's army—like Napoleon's at Borodino—never recovered.

In Tolstoy's view, power and the movement of peoples were generated not by the orders of leaders but "by the activity of *all* the men taking part in the event." So it seemed at Stalingrad, as the captured diaries and letters of German soldiers show:

September 1942: "Tremendous casualties from Russian Katyushas—Lucky are the wounded; they . . . return home." *November 30:* "Food of horsemeat without fat." *December 8:* "Food made of rotten potatoes." *December 17:* "The ring of encirclement becomes smaller and smaller." *December 26:* "The first time . . . I've eaten a cat." *January 1, 1943:* "The New Year—the Russians give us no rest. Very low spirits. No trust in God, no belief in people."

The Germans were not alone in their suffering. In the Defense Museum, I copied these words written on the passport of a Dr. Ponomarenko: "I'm writing this with my blood because there is no ink in Stalingrad . . . I'm badly wounded. The blood saturates the bandage. I feel I'm dying. I do not want to die because I'm only 26. . . ."

Name any dominant landmark of this slender strip of a city—one to six miles wide by more than 46 miles long—and a violently heroic story looms behind it: for example, the tractor factory ("yes, we built tanks there—and drove new ones straight into battle down the road"), the grain elevator ("Germans said the defenders were superhuman"), and Mamayev Hill ("each square meter received up to 1,200 fragments of shells or mines—when the first spring came, Mamayev's iron carpet prevented the growing of grass").

But the wide-screen horror of Stalingrad is matched by the poignant, diminutive detail. For example, Luiza Dmitrievna Ozhogina told me her own memories one day: "I was a small child when my mother and I were evacuated from Stalingrad. That was August of 1942. Mother carried one bag—all we could take from our apartment. I had my doll, a heavy one. And as we crossed the Volga we were bombarded by German planes. I don't remember the fear that day. But after the war, I always cried when I saw an airplane.

"When we arrived on the east bank, we asked strangers to take us in. We had no food, so we went to the fields and picked sunflower seeds to eat. I remember the husks on the ground! You must eat many seeds not to feel hungry.

"We walked more, and we were both very tired. I begged Mother to carry my doll, but she said she could not; I must carry it—or throw the doll away. I cried. But the doll was too heavy. I wept, and then threw my doll into the field with sunflowers."

As a war casualty a doll is very small; for one little girl, it was only everything.

Retired Air Force General Leonid Karpovich Chumachenko has larger memories. A hearty man now in his late sixties, he saw the battle from the sky: "I was commander of a regiment of Ilyushin 2's—Germans called them black death. Yes, dive bombers—but we had machine guns, too . . . steel-armored. They were good planes! I was 35 then and a lieutenant colonel.

"While Paulus was advancing, our dive bombers tried to slow him down. Heavy fighting began on July 17. Hot! It was 40° to 45° C. [104° to 113° F.]. Water turned to steam. We flew in our underwear—six raids a day, often with no time for meals. Then on August 23, big German raids began on the city. Panic raids. Earth was hell. Dust rose 300 meters—we couldn't see whose soldiers were below us, so we couldn't use machine guns. Fires everywhere—oil spills on the river caught fire. Smoke 1,300 meters high! One general wrote, 'Land, water, and air were burning. Nothing to breathe upon the earth.' And the soldiers in Stalingrad took an oath: 'There is no land for us across the Volga.'"

General Chumachenko shook his head, eyes narrowed: "Ruins, cadavers. In one day our railroad station changed hands four times."

As he talked, the general became a young man again. There was the time he shot down a German ace (slyly, "but I was an ace myself"), and the time his damaged plane barely made it to the Soviet lines ("oil covered me—so that Russian troops took me prisoner until they could wash me enough to see I was a Soviet pilot!"). With a boy's roguishness, he turned off my tape recorder to quote some resonant oaths of his youth, and he turned into a laughing, exuberant warrior as he described his comrades' dive-bomber exploits: "Sometimes they broke the discipline of flight. Some were so passionate they'd go very low—flying through our own bomb concussions. Yes, as the explosions hurled supplies and bodies of Germans into the air, our planes flew *through* that debris. After the flights our mechanics had to clean blood from the propellers—you could not call them German bodies, only *meat*. As they wiped the props, the mechanics would swear and say, 'Ach! Germans!'

"I had one pilot—Lieutenant Zhinzhikov—his hands and face badly burned, all but his eyes, where he had goggles. He landed and refused to go to the hospital. 'Let me go on another raid!' he said. He went out again with his wounds. That's the Russian soul."

The old general grew thoughtful: "We are all living history. No veteran will say, 'Let's go to war.' Only those a cosmic distance from war will say that. . . . My pleasure now is seeing Volgograd reconstructed. I see happy children here. I fought not in vain."

I agreed with the general that Volgograd is an attractive and friendly city. One summer Saturday evening, I found a bench on the leafy promenade of Lenin Prospekt; there I sat to read and watch the human parade of young Volgograders. Boys generally wore jackets but not neckties; girls carefully wore stockings and heels. Some listened to transistor radios and nibbled at ice cream. As girls passed, boyish heads turned like iron filings near a magnet.

Two young men, both 20, struck up a conversation with me, to ask

Dogfight remembered: Hands become warplanes as retired Air Force General Leonid Chumachenko relives the moment he shot down a German ace during the siege of Stalingrad (now Volgograd) in 1942-43. Then a lieutenant colonel, he flew as many as six missions a day throughout the bitterly fought six-month battle that finally stopped Hitler's eastern advance.

about the latest records of Bob Dylan, David Cassidy, Elton John—then invited me to share a bottle of wine at a riverside pavilion.

We toasted big rivers and rock music. Then Vadim and Igor told me some Russian jokes. All of us tried hard, pooling our vocabularies and riffling my dictionary, and laughed heartily—even if in translation the punch lines suffered beyond all communication.

"Where have you been?" Gena asked when I returned to the hotel. "I've been worried." His concern was genuine; I could have fallen among hooligans, dissidents, or black marketeers, of course. But the protective Gena underestimates his countrymen.

Whatever its other heroic qualities, Volgograd remains, as its name translates, City of the Volga. Aboard a riverboat one afternoon I talked with Ivan Pavlovich Podshivalin, an engineer with the local port authority. For a while, since he was an engineer, we visited in vital statistics: the 72 passenger boats belonging to the Volgograd port, its 2,500 employees, the 15-day round trip to Moscow, Volgograd's rank as a major river port, its number-one position as a tourist attraction. Then nostalgia took over: "My father was a Volga River captain for 40 years," said engineer Podshivalin. "And as a boy I went with Father on his boat every holiday. Always in the captain's cabin. At the end of the first summer, I knew every boat by its whistle. No dams then. The river flow was natural—as it had been for a thousand years, with many shallows and sandbars. And in storms, we tied up to wait it out. In autumn we had dangerous fog. We had many old paddle-wheel boats—but now only three are left.

"But things are better—riverboat engineers retire at 55, and those who stand on the captain's bridge at 60. It's good work. On tankers, because of extra risk, engineers make 300 rubles a month plus 40 percent bonus. Captains make about the same.

"Yes, I miss the river since I became a port engineer. But last summer my 14-year-old daughter Svetlana joined me for her school holidays and we went to Moscow on a riverboat. Cool weather on the river. Good for my heart trouble. Now Svetlana wants *(Continued on page 148)*

Eighteenth-century trilogy in wood—an unadorned bell tower, the many-tiered Church of the Transfiguration, and the Church of the Intercession (at right)—towers above a log pali-

sade on Kizhi, an island in Lake Onega northeast of Leningrad. Wooden pegs and precise
workmanship, not nails, keep these examples of old Russian wood architecture intact.

BATTLEFIELD AT BORODINO

Stage for decisive and bloody fighting in two wars, the countryside near Borodino bestowed hollow victories on both Napoleon and Hitler. Today, visitors stroll the quiet fields while guides with battery-powered megaphones (right, above) point out battle lines and describe tactics. Paintings in a nearby museum depict the Napoleonic battle (right) that inspired Tolstoy's War and Peace and Tchaikovsky's 1812 Overture. Napoleon took Borodino in 1812—at a cost of 55,000 men. The shattered French army never recovered; although it advanced to Moscow a week later, it soon withdrew from the deserted and burning city, and suffered additional catastrophic losses during the retreat to Paris. Hitler's invading regiments followed Napoleon's route 130 years later—and also sustained heavy casualties at Borodino. German troops captured the town and nearby Mozhaysk, but never quite reached the capital.

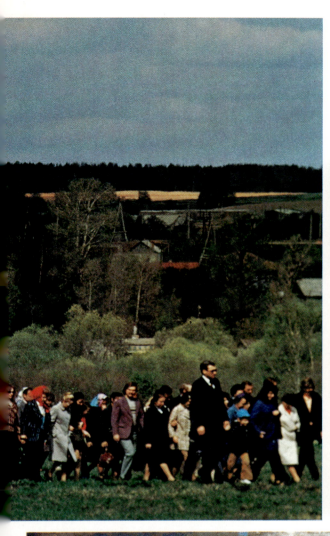

TIMELESS NOVGOROD

Sun-loving farm workers rake hay in a field near the medieval town of Novgorod. Spared from Mongol invasion by its northern location, Novgorod became an important trading center and enjoyed almost uninterrupted development of distinctive artistic and architectural styles. The Church of Our Savior (upper left), built in 1374, marked the flowering of a new trend to decorate a building's exterior while maintaining a clear and simple structure. Restoration after extensive World War II damage has preserved the church's few remaining frescoes; that at far left demonstrates the muted color scheme and bold brush strokes typical of 14th-century artist Theophanes the Greek. G. M. Shtender, chief architect of Novgorod's restoration, describes an exhibit in the town's museum. The golden tabernacle formerly held the consecrated bread and wine in a Novgorod church.

PALEKH'S ART

Fanciful troika—three-horse team and sleigh—races across the lid of a lacquered box, one of 20,000 decorative pieces produced each year in Palekh, northeast of Moscow. For 400 years the village enjoyed widespread fame for its icons, such as those in front of the altar of Palekh's Cathedral of the Holy Cross (right). But after the Revolution, Palekh artists turned to lacquerware, drawing their themes from Russian history and folklore. Today, a five-year school teaches the craft, from shaping papier-mâché boxes on wooden molds to applying the lacquers and bright-hued tempera paints (right, below). About 240 artists now work in Palekh. Their finely detailed creations bring such high prices that most lacquerware goes to the export trade.

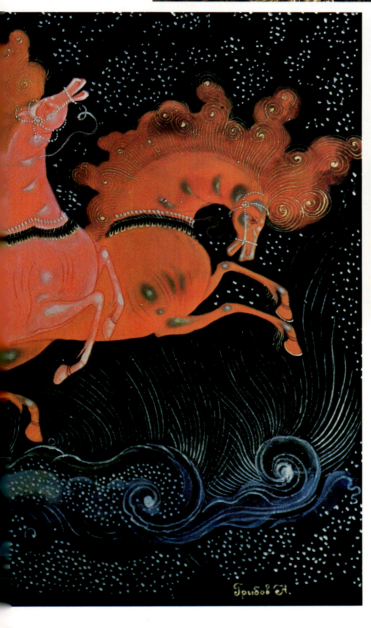

WINDOW "DOILIES"   *Gaily carved window frames of a rural house flank a white-*

barked birch, the national tree of the Russians and a favorite theme in their folk song and verse.

FAMILY GARDENS

Huge collective and state farms command most cultivated land, but millions of Soviet people such as these living near Suzdal still work an acre or so for personal needs. They may sell their produce in the state-run markets, where its quality generally brings a premium price. An estimated 20 to 25 percent of the food consumed in the Soviet Union comes from private plots, which occupy only about 3 percent of the land under cultivation.

STALINGRAD

Massive war memorial to Stalingrad's defenders, Mamayev Hill marks the site of some of the fiercest fighting of the siege. Effigies far larger than life, chiseled from the ruins, symbolize Soviet soldiers who took shelter behind such rubble and vowed to fight to the last man. The Battle of Stalingrad claimed nearly a million lives. Memories of such staggering losses still bring tears to the eyes of visitors as they near the heroic sculpture "Stand to the Death" (above) or the sword-wielding "Motherland." At the Hall of Military Glory (below), brides place their wedding bouquets before an eternal flame.

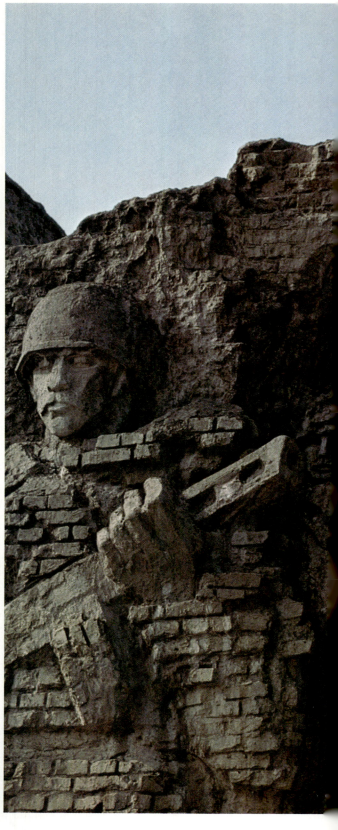

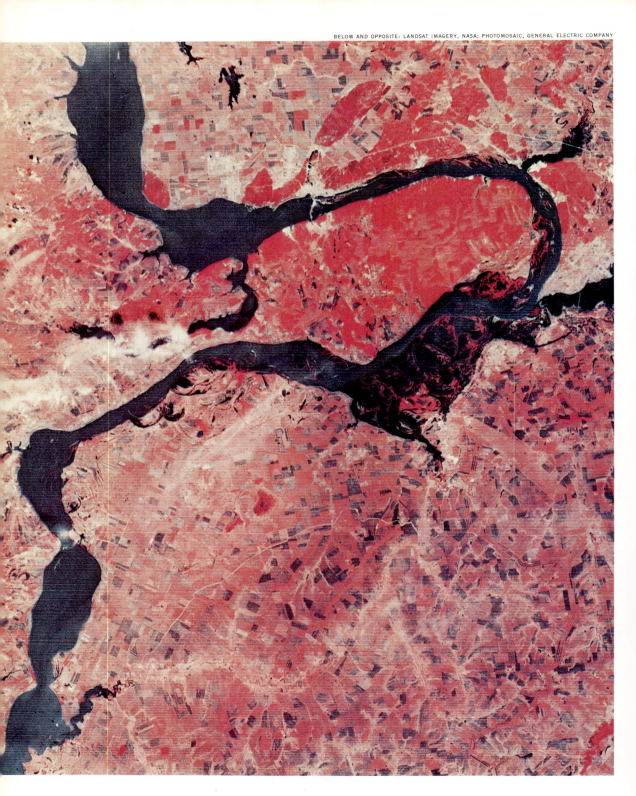

1974 *Both fat and lean of the land show plainly in satellite infrared images recorded a year apart. Healthy vegetation appears pink or red. A 1974 photograph (above) attests to ample rain: a full reservoir, the Volga River whipped white by the Lenin Hydroelectric Power Station near Togliatti,*

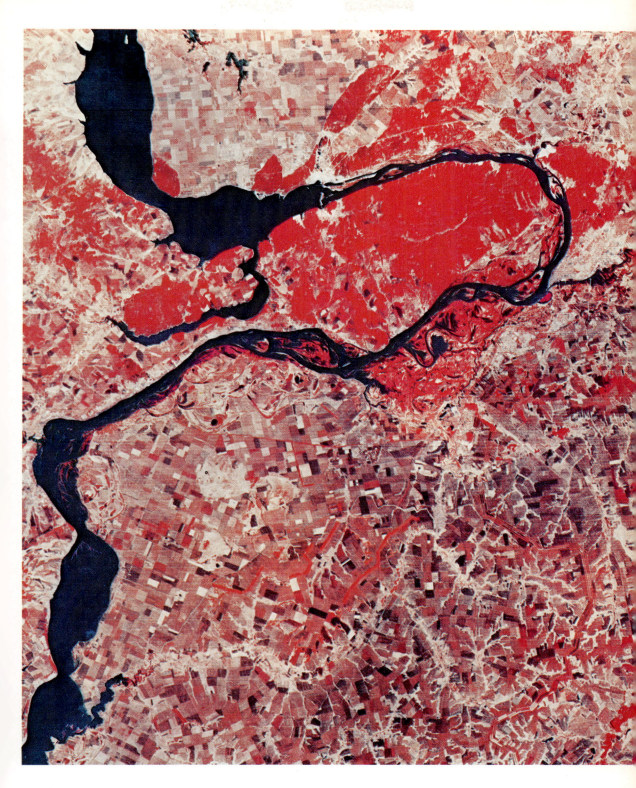

1975 *and fields rich with wheat and barley. But a similar view in 1975 reveals many defoliated areas and a river dramatically shrunken by drought. The diminished grain harvest—resulting in the purchase of American surpluses—ran 28 percent behind that of the previous year.*

DETROIT ON THE VOLGA

Wide shopping malls and a new cinema characterize Togliatti, a Volga River city renamed in 1964 for the longtime leader of Italy's Communist Party. Formerly an agricultural town known as Stavropol, Togliatti owes its recent growth to industry—primarily an 800-million-dollar automotive factory designed and built by Fiat of Italy. Its product: the Zhiguli, a revised version of the Fiat 124. Two inspectors (far right) discuss assembly-line schedules that turn out 660,000 cars a year. Despite a huge domestic demand, much of the plant's production goes for export—at a very competitive price. The least expensive model costs 5,600 rubles ($7,420) in the Soviet Union, but as little as $1,900 outside the country.

LENIN'S HOMETOWN

Even in the rain, visitors queue up daily before a frame house on a quiet, tree-lined street in Ulyanovsk, formerly Simbirsk. Their goal: to tour this boyhood home of Vladimir Ilyich Ulyanov—better known as Lenin, father of the Bolshevik Revolution. Lenin lived here a century ago, in comfortable surroundings befitting his father's respected position as director of public schools. Books fill many of the shelves, and the restored dining room (right, above) includes authentic period

furnishings, some of which belonged to the Ulyanovs. The revolutionary leader's high school also remains, as well as his desk, textbooks, and grade reports—straight A's, with only one exception (in Logic). A tombstone in a nearby park marks the grave of Lenin's father. In 1970, on the centenary of Lenin's birth, his hometown erected a Commemorative Center that contains a hotel, theater, art gallery, museums, a teachers' college, and government offices.

to finish secondary school and go to the Institute of Water Transport Engineers in Gorky—to become a river sailor."

I wondered how many riverboat whistles Svetlana could recognize.

One of the men who issues orders to the Volga and regulates its flow is E. S. Kulgussky, chief engineer of the hydroelectric plant outside Volgograd—the largest in Europe. While his 22 generators are producing 11.5 billion kilowatt-hours of electricity a year, the dam is also serving as a major traffic corridor across the mile-wide Volga, for the nearest bridge is 200 miles away.

"We also offer another sort of bridge—one for fish," explained engineer Kulgussky. "Some 90 percent of the world's sturgeon live in the Caspian Sea, and they swim up the Volga to spawn. Since they can't pass through a turbine, we help them by means of a kind of 'fish elevator.' The fish enter the canals on a swift current; then a system of vertical and horizontal wires in a shaft filled with water lifts the fish into the upper basin. The automatic lock cycles occur every two hours between May and October—that means we can lift 40,000 to 60,000 sturgeon and half a million other fish each season. Perhaps another quarter of a million sturgeon lay their eggs below this dam. And some go upstream in the ship canal locks—we don't know how many.

"This last May, a technician reported to me that he couldn't raise the lift. When we checked it out, nothing was wrong; it was simply full of fish—six layers of heavy sturgeon. *We had 30 to 40 tons of fish!*"

The Volga falls some 900 feet between its source and the Caspian Sea—a distance of about 3,700 kilometers, or 2,300 miles. Its waters are used intensively by a series of seven hydroelectric stations, and an eighth is being constructed. Moscow coordinates the flow of water and power. "When people use their television sets," said Kulgussky, "for, say, a big hockey game or a movie like *Seventeen Moments of Spring,* we must react at once with more power."

Engineer Kulgussky can grow philosophical about the hardworking, south-flowing Mother Volga, and refers to "a natural geographic injustice: In the European part of the U.S.S.R., we need more water moving south; at present large quantities flow north, where there is an excess. We have several projects to divert some northern rivers. This will require enormous investments, which we intend to provide in the not-too-distant future. We could have accomplished this sooner, were we not obliged to allocate considerable sums of money for national defense."

We followed the sturgeon to other points along the Volga. On the west bank, just below the dam at Kuybyshev, we saw the settlement of Morkvashi. In the 19th century this was already a 600-year-old village, and it was here that the artist Ilya Repin found the inspiration in the 1870's to express visually the song of the Volga boatmen in his "Haulers on the Volga," a painting that has been called "the icon of populism." Lenin's personal secretary noted that young revolutionaries "swore vows in the Tretyakov Gallery on seeing such pictures." But at Morkvashi I saw no boatmen—only a uniform wall of high-rise buildings facing the river.

Just upstream stands Togliatti, named for the longtime Italian Communist Party chieftain Palmiro Togliatti. The nationality honored is no coincidence: Italian capitalists of the Fiat company contracted to build the giant automobile plant here. Each year the 111,000 employees of the VAZ enterprise build 660,000 cars trademarked Zhiguli, their design adapted from the classic Fiat 124 of 1966.

Igor Nikolaevich Dzubin, executive engineer, is proud of the way Russians took over from the 800 Italian specialists who started here in 1967. "Production began in August 1970," said Dzubin. "And now we have no foreigners here." But Italian memories remain. Some 40 Italians found wives here and some return for family visits. Our Togliatti hotel —not an Intourist establishment—served the best food I found in the U.S.S.R.; several snack bars in the auto plant still offer lasagna. And on the streets, the youthful population (average age is 28) sports clothing and haircuts with Italian dash.

There is even a touch of the West in auto marketing: Prices of the exported Zhiguli—30 percent of production—will fluctuate with world markets, and cars will be sold in 19 different colors to tempt international tastes. And what is the favorite color among Soviet consumers? "It's hard to say what is a favorite here," Dzubin explained, "because demand is so great. But in the future, we hope to determine preferences."

At a meeting of the International Friendship Club one night, I polled some 30 members present; four already owned automobiles. "And of our 400 teachers," one school administrator told me, "83 own Zhigulis. By 1980 we estimate half the families will have cars. No, employees do not get discounts. Unfair! Loyal workers and dedicated Party activists, of course, deserve cars first."

Already Togliatti has come a long way. "I'm an early settler," one man said. "In 1952, we had only a few thousand people. And when your Henry Ford visited our plant, he rode on our bad streets, and said, 'You don't need test roads.' "

"We are still close to nature," a girl remarked. "Two weeks ago on Belorussia Street I saw two elk."

"But we are mostly proud of our River Volga," said conservationist R. V. Kazakov. "We have a fish hatchery, a biological station, and VAZ has a unique purification system. We are patriots of our town."

Upriver from Togliatti, we stopped at Ulyanovsk, once called Simbirsk. The new name honors the city's most famous son, Vladimir Ilyich Ulyanov, later known as Lenin. Ulyanovsk boasts three houses occupied by the Ulyanov family. The one at 58 Lenin Street tells the most about the Ulyanovs, who lived here during Vladimir's formative years, 8 to 17.

Decor is intellectual-bourgeois: a grand piano in a somewhat stuffy parlor. A visitor can picture the young Vladimir, nicknamed Volodya, with his large red head and intelligent face, practicing Tchaikovsky, Bach, and Beethoven—"his favorite composers," explained museum director Lyudmila S. Rudneva. "The tree stood there at New Year's." No one calls it a Christmas tree today, although the Ulyanovs celebrated a German Christmas and regularly attended church. The father, director of schools of Simbirsk Province, was awarded a title of minor nobility, *dvoryanin*, before his death of a stroke at age 55. We see the father's writing set and mother Ulyanova's sterling silver and samovar.

The Ulyanovs had six children, a nursemaid to care for them, and sufficient leisure for the youngsters to pursue revolutionary ideas. Director Rudneva pointedly displays a book Vladimir's contemporaries

studied in school, *Taras Bulba*, by Gogol. I thumbed the pages to find Gogol's characterization of the hero:

"Bulba was terribly stubborn. His character was one of those which could find its origin only in the harsh and cruel fifteenth century . . . when all Southern, primitive Russia . . . was ravaged . . . by merciless hordes of Mongol plunderers; when man, despoiled of roof and home, grew daring, and settling on smoking ruins, in sight of terrible neighbors and continual danger, inured himself to look them straight in the eyes, forgetting that there was such a thing on earth as fear; when the old-time peaceful spirit of the Slavs was clothed in the flame of combat, and the Cossack brotherhood arose—that embodiment of the broad, rioting sweep of the Russian nature. . . .

"Taras was one of the old, genuine chieftains; he was created body and soul for the turmoil of battle, and was distinguished for the rude sincerity of his character. . . . He loved Cossack simplicity. . . ."

Volodya's room shows the same antique simplicity: a plain bed, yellow wallpaper, a wall map of the world he would one day shake.

Across the street from the city's new Hotel Venets (meaning crown, for its location on high ground), a modern civic center incorporates the two other Ulyanov houses—restored and floodlit—along with birch trees, planted by Soviet leaders to symbolize their homeland. And down Soviet Street stands the former Simbirsk high school where Vladimir studied. The headmaster evaluated the young man this way:

"Very gifted, always neat and industrious, Ulyanov was first in all subjects. . . . Neither in the school, nor outside, has a single instance been observed when he has given cause for dissatisfaction. . . . Religion and discipline were the basis of [his] upbringing. . . . Looking more closely at Ulyanov's character and private life, I have had occasion to note a somewhat excessive tendency towards isolation and reserve. . . ." The headmaster signed his name, Fyodor Kerensky. One day his son Alexander Kerensky would head the provisional revolutionary government of Russia and be overthrown by the gifted, industrious Ulyanov. Thus the fate of two provincial educators and their sons.

What of this tradition of schoolmasters today in Ulyanovsk? We put that question to the family Khmarsky, the father Ivan Dmitrievich an assistant professor in literature, the mother Maria Fyodorovna a teacher of mathematics, and their 20-year-old student son Sergei, born on November 7, like the Revolution, "and so a Bolshevik by birth. Yes, we stand in the local tradition," laughed the professor. "Hobbies? Oh, I paint with watercolors—mostly still lifes—and play piano. I have even played Beethoven's *Appassionata* in concert—it's my favorite, as it was Lenin's. Unfortunately, we sold our piano when we moved here."

The sale was no loss for Sergei, who plays an electric guitar and likes the records of the Beatles and the Belorussian Beat Group.

"I tell my father, 'Don't listen to so much classical music,'" said Sergei, "'it can spoil your taste.'" Father and son now sometimes play guitar duets: Sergei on a six-string guitar and the professor using seven strings. "We play many Gypsy songs—people like them at parties."

Over tasty Russian food in the Khmarsky apartment, we talked at length about boyhoods and books—from Tolstoy to Steinbeck—about swimming in the Volga, and table tennis, and mushroom-picking on holidays when the Khmarskys drive to the country in their automobile, a Zaporozhets. We laughed about Sergei's late hours on weekends. Whatever the other traditions in the pedagogical household, I found no excessive tendency toward isolation and reserve.

We ran into other regional traditions in Ulyanovsk. At the machine tool plant I met an assembly fitter named Vadim Ragimyanovich Fogin. He was a Tatar, from a village in the Tatar Autonomous Soviet Socialist Republic 80 kilometers away.

"Tatar customs? My parents keep the old ways in the village," said Fogin. He was short and sturdy, with dark hair and level green eyes; he spoke in a direct manner, friendly yet unsmiling. "We have a special season at this very time—we call it *Uraza*—and even I remember it." He described the Muslim holy month, ninth of the year, that Arabs call Ramadan, though Fogin did not recognize the term and seemed vague about the religious meaning. "My mother and mother-in-law observe a fast. They only eat before dawn and after sundown. By the lunar calendar Uraza goes on for a month, then after it we have many pies and pastries at a feast—but nothing with alcohol.

"In springtime we have a holiday called *saban tuy*, which means in Tatar 'festival of the plow.' After spring work in the fields, we have a festival with horse races—and lately we have added competitions like wrestling and motorcycling. The young take part and the old watch. We eat *lapsha*—homemade noodles—and roasted sheep. Of course the old lunar calendar is inaccurate—each year it's about 11 days sooner. Once, I believe saban tuy was an autumn holiday.

"Religion? Many of the old Tatars still believe. I know the ceremony, and my children also know it, but I don't go to the mosque regularly. And I do not fast now—I'm a worker!

"The Tatar language is another thing. My son knows a few words, but not my daughter.

"Yes, as a boy I rode horses. I was good. Of course, my son cannot ride a horse at all. In an apartment," Fogin smiled for the first time, "it is hard to keep a horse!"

Scratch a Tatar, find a Russian.

Social homogenization is even more apparent in the newer cities of the Russian Federated Republic. Murmansk, for instance. Though Murmansk perches on the 69th parallel, well above the Arctic Circle, the harbor is warmed by the Gulf Stream, so ships are never icebound here. The all-weather nature of the port was, of course, a reason that the imperial government built a railroad here during World War I and thus founded the town.

A train is still the appropriate way to reach Murmansk from Leningrad in winter, though the trip is less comfortable than travel on the Trans-Siberian Railroad. North of the flat, wide stretch at Lake Ladoga, the roadbed has settled a bit, and the ride is rougher. The diner is neither as fancy nor as neat as those on other Soviet trains. Passengers bound for land's end—sailors and soldiers, fishermen, wives—pass the time with food and drink: "beefsteak," actually hamburger with chopped onions, Hungarian goulash, kefir—sour milk—and enough wine and cognac to turn the diner into a bar car. A few passengers laugh noisily, and others sing.

Outside frosty windows we watch a snowscape by the pale, slanting light of arctic midday. Villages grow smaller and farther apart. The forest loses its grandeur, shrinking into bushy trees. Night settles early and holds on late with a blue, reluctant dawn. Then a pink, cloudy sunrise reveals the Kola Peninsula with its steep, stubby little hills famous for windstorms.

The train moves slowly as we pass a power station, a labor camp, a body of slate-colored water, some unhealthy birch trees with white bark soiled, and then a large sign: "SLAVA RYBAKAM!" GLORY TO FISHERMEN! This is Murmansk, population 368,000, metropolis of Soviet Lapland. (The name itself may be Lapp: from mur meaning sea, and ma meaning land.)

"But we now have very few Lapps," said Simon Tivilov, a Jew transplanted from the Caucasus. "It's a very mixed population. Naturally, we get special incentives to live in the Arctic—at first, a 40 percent increase in salary; after six months, another 10 percent. It's graduated so that within five years we make more than twice our regular salary elsewhere. And we get vacations of 42 days a year; every three years we have a free round-trip rail ticket to any place in the U.S.S.R. Where? The Black Sea is popular, but not Soviet Central Asia—after this, it's too hot!"

Townsfolk seem well adapted. We saw big, new apartment buildings linked together to provide windbreaks. "The Great Chinese Wall," people call them, but the arrangement shields playgrounds from the prevailing southwesterly winds, and every apartment gets sunshine whenever the planet permits. Regardless of weather, the world's northernmost trolley cars run through Murmansk streets. Out from town at the Valley of Comfort, builders are raising a ski jump. Here on the last Sunday of March, the city sponsors a festival with reindeer races, and visitors fill the Hotel 69th Parallel. Meantime, a sign exhorts the populace: "EVERY MURMANSK CITIZEN SHOULD BE A PARTICIPANT OF THE COMPETITION. SKI TRAIL AWAITS YOU."

A different kind of adventure awaited a man named Ivan Stepanovich. We met him, a bald old fellow in bathing trunks, as he broke enough ice off a pond to plop in for a swim. Gena and I yelled to ask him why. "A crazy story," he shouted back, his words visible with steam.

"My wife was out of town four years ago and I was bored. I'd read about people who swam like this. So I tried it. And now I swim here every day. See the posters?" He pointed a dripping, steaming finger to a sign that read: "WALRUS SECTION! *We've forgotten sore throats and bad moods in winter with Swimming Club, our secret of health.*"

Ivan Stepanovich was now treading water: "It's only cold at first!"

Obviously, temperature is not the big hardship here. It's the absence of the sun. "Our polar night lasts about 60 days," said Simon. "And then we have a period that resembles dawn from noon to 1 o'clock. You can turn off the lights, but it's only gray. At the merchant port, sailors have sunlamps in the shower areas. And schoolchildren get regular lamp treatment."

Murmansk is a salty city. Settlers boast about streets named for fishermen and "the only state market in the U.S.S.R. with live sea fish every day." At the fine local theater, director V. A. Minin observed that "we always search for plays to reflect the labor of fishermen."

Trawlers even today drag up bits of Liberty ships sunk in World War II. And some Murmansk residents recall the ocean drama from their own experience. Like S. N. Dmitriev, who was the commissar here in January 1942 when the first convoy of U. S. and British ships arrived: "We organized 150 brigades of workers to unload the ships. And many came to greet the sailors—but the Nazi bombardment was bad.... In April of 1942, we once had 65 air raids in one day, and in June that year the whole town was set afire. Impossible to escape. Some people burned in the streets. Afterward it was hard to find a place to live; people dug out temporary shelters, simple holes."

A port pilot, Captain M. I. Suchkov, remembered that fog was the greatest danger for convoys entering the difficult harbor. "I once brought three American ships in," he recalled. "Fog was terrible, and it was polar night. Everything invisible! But worst of all—we had no compass. German planes had destroyed the ship's gyrocompass, and I found that the magnetic compass was frozen! No radar or sonar then. Well, in the bay, I had to *listen, only listen* for buoys and diaphones. And to guess the distance. We were on the east passage—narrow and difficult near Salni Island and very changeable current. But we made it to port." And were the American sailors scared? The captain's blue eyes sparkled. "Well, they gave a wonderful party afterward!"

The Murmansk waters bring other worries today. The 16,000 workers attached to the fishing fleet and the 5,000 cannery workers (mostly women) depend on productive ocean waters, so Murmansk has a vital environmental concern. At the Polar Research Institute of Marine Fisheries and Oceanography, V. P. Kilezhenko keeps close watch on pollution. "Oil pollutants are brought to our waters by the currents," he said. "One of the reasons is the new oil explorations in the North Sea. Renewal of the Barents Sea is slow; the cycle of self-cleaning is about 15 years." A colleague voiced the fear that new drilling planned by Norway could cause such pollution of the Barents Sea that all fishing there would cease.

Whatever the catch in the Barents Sea, the Murmansk fishing fleet, one of the largest in the U.S.S.R., ranges far from home. We were standing on the docks among swarms of noisy, begging seagulls, when the trawler *Karpaty* returned from waters off Labrador. "How long were you gone?" we shouted. "Five months!" a fisherman answered. "At home it will be like a wedding again!"

We inspected the new East German-built trawler *Wilhelm Pieck* fresh from Georges Bank. "We saw New York television," reported 33-year-old Captain Nikolai M. Krasnikov. He proudly showed his ship to us, from the gleaming bridge to a well-lighted library with much-thumbed novels and bindery-fresh *Collected Works* of Lenin. "And this is our operating room," said the captain. "The surgeon used it on our last trip for an appendectomy—a stewardess from the buffet. We were off Labrador with an 8-knot wind, so we went into the ice—not thick ice, just for shelter to keep us from pitching and rolling.

"Everyone on the ship worried. As soon as the patient went into the recovery room, we announced the success over loudspeakers. In four days the sick woman watched movies with us. She was well by the time we came home."

Statue of Yuri Gagarin, world's first space traveler, stands tall in Zvezdny Gorodok, or Star City. The Moscow suburb serves as training base for all Soviet cosmonauts, and home for military cosmonauts and their families. Onetime dwellers in its high-rise environs: members of the Apollo and Soyuz crews that took part in the first joint American-Soviet space effort.

Homecoming is a theme that runs deep in Russian life. And in one way, home means Moscow. During our travels, even Dean and I came to think of Moscow as something like a place of solace, the spot we could thaw out from the Far North, visit friends and regroup with luxuries not found in the provinces.

One of those Moscow luxuries was simply walking the streets without an official entourage. I never feel that I know a city until I have walked it: digressing from the landmarks, stopping, detouring, watching people and traffic. I like Moscow's ironies—like the address of the Chase Manhattan Bank in the Hotel Metropole at No. 1 Marx Prospekt, and heavy stone facades on Gorky Street that were brought to Russia by Hitler for the monument to his conquest (so guidebooks say).

But the walking visitor in Moscow can make smaller discoveries—on obscure Moskvin Street, for example. It is named for a famous actor, and there is a branch of Konstantin Stanislavsky's Moscow Art Theater. Across the street stands the ornate mansion of the Baron Korsh; here Maxim Gorky set up offices for a magazine now called *Soviet Union*. Down the street a plaque identifies the residence of lyric poet Sergei Yesenin, once married to dancer Isadora Duncan. At the end of the street stands an active church, still humming with hymns as ladies with head scarves bob in and out. I recommend, too, a walk through the Moscow Central Market, where life is as real as the smell of produce, poultry, and fish.

Sometime, in every city, the stroller should lose his way. Not until you throw yourself on a city's mercy can you judge its human response. I first got lost alone in Moscow at 3 o'clock one Easter Sunday morning, returning afoot from midnight service. Subway trains had long since stopped running, so I asked passersby what trolleybus to take and what direction to walk. Every person was helpful. A swarthy Georgian, however, outdid all others: He flagged down a tired, reluctant taxi driver and overpowered him with sheer oratory. "Friend!" he called him. More verbal persuasion. Then "Brother!" The driver surrendered; I rode back to my hotel in a grateful glow. The diverse folk of Moscow easily pass the humanity test.

The intellectual life of Moscow has a spice of adventure. "Could you bring me some records of John Cage's music?" a young composer once asked me. "Next time, if you could find a book on Zen Buddhism — in English or French — and more by Nabokov. . . . And a pair of jeans! I'll measure my waist on this string." So on my trips from the West into Moscow, I brought Western booty — nothing illegal, but things usually unavailable in the U.S.S.R. In exchange, I enjoyed many an evening of good food and talk.

Tanya, for example, restored old icons for the museums; her apartment was a single room with a hot plate and a shared bath, but she had decked the walls with portraits of her friends and festooned the ceiling with serpentine streamers. The place was a festive, delightful dump. But not Igor's. He lived in his parents' shining 14th-floor apartment — a new building near the center of Moscow. Igor was studying music for his debut as a concert pianist; the parlor was large enough for two pianos — an upright and an East German baby grand — under a large chandelier of Czechoslovakian crystal. "Perhaps I should not discuss my father's position with a Western journalist," Igor said.

Then there was the old antique-filled apartment of a retired actress. She was crippled and lived on a pension, but with the help of neighbors, who ran her errands, she still managed to preside over a frugal semi-salon. And so on. Behind the gray facades of its buildings, Moscow has a rich human variety. And endless talk — in every mood, on every kind of subject — as suggested by fragments from dozens of late-evening conversations:

"When I drink two bottles of vodka I am a new man — and that new man wants *his* two bottles."

"My father told me how the Germans shot up barrels of red wine — rivers of wine flowing in the village streets. All the dogs were drunk and could not move."

"The music of Richard Wagner? It's merely Tchaikovsky with Nietzsche added."

"But percussion! We already have too much percussion in this life!"

"That Estonian boy labors in a factory, and the workers in his dormitory want always to drink. He is trying to study at night, so he sleeps here on the couch."

"No, I did not understand *Finnegans Wake* — but that is just as well. I fill it with my own content."

"Bite into this cake — *there!* A sour gooseberry inside the sugar."

"Marc Chagall came to see her and fell to his knees in tribute. And she said, 'I knew his age, so I was afraid he could not get up.' "

"You can always tell Moscow icons from those of Pskov. Moscow's have brighter colors and are more ceremonial, like Moscow itself."

"The thin young man Mitya — his fate was very bad. When he was ten his father hanged himself. Now his mother lives in the other room, sharing the kitchen with his wife, and always there is much tension between them."

"Suffering brings its reward. I believe in the proverb, 'For one beaten person, I'll give you two unbeaten people.' "

"And the bearded young physicist — would he be a good husband?"

"When you speak to the Arctic, you must be polite."

"Perhaps this is not an age of Romanticism. Still, his poem seems so."

"But it's only 2 a.m. And Russian parties never end this way! We must first run out of vodka and then drink all the ladies' perfume!"

ICE-FREE ARCTIC PORT

Home from harvesting the world's oceans, trawlers and larger factory ships tie up at Murmansk. At top, a factory ship off-loads boxed, frozen fish to waiting railroad cars. A clerk oversees port traffic beside a notice addressed to "Comrades, Port Workers!" Murmansk stays ice-free because of the warming Gulf Stream—a vital factor during World War II, when Allied convoys defied German U-boats and bombers and bitter gales to deliver lend-lease goods here.

THE FAR NORTH

Largest city north of the Arctic Circle, Murmansk offers abundant opportunities for both skiing and snowballing. Temperatures rarely dip below 10° F., only slightly colder than Moscow; yet the long, dark arctic winters mean higher salaries, longer vacations, and earlier retirement for its 368,000 citizens. Because the winter darkness can retard normal development, Murmansk schoolchildren receive—along with extra vitamins—a periodic dose of ultraviolet light.

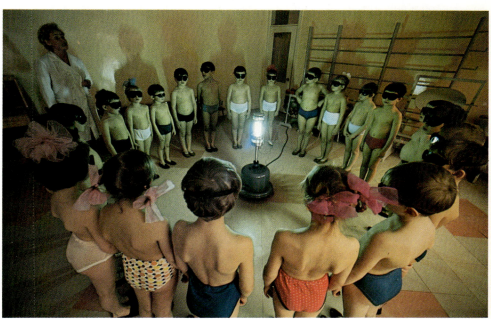

Timeless atmosphere of old Russia survives in quiet rural villages

such as Sverdlovo, on the Volga River about 75 miles north of Moscow.

5

THE WESTERN PERIPHERY

Goose-stepping young-sters advance the flag of the Communist Young Pioneers at a school in the Ukrain-ian port city of Odessa. During opening-day ceremonies, the older pupils welcome the newcomers; then, to the music of a mili-tary band, the chil-dren march to their classrooms and pre-sent their teachers with bouquets.

FOR CENTURIES the royal title was "Tsar . . . of all the Russias." *All the Russias* referred to three: that vast heartland of Muscovy known as Great Russia; the land we call the Ukraine and then known as Little Russia; and finally the flat, westernmost region called Belorussia, or White Russia. South of the Baltic, the western periphery of the U.S.S.R. thus comprises the small constituent republic of Moldavia and two of the old Russias.

"And why are we called White Russians?" rhetorically asked journal-ist Anatoly Ivanovich Stuk. "We have too many explanations. Perhaps our blond coloring." Stuk himself is blue-eyed and pale-haired. "Per-haps because the Golden Horde stopped short of our lands — our border was the white line."

Tatars were among the few conquerors who failed to make Belorus-sia a battlefield. Armies of Poles, Swedes, Lithuanians, Germans of several sorts, and Great Russians have all traversed this flat land. The capital, Minsk, shows the results: Its boxlike buildings stand with recent uniformity. "Undoubtedly," said Stuk, "in the Great Patriotic War, Belorussia suffered the most of all the U.S.S.R. When the Red Army retook Minsk in July 1944, only 40,000 people — of a prewar 237,000 — remained. And the Germans left only a few buildings intact."

Today some 1,189,000 people live in Minsk. They manufacture watches ("3.8 million a year — we raised productivity 24 percent by abolishing the conveyor belt so each girl regulates her own speed"); ceramics; bicycles; and trucks ("sorry, but foreigners cannot visit the truck factory").

The chef at the Hotel Yubileynaya, G. I. Kukareko, counseled us on the gastronomic side of his native land. "Our most important food is the potato — we call it our second bread. We even have Belorussian songs

BELORUSSIAN
S.S.R.

★Moscow

MOLDAVIAN
S.S.R.

UKRAINIAN
S.S.R.

about the potato. And our most inflaming folk dance is called the Bulba, meaning 'potato.'

"Annually, Belorussia produces 4 to 5 percent of the world's total potato crop. Peter the Great introduced the potato to the country. And the Russian Senate in 1765 *decreed* the planting of potatoes." The compulsory crop became a favorite food.

"We have more than a hundred recipes for potatoes in Belorussia—salads, soups, hot dishes, smoked, dried, with sauces. . . ." The chef's talk grew technical ("boil on a moderate fire to heat evenly"), yet it was still the single most animated discussion I heard from a Belorussian.

Perhaps Belorussians are not easy to understand on short acquaintance, but we got help from officials of the Institute of Art, Ethnography and Folklore. "Our language differences appeared between the 13th and 15th centuries," one of our hosts explained, "and certain customs disappeared in Great Russia then—because of the Tatars, of course. But old Slavic customs remained in Belorussia." In their alphabets, for example, the Ukrainians and Belorussians—unlike Great Russians—use a dotted Latin *i*. "Our material culture differs, too. By tradition, our houses have only two windows viewing the street—Great Russians had three. And plows—our muddy soil needed the lighter *palesk* plow pulled by two mules. Russians used a more massive plow.

"The Lithuanians and Poles brought a Roman Catholic influence—in the western part, we have 30 percent Catholics even now. So our national character tended to be formal during a long history. Most people say we are quieter than Russians or Ukrainians—a little more reserved. Why not? To survive, we needed reserve. You'll never find a severe quarrel over money here. The Belorussian is calm, quiet, reasonable."

His colleague discussed folktales. "Ours are vivid and poetic, but do not have long descriptions," he said. "The bear is a popular hero in legends, a friend of man. We even have a bear holiday called *Kamayedi-tsa*—people eat a dish of potatoes and beans and lie on the grass, imitating the movements of a bear."

A green-clad forest ranger supplemented the ethnology. In the Berezina Reserve, 120 kilometers from Minsk, chief forester Y. M. Petrov speculated about the toughest character in the Belorussian forest: "Well, the strongest is the bison—our *zubr*—but the toughest? Probably the bear. In 1974 a forester was attacked by a bear here—his leg injured. It's hard to understand a bear's character. In a minute he can change from kindness to cruelty."

The pine forest itself has seen its share of kindness and cruelty. In the swamps around Lake Domzhereskoye, wartime partisans built camps that served as bases. "In all, some 15 partisan brigades functioned here—they even built a hospital—under the Nazi nose," Stuk told us. He spoke sparely in laconic Belorussian style but with pride, for he himself had served as a partisan in the Great Patriotic War, helping to publish four clandestine newspapers behind German lines. "We used broken type for printing and made our ink with kerosene and chimney soot," he said. "Our editors were often executed. But that was not unusual: *One-fourth* of all Belorussians died in the war."

Belorussia seems haunted by its wartime trauma. At the Khatyn monument, memorializing the burning of that famous village and the massacre of its people, plaques list an inventory of total destruction: 209 towns and 9,200 villages extinguished, 2,200,000 people killed. Since 1945, however, Belorussia has grown in population to 9,400,000.

South of Belorussia and still on the Soviet western periphery spreads the land once called "Little Russia"—smaller certainly than Great Russia, but nevertheless three times as large as Belorussia. If wartime devastation was less concentrated here, it was no less intense, for the Ukraine was repeatedly a battleground and was completely occupied by the invading Germans.

Retired Commissar I. T. Kmeta showed us through the tunnels of a limestone quarry in Odessa, where a party of 35 officers of the secret police fought, literally, in the underground. They even waged one three-day battle with Germans inside this dark, cold labyrinth.

In Kiev, avid Ukrainian soccer fans like my sportsman friend Igor Zaseda still tell about a grim 1942 match organized by the Gestapo during Kiev's occupation. "If you win, you'll come to grief," a Gestapo officer warned the Ukrainians. "But our Kiev team still beat the Germans, 5 to 3, and"—insists Igor—"next day our team was put to death."

Horror stories are commonplace in Ukrainian history. Wrote Taras Shevchenko, the 19th-century national poet:

> *My beautiful country, so rich and resplendent!*
> *Who has not tormented you?*

Resplendent Ukrainian farmland has always been a prize of war. So it was natural that the Russian civil war from 1918 to 1921 should have been especially hard for the Ukraine. Curiously, though I have seen dozens of monuments to World War II throughout the U.S.S.R., I have seen only a few that commemorate events of the civil war.

But schoolmaster I. D. Khmarsky remembers that struggle. "It coincided with my childhood. Once when the White Guard division came, my mother and I hid in the cellar. We lived near the railroad, and I recall seeing troops shoot at each other. I heard bullets whistle through open windows. Later, with other children, I went to gather shells and sabers. Suddenly, we were horrified to see a hillside covered with cadavers! Of course, we ran home. . . .''

Though Professor Khmarsky left the Ukraine in 1934 to attend school in Moscow, he still thinks fondly of his homeland. ''The language differs somewhat,'' he said. ''It's pronounced more softly. We have a rich tradition of songs.'' He laughed shyly. ''And we Ukrainians have a reputation for moving slowly and tardily. A joke is told about two Ukrainians at a train station. The bell rings for the train, and one Ukrainian says, 'Not our call.' It rings again, and he repeats his comment. Then the stationmaster comes out and shoves both Ukrainians onto the train just as it pulls out, and the Ukrainian says, *'That's* the signal for us!' ''

Slow and tardy, perhaps, but the Ukrainian reputation stops short of passive. ''Women of the Ukraine are even known as husband-beaters,'' a Russian ethnologist told me in Moscow.

I questioned Ukrainian friends about it, and they admitted, ''Well, yes. Some wives beat their husbands. But they don't do it systematically!''

Except on stage: In the classic Ukrainian opera *Zaporozhets za Dunayem,* a wife socks her Cossack husband with her own effective fists.

Gena nodded. ''When a man seems timid, afraid to make a decision, we Russians say, 'He has a Ukrainian wife.' ''

In Kiev we encountered a relative rarity for the Soviet Union, a woman taxi driver; we even drove head-on into another Ukrainian legend. ''We have an all-woman taxi stand here,'' a driver told us proudly. ''Fewer accidents than men. Women drink less and are calmer.''

''And our Dynamo soccer team,'' said Igor Zaseda, of Kiev, ''you know why they are champions? The wives of the players say, 'Win or we shall beat you!' ''

I don't believe it. An old lady in Odessa scolded me in church once when I was talking too noisily with some sailors, but she did not seem dangerous. And most of the Ukrainian women I saw were round-faced, open-mannered, and friendly—as a group, friendlier, I think, than the Great Russians.

Perhaps a warmer climate invites the open manner. Odessa, for example, is a city of street life. In summer old people move their chairs outside onto the tree-shaded walks. Children kick soccer balls, mothers push perambulators, vendors peddle private-sector melons and fresh-caught fish, and neighbors with shopping bags lean on doorways to gossip with friends indoors fixing meals. As a visitor moves along the walk, people nod and smile and stare in friendly curiosity.

Pushkin described Odessa's weather: ''There for a long time skies are clear.'' But a demurrer comes from the chief of the 89-man meteorological department for the Black and Azov seas, P. I. Melnik: ''Pushkin preferred autumn—and here autumn is soft. No wind. And because of the dry Siberian air, no rains. I prefer autumn, too. Passions subside. Harvesting is over.

''But the Black Sea region has specific geographic characteristics— surrounded by massive mountains except to the north. A special climate indeed. Northeasterly winds, frequently stormy, are characteristic

On the first day of class a proud first-grader wears a lace collar and cuffs to embellish her Ukrainian schoolgirl uniform.

of the winter weather. Because of these winds the winters can be very cold, with frequent snow squalls and a heavy billowing sea. Summer is the opposite, usually with calm weather conditions and local breezes along the coast. In the periods of transition—spring, early winter—fogs are not rare on the Black Sea. And we can have rainy, windy weather then—sometimes strong northwesterly and northerly winds.

"The Black Sea is extremely rough. Some say it was called *black* for its storms. This is an anxious sea! Waves aren't long, but high. I'm a seaman myself, and know that waves eight meters high in the Atlantic are less dangerous for steamers than four- to six-meter waves in the Black Sea. But also, the bottom of the Black Sea is dead. Lack of oxygen, little marine life. Perhaps that is the reason for its name."

Weather is no problem for Odessa port workers. "Never in all my years here have I seen the port empty because of storms," says 38-year-old dockworker A. P. Tkachuk. "Mechanical reasons, well, that's different. With new equipment here, we have laid off one third of the dockworkers—retrained for other work. Two became lawyers. I myself have taken a course in crane operation." Dean offered Tkachuk an American cigarette. "Oh, a Winston," smiled Tkachuk. "I know them well. After all, Odessa is a port town."

On September 1, like every pupil in the U.S.S.R., we went to school—specifically Odessa's Public School 54. A 12-piece military band provided the music; people, costumes, and banners did the rest. Each uniformed youngster carried a bouquet of flowers for the teacher. Over the doorway a sign exhorted, "STUDY, STUDY, STUDY!"—Lenin's advice about the main task of the young. After a few memorized speeches—one of them blushingly forgotten—serious flag-bearers goose-stepped forward, and the tense first-graders took their places in front. One girl dropped her book satchel and gigglingly retrieved it; another, with hands full, tried to scratch her nose, gave up, and wiggled it like a rabbit. Four accordions (especially popular in the Ukraine) accompanied a chorus of singers: "Today we're Soviet children, tomorrow we're Soviet people." A father in an Aeroflot uniform near me called out, "Natasha!" A very little girl saw him and smiled. The father whispered to me, "She couldn't sleep at all last night. Too excited."

More speeches followed, all punctuated with exclamation points. Finally, as the band played limpingly, as parents and neighbors clapped in cadence, the 1,860 students of School 54 marched inside.

We met the principal in the teachers' lounge, a plump blonde woman with laughing eyes. "Here," she said, "for *you!*" and handed Dean and me flowers enough for a Derby winner. "Disposing of flowers is the problem on the first day!"

We went on a quick tour of the school ("not the worst in Odessa—our Young Communist League is one of the best"), especially the well-equipped English language laboratory. The blackboard was heavily chalked: " 'A FOREING [sic] LANGUAGE IS A WEAPON IN THE LIFE STRUGGLE'—K. MARX." Then we returned to the lounge for a breakfast of Ukrainian peaches, grapes, caviar, and cognac ("of course, the children have to drink milk!"). After toasts ("one cognac does not count!"), I told the principal about little Natasha, too excited to sleep.

"I couldn't sleep either," she laughed. "A pleasant anxiety—after 25 years of teaching. This was also my son's first day as a teacher. He got up today and said, 'Good morning, colleague.' "

Our principal was still smiling, but with a sad fondness.

Most visitors comment on the openly demonstrative nature of Ukrainians. A close soccer game brings big cheers for the Ukrainian home team—not with the abandon of a Brazilian or Mexican stadium throng, but a noisier enthusiasm than I found in Great Russia.

Baptist churches in Moscow and Odessa showed a similar contrast in atmosphere; the Ukrainians seemed to me far less restrained. I attended the Odessa Baptist Church on a hot August Sunday, for the hundredth anniversary of the church's foundation. Official discouragement of religion had not prevented a thousand perspiring worshipers from crowding into the simple church building, nor hundreds of others from standing outdoors, listening to a public address amplifier while seeking the sparse shade of a grape arbor. In spite of the heat, everyone wore formal Sunday best: long-sleeved white blouses for women and kerchiefs for their heads, dark jackets and neckties for men.

We crammed ourselves into balcony pews, looking down upon the baptistry and pulpit decorated with dahlias and asters; framed signs overhead said "GOD IS LOVE" and "WE PROFESS THE CRUCIFIED JESUS CHRIST." If Norman Rockwell had painted in the Soviet Union, these Ukrainians would have been his models: unselfconsciously unfashionable people with open, honest faces and work-hardened hands clasped for prayer. We listened as they sang hymns, harmoniously, fervently; some turned their eyes heavenward, some wept. One youngster idly rolled up a sheet of paper to make a spyglass.

From the pulpit, visiting clergymen and deacons recalled the church's hundred-year history. "This is the centenary year not only for our church," said one minister, "but also in 1875 Brother Lisitov was crucified in a village not far from Odessa. Still, God took care of us. . . ."

We heard how "15 believers met and formed a church when they read from the Gospel, John 3:16, '. . . for whosoever believeth in Him shall not perish but have everlasting life.' Because they did not follow the established Orthodox faith, they were persecuted by the tsarist police as well as by hooligans. During services in one house, the grandson of the owner stood guard, so that he could warn the worshipers. . . . The revolutionary movement of 1905 caused the government to permit religious freedom, so we then had a chance to meet freely. . . ."

We listened to some poems by Odessa Baptists, then closed our eyes for prayers that "in Heaven we shall meet those brothers and sisters who shall have gone ahead of us."

The same Ukrainian strength and goodwill find secular expression in a famous Odessa institution, the Filatov Eye Clinic. There we met the head physician, a kindly woman named Yevdokia Antonovna Budilova. She talked proudly of her home city ("Odessans are enthusiastic, full of fun and the joy of life") and of the 40-year-old Filatov clinic. The medical staff has an impressive record, seeing a quarter of a million patients and performing 10,000 operations a year, a thousand of them corneal transplants: "We always need corneas, and have no eye banks here. But we have the right to get corneas from the dead even without permission of the relatives, provided it will help others. Eyes live seven days after death, you know, so the corneas are flown to us from Moscow and

Immortalized by dozens of streets, parks, and theaters throughout the Ukraine, Taras Shevchenko lies buried near the town of Kanev. A small museum honors the 19th-century poet and Ukrainian patriot, displaying this bust, other sculptures, and several exhibits describing his life and work.

Leningrad. Pilots, though, are superstitious about having anything dead on board the planes. They tell us, 'We brought you *sight*.' They never use the word *eyes*.''

We followed Dr. Budilova through the wards, looking into eyes newly restored to sight, meeting patients awaiting operations.

"You can't imagine the streams of unhappiness coming here. It's hard for healthy people to know how terrible blindness can be. And how slowly people learn to see after a successful operation.

"A 48-year-old woman came here who had been blind since the age of 30. Her little son was only 3 when she lost her sight, and now he was 21—and the young man told me, 'I lost my childhood because my mother couldn't see me.' The woman seemed old, old—with a face of constant sorrow. She dressed in black, indifferent to her appearance.

"We did a corneal transplant, and she had her sight completely restored. 'I want to see my baby!' she said, very emotionally. She was happy and began to dress well and use cosmetics as though to turn back time. 'I want my son to see me as attractive,' she said.

"Well, the son came to see her at last. She heard he was here and rushed downstairs from the third floor to see him. He was coming up and saw her on the stairs. He stopped, unable to speak, and she did not know him. 'Is something wrong?' she asked—and approached him. 'Where is my son?' And still the young man could not speak. But then he gasped—and she recognized the sound. She closed her eyes there on the stairs and felt his face with her fingers. All of us wanted to weep. Even some foreigners who could not understand the words—they sensed the human drama. That's what it means to get your sight.

"Sorrows come here—but more than 86 percent of our patients get to see again." Dr. Budilova's own kind eyes were shining now with tears.

On our last morning in Odessa we were breakfasting in the hotel restaurant when a woman entered, leading a blind boy by the hand. She read the menu to him and arranged his dishes when the meal arrived.

"Filatov Clinic!" the waiter whispered to us. "Out-of-town patient." And a sad moment became hopeful.

At the height of the tourist season, with Black Sea beaches paved in bare bodies from the whole Soviet Union, the Crimean Peninsula does not seem at all like a part of the Ukraine. For many years it was not; but in 1954, to observe the 300th anniversary of a treaty of union between Russia and the Ukraine, the Crimea was formally ceded by the Russian Federated Republic to the Ukrainian Republic.

Only a few years earlier, the Ukraine had received other special considerations. In 1945, Allied leaders agreed to a special concession for both the Ukraine and Belorussia: Each republic would have full sovereign representation in the General Assembly of the soon-to-be-organized United Nations, thus giving the U.S.S.R. three seats. The meeting place for that 1945 Allied conference was the small Livadia Palace, one of several tsarist retreats near the Crimean resort of Yalta.

We visited the palace—now a museum—on a gray day. "Too bad," said curator G. S. Perepelitsa. "The weather was good in February 1945. When we now have winter sunshine, we still call it Roosevelt weather."

The palace perches high above the Black Sea, but the building seems to pull back from its lofty view to look inward toward its own patio: a diffident, passive palace. The architecture thus matches some

Furnishings of the Livadia Palace re-create the setting of the historic Yalta Conference held in February 1945. In this banquet hall Joseph Stalin, Franklin D. Roosevelt, and Winston Churchill met to discuss anticipated problems of postwar Europe. The palace, built in 1911 in the mild Crimea as a retreat for Tsar Nicholas II, became a sanitarium after the Revolution. Now a museum, it commemorates the Big Three meeting.

qualities of the first owner, unlucky Tsar Nicholas II. Some 2,500 workers built this limestone summer retreat during 17 months in 1910-11; the tsar had little chance to use it before he lost his throne and his life.

The palace smelled of fresh plaster and paint, for the museum is still new. "This was a dining room last time I was here," said Dean, "when this palace was a sanitarium." He referred to the formal meeting hall, "a room in Roman style," the curator noted. "Each of the Allied delegations had a palace for its own headquarters. Because of Roosevelt's health, the meetings were held here at his palace, in this hall.

"A filmmaker who was here for the conference told me about the first meeting. At that door, he saw a cigar! Then Churchill entered with his daughter. Next Stalin came in, very slowly . . . and finally Roosevelt in his wheelchair. The atmosphere was very pleasant."

For me, the Yalta atmosphere seemed pleasanter on the pebbled, populated beaches and on the seaside walkway of Lenin Street, regally landscaped with royal palms. Here polyglot vacationers strolled in bikinis and bathing trunks, the men sporting cowboy-style straw hats, older women avoiding sunburn with cotton house dresses.

The resort atmosphere of Yalta has lately been augmented by a Riviera name—the Nice—for a people's nightclub. The floor show featured nine Gypsies, complete with guitars, coin necklaces, wild hair, flashing eyes. One number included a kind of belly dance, which surprised Dean—not for its mild shimmying, but for the fact that such goings-on were now tolerated in this nation of prudish atheists.

For all its seasonal frivolity, Yalta provided one spot with gentle memories; the house of Anton Chekhov. Here the tubercular dramatist came seeking a healthful climate. His nine-room house, next to an old Crimean Tatar cemetery, sits surrounded by trees planted by Chekhov himself—magnolias, loquats, Indian lilac, but no cherry trees, although he wrote *The Cherry Orchard* here.

"He wrote his wife that this view 'baffles all description,' " noted Y. S. Turchik, a Chekhov scholar in attendance at the museum. "But two years later Chekhov wrote, 'I'm sick and tired of this view from my window—and long to see you.' His wife was an actress who had to work in Moscow, and Chekhov often felt himself a prisoner in Yalta. Yet, as a trained medical doctor, he found time here to help some local people.

"Now in Yalta," said Turchik, "we have a 400-patient tuberculosis sanitarium named for Chekhov. It seems proper. He knew the secret of hope and love for mankind."

For mankind and for Russians—but Chekhov, though born on the Sea of Azov near the Ukraine, was not Ukrainian. To approach the atmosphere of the real Ukraine, we needed to go to the land of poet Taras Shevchenko, to the rolling wheat fields and rich truck farms southeast of Kiev. There we watched the last of the season's threshing. Plows and disks were now peeling up gold wheat stubble to expose the black, rich, coveted Ukrainian topsoil. This is the breadbasket of the Soviet Union, producing wheat, corn, and rye—along with peas, sunflower seeds, sugar beets, and beef cattle. Even political symbols reveal the farm touch: Here the Communist Party hammer-crossing sickle shows a blade serrated in Ukrainian farm style. Each time Dean stopped to take pictures, farm workers grinned a greeting. At one stop, sunburned women on a flatbed truck roared with coy laughter and cheerfully chucked fresh-picked cucumbers our way as a goodwill gift.

At New Tsibly we stopped at a model 2,700-hectare collective farm and met the chairman, A. A. Lepyakha. "Last year was a profitable year—we grossed 2,400,000 rubles and made a net profit of 726,000 rubles," he told us. "But this year—dry! It won't be good."

We talked about the earnings of his 650 workers ("technicians average 4 to 7 rubles a day") and their hours of work ("10 hours a day in summer"). Judging from the people I saw in other fields, I would guess those hours longer than most. Even in August, few farm hands seemed to work on collective lands after 5 p.m. I asked Lepyakha about these remarkably short work days; he shrugged. "Of course, our people also have private garden plots—an area of .32 hectare per family. Families may sell their produce in the public market." This touch of private enterprise seems to serve collective farmers well; some reportedly have made 2,000 rubles a year from such sales.

"Come, I'll show you at our savings bank," said the chairman. He forthwith told the savings-bank teller to show us her records.

She refused. "Illegal," she said.

"Nonsense!" said the chairman—and a bit more. The teller then complied, showing us several of the 1,261 accounts—but she kept the names carefully covered. One indicated a balance of 2,202.86 rubles, another 5,131.92—and savings here draw interest of 2 to 3 percent, depending on the terms of deposit.

I had no way of knowing whether this argument over legality was genuine; in the land of Stanislavsky, talents are abundant. But my own strong capitalistic impression is that it was real.

Certainly the people we met were real—people like Mikhail Sergeevich Boyko, age 49, collective-farm member. He showed us two pigs fattening in pens behind his 7,000-ruble house. "I sell hogs in winter, at Christmas, usually. And I average 200 rubles apiece for the hogs—of course, the price is regulated." Near the pigs a motorcycle was

Triple-decked side-wheeler leisurely ferries travelers up and down the Dnieper River, the Ukraine's main waterway. A dam built in 1933 to submerge a stretch of rapids opened the river to regular cargo and passenger service.

parked. "Yes, it's ours," said our host. "But we don't use it in winter."

Boyko invited us inside to see his wife's handiwork. Her *rushnik,* typical Ukrainian embroidery, bloomed like a garden throughout the house. Embroidery curtained doorways and festooned picture frames; doilies decorated tables, chairs, and the television. Flowerpots wore embroidered skirts. "My wife stays busy in winter," boasted Boyko.

The whole Boyko family stays busy year around, in fact. I asked our host his schedule for the day before: up at 5 a.m. to feed his pigs, chickens, and ducks; a breakfast of soup, potatoes, tea, milk, eggs, and meat ("we are farmers—it depends on how you feel, but fat meat is popular"). Generally his wife cooks, "but if she's busy, I do—after all, she works in the fields and must leave at 8; and sometimes she works until 8 p.m. at harvest time. Women carry their lunch into the fields, though combine-operators get free food brought to them. I, too, worked in the fields—for 26 years, starting at age 13. Now I am a fireman.

"In the evening, our cows must be milked. We have two cows and one calf. We sell milk to the collective farm. No, I never milk—that is *women's work!*

"For supper last night we had hot Ukrainian borscht, cucumbers, tomatoes, milk, and pastries. Then, usually, we watch television before bedtime, but last night we were sleepy."

Back at headquarters, I checked the collective-farm bulletin board: cartoons against excessive eating and drinking and the wasteful spilling of grain out of wagons. I asked the chairman the farm's official name. "Oh, it's named for Shevchenko," he answered. "You know his poetry?"

I did. Taras Shevchenko's statue stands less than a dozen blocks from my office in Washington, a statue raised by Americans of Ukrainian descent still nostalgic for the old country. He is loved no less in the land of his birth. Shevchenko lived between 1814 and 1861, and by virtue of pure genius he rose from serfdom to high acclaim, first as a painter, then as a poet fiercely dedicated to freedom for his Ukraine.

"It's sometimes hard to tell folklore from his poetry," said V. S. Borodin, of the Shevchenko Institute of Literature in Kiev. "You should see his grave at Kanev."

We took Professor Borodin's advice, traveling down the wide Dnieper to Kanev by hydrofoil. Time and again along the way we passed paddle-wheel steamboats reminiscent of the old romantic Mississippi. One paddle-wheeler bristled with television antennas. The riverboats recalled the words of Shevchenko himself:

Skimming above the Dnieper's surface, the Meteor-6 speeds between river towns at 45 mph. Ski-like hydrofoils lift the hull free of the water. The largest Soviet hydrofoil vessels can carry 300 passengers.

Oh, great Fulton and great Watt,
Your child grows not by the day but by the hour
And will soon devour whips, thrones, and crowns . . .
What encyclopedists started in France
Will be completed on our planet earth by your colossal
    and genial child.

Those words, written in 1857, today enscribe Shevchenko's gravestone. He is buried atop a windswept bank with the broad Dnieper below, and on the horizon, fields of Ukrainian grain.

Between the southern Ukraine and Romania, of which it was once a part, lies the Republic of Moldavia, only 33,700 square kilometers. Most of this area—350 kilometers long by 150 kilometers at its greatest width—was formerly called Bessarabia, a much exchanged land of scenic green hills.

The four million Moldavians are generally dark-haired people who raise grapes, make wine, cure tobacco, and write poetry in the only Romance language native to territory of the Soviet Union.

What are Moldavians like? "On a scale of temperament," one friend had remarked in the Ukraine, "Moldavians would rank somewhere between Italians and Gypsies." I strongly disagree. Moldavians, like their Romanian cousins, look like Latins, but to me they have a kind of rural restraint, the patience of gardeners and shepherds. Once we passed a minor auto collision on a side street of the capital, Kishinev. A truck had crunched into a taxi, and the drivers—along with witnesses and passersby—were debating the fault with broad gestures. Everyone showed animation, but the decibel count was not even half Italian.

Kishinev itself shows the same gardener's calm. Parks and plants flourish everywhere, and native Moldavian taste gives the city a special flair. Its name—"springs of water" in Moldavian—is mentioned in documents of the 15th century, but wars with Tatars and Turks erased early landmarks. In 1812 Bessarabia became Russian, and Pushkin, exiled here a few years later, wrote a bitter poem about the city with language too strong for family libraries. In 1944, Axis armies retreated through Kishinev, and three fourths of the buildings were blown up.

"Now we are trying to preserve the national character of those buildings left in the center of the city," said S. B. Lebedev, chief architect and city planner. "Our soil here is valuable—every piece can be used for vineyards or orchards. So we try to conserve it in our Botanic District, where green strips enter the city like spokes of a wheel. We also have three green belts around Kishinev. We have even created microclimates with artificial ponds, like the 100-hectare Gidigich Lake."

Exploring the city, I kept track of the statues. The largest one I found was of Kotovsky, a Moldavian civil war hero. Next largest belonged to King Stephen the Great, who fought 46 wars "and was mostly the winner," as Moldavian poet Viktor Gavrilovich Keleuka put it when he showed me around the Alley of Classics in the park. (The king, I noticed, had collected five bouquets on his pedestal.) Third largest was Lenin's statue, carved in red stone. Pushkin trailed way down the list, with merely a bust; even so, citizens of the town he had so poetically cursed had recently brought him two spontaneous bouquets.

"Poets are respected here," explained Keleuka, who is not only a leading poet himself but also editor of the weekly *Kultura*. "When a people is small and proud, it can create a great culture. For 300 years we fought the Turks, who took away the most beautiful things. We had to defend our beauty. For ages we had no written language, so each poet added to our oral literature. Our ballad, the *Mioritsa*—it has 118 versions! Each song starts with the words, 'Green leaf of oak' or 'of grape.' The leaf is symbolic. We were preserved only in the forest. Only when trees are leafed out can men find a hiding place. An oak leaf stands for courage, a grape leaf for beauty.

"Loneliness is a strong theme in our songs and poetry. I was once with a friend in the hills of northern Moldavia. All was silence, but my friend asked, 'What do you hear?' 'Nothing,' I said. 'I hear songs,' he said. 'Here songs are growing.'

"Almost all our writers were peasants, and so they came to poetry with the wisdom of country life. We worked as children. When my father and brother went off to war, I was a man at 13. We poets have the hands of workers."

We followed Viktor's advice and went to the country where songs were growing. Instead of silence, we found the most densely populated constituent republic in the U.S.S.R.—109 people per square kilometer. We also found tobacco plants (40 percent of Soviet tobacco comes from Moldavia), apples, plums, and the grapes that earn half of all Moldavia's income. We arrived, in fact, during the grape harvest at the 1,000-hectare Kishinev State Farm School of Winery and Grape Growing.

"It's Moldavian autumn," an attractive blonde woman said as she filled crates with bunches of fine white grapes. "Sunny, dry—good for harvest. Pensioners are working here along with students. Everyone." Her name was Valentina Dmitrievna Zubchenko, and she had recently served as a Deputy of the Supreme Soviet of the U.S.S.R. She left her crates to show me around.

Munching grapes, I asked about the deputy's duties as a member of the Supreme Soviet.

"Well, I am retired now; I served from 1970 to 1974. My duties required one full working day each month—for mail and visitors and such. For the two sessions each year, I had to go to Moscow, and each session lasts two or three days. One session is entirely a discussion of current events and problems. The other is a discussion of the budget for the coming year." The Supreme Soviet did not demand so much time that Deputy Zubchenko lost her pastoral perspective.

Aiming a powerful kick, a member of Kiev's champion Dynamo soccer team drives toward a goal in his home stadium. Soviet fans follow soccer as avidly as Americans do their own version of football. A title match may draw more than 100,000 spectators.

The same rural viewpoint pervades Moldavian folklore, where the lamb is a favorite hero. One recurring theme is a shepherd named Fet Frumos; a lamb warns Fet to expect death, and the shepherd accepts his fate, asking the lamb to tell his family to bury him in the sheep shed. Modern readers can speculate at length about the historic origins and psychology of the sad and passive Fet Frumos. But today he is memorialized, not in a sheep shed, but as a brand name for cigarettes.

Moldavian folklore includes no bears, but the Slavic influence has been strong in the culture. Some 30 percent of Moldavian-Romanian words are Slavic (borrowings from Russian, Bulgarian, and Polish) along with 2 percent Turkish and a scattering of Hungarian. Two thirds of the words come from Latin. Professor A. I. Chobanu, head of the Romance language department at Kishinev University, notes that "before the Revolution we had only one style—literary. Now Moldavians are also getting a scientific language and a political-administrative language. In this way Moldavian is enriched. Our new dictionary includes 100,000 words, and we are able for the first time to translate the great works of Marx and Lenin."

Yet the old language remains close to the people. "When my poems are read on the radio," said Viktor, "I get letters from the country people —and from Romanians across the frontier."

Moldavian wines speak the same Romance tongue. Visiting a winery, we tasted some typical vintages. Dry wines are the most popular here—and those with the savor and bouquet of the country. "This Riesling smells of newly cut hay," one vintner said fondly. "The two-year-old Dniestrovska—when you drink it, *the moon rises!* And this Gratieshty has the scent of fresh bread."

Simple, poetic metaphors close to the earth and life of Moldavia. Fondly, I packed a bottle of Moldavian Cabernet in my bag next to Novosti booklets on the small republic.

But baggage compartments on Aeroflot domestic flights are not pressurized. My bag arrived with the bottle exploded, my clothes smelling of Moldavian grapes, hay, and moonrise . . . and the Novosti booklets appropriately tinted red.

Grim monument to all the Belorussian villages destroyed during World War II: In bronze,

a lone survivor holding a dead child recalls the slaying of 149 inhabitants of Khatyn.

THE WINES OF MOLDAVIA

One of the smallest of the Soviet Union's 15 constituent republics, Moldavia ranks first in wine production. At the Kishinev State Farm School of Winery and Grape Growing (below, left), a student carries a crate filled with freshly cut fruit. Wires strung from concrete posts support the vines and leave them open to the rays of the sun. Wide pathways between rows allow mechanized cultivation, fertilizing, and spraying in the vineyards. Inside the cool cellar (right), wine ages in numbered wooden casks until the proper moment for bottling. Ready for tasting, an assortment from the winery offers a variety of brands: delicate, dry white table wines, heavier dessert wines, sparkling champagnes, and a ruby Cabernet. Each bottle bears the symbol of first-quality Moldavian wine: a flying stork with a cluster of grapes.

COLLECTIVE FARM

Plowing wheat stubble back into the earth, a Ukrainian farmer prepares the soil for another planting. The Ukraine supplies more than a fifth of the Soviet Union's agricultural commodities. Mikhail Boyko and his family (top, left), members of the Shevchenko Collective Farm at New Tsibly, have their own small house and some pigs, chickens, and ducks. At the farm's cooperative savings bank and post office (above), savings earn interest at 2 to 3 percent.

HOME IS THE SAILOR

*Broad smiles welcome seafarers home from a nine-month voyage.
Odessa's large fishing fleet and canning industry make important
contributions to the city's maritime-based economy. At the bottom of
the Potemkin Steps, a new passenger dock (right, above) accommodates the cruise ships that visit the Black Sea resort in increasing
numbers. The terminal provides for cargo movement on the first
floor, passengers on the second, and a rooftop restaurant on the
third. At Ilyichevsk (right), about 15 miles southwest of Odessa,
cranes load barges with coal. One of several facilities recently built
to handle both foreign and domestic cargo, Ilyichevsk serves as port
of entry for most shipments of North American wheat to the U.S.S.R.*

BAPTIST CENTENNIAL

Speaking before an emotional congregation, a Baptist minister leads a Sunday service in Odessa. About a thousand worshipers crowded into the sanctuary—women on the right (below), men on the left—to celebrate the founding of their church a century before. A few recorded the service on tape, perhaps for absent friends or relatives. Outside, hundreds more gathered in the August heat to follow the hymns and prayers on a public-address system. Established in 1875, the Russian Baptist

Church merged with a similar sect in 1944; the resulting Union of Evangelical Christians and Baptists today claims a membership of about five million, the largest Protestant denomination in the country. Like other conformist religious groups, the Baptist church officially supports the government. In return, its members may publish an edition of the Bible and certain other materials, train ministers, and participate in international congresses.

ODESSA OUTDOORS

Odessa impresses most visitors with its youthful, friendly mood. The gregarious townspeople spend much of their time outdoors, playing, chatting, or strolling along tree-shaded cobblestone streets. In the old quarter, a corner market (right) lends a Mediterranean flavor. Apartment dwellers (left) pull their chairs out to the sidewalk to enjoy a warm summer evening. Wearing fashionable long skirts, teenage girls pause for a "mineral," or carbonated soft drink, dispensed from a streetside vending machine. Running water and brushes in the machine clean the community glass after each use.

187

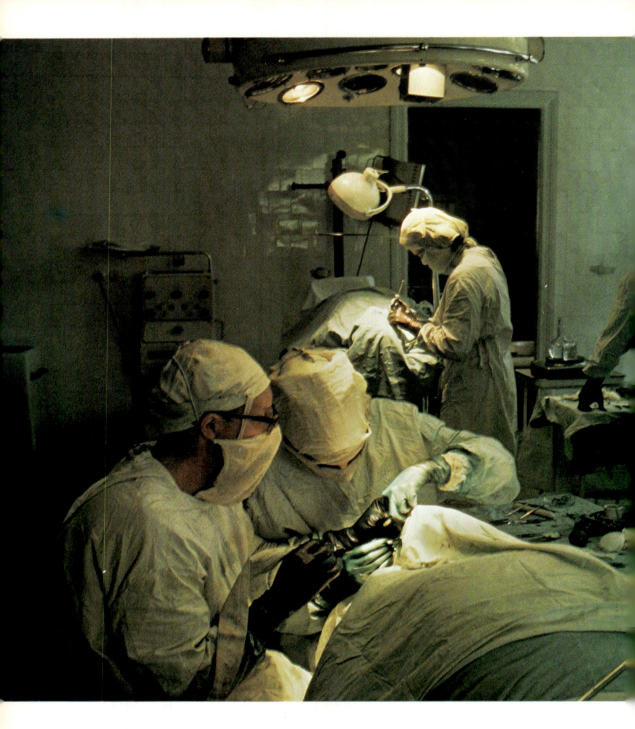

HOSPITALS AND SPAS

Surgeons at the Filatov Eye Clinic in Odessa perform a corneal transplant. While Dr. S. V. Filatov (at far left), son of the institute's founder, completes the operation, a nurse prepares the next patient. The late Vladimir P. Filatov developed many new methods of combating diseases and treating injuries of the eye. A large staff of his followers and former students now operates the research hospital and laboratories where a quarter of a million people from all over the Soviet Union receive care each year. In the recreation room (right, above), patients recovering from eye surgery play checkers. At right,

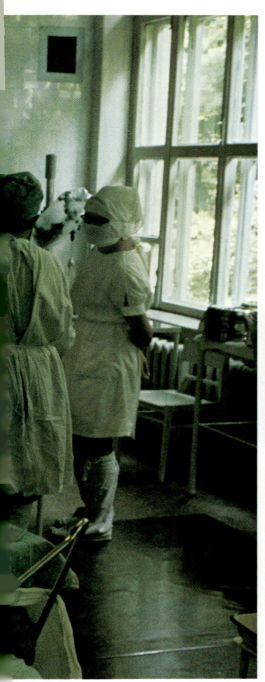

a woman at a Yalta sanitarium inhales medicated mist to relieve bronchial congestion. Health spas and resorts abound in the Black Sea area, attracting foreign tourists and Soviet vacationers as well as people with chronic illnesses.

BLACK SEA HOLIDAY

Where Crimean mountains meet the sea: A water-skiing instructor from the Sputnik Pioneer Camp near Yalta cuts through the wake of his tow boat. Sanitariums and resorts dot the hillsides. Many youngsters from the Soviet Union and other eastern European countries spend their summer vacations here on the Black Sea in camps operated by the Young Pioneers, the Soviet organization for children 10 to 15. Artek, a series of ten Pioneer camps, extends four miles along the coast.

190

6

SHORES OF THE BALTIC

Town-hall spire rises with Renaissance grace in Tallinn, Estonia. Behind the Old Town's facade, almost unchanged over the centuries, modern shops, cafés, and artists' studios flourish; the apothecary at right occupies a renovated guildhall. But a scarcity of metalcraftsmen, stonemasons, and heraldry experts slows restoration efforts.

IN THE BALTIC REPUBLICS, I frequently argued with our longtime traveling companion Gena Sokolov. His viewpoint was Russian and Soviet; mine was influenced by friendships with Americans of Estonian, Latvian, and Lithuanian descent.

"Your government still does not recognize the Baltic republics as part of the Soviet Union," Gena said in honest sadness. And he tried to correct my bourgeois wrongheadedness with a booklet by Mikhail Kulichenko: "The nationalities question is not an eternal one. Its existence in mankind's history covers the period from the removal of the feudal-absolutist obstacles in the way of the emergence of the first nations to the triumph of socialism. . . ." Policies are "based on the Marxist-Leninist theses that nations and national relations are transient phenomena in human history."

Our political differences would be out of place here. At least Dean, Gena, and I agreed on one important point: All of us liked and enjoyed the three Baltic republics. Though similar in climate and atmosphere, each has a distinct individuality.

Estonia reminded me of Finland—and should have, since Estonians belong to the Finnic language group. "Yes, we watch Finnish television, and understand it easily," said Ferdinand Kala, a specialist at an experimental farm. "We see many advertisements and even U. S. programs. Your detective Cannon has done more for the U.S.A. in Estonia than many American Presidents."

For us, language presented a greater problem, since few people we encountered spoke Russian. When Gena ordered a tomato salad in Russian, we got sliced eel. I tactfully switched to an Estonian *palun* and *tanan* (for "please" and "thanks") and traded my painfully practiced Russian for English mixed with German.

Kaliningrad
ESTONIAN S.S.R.
LITHUANIAN S.S.R.
LATVIAN S.S.R.
★Moscow

The whole Estonian ambience is un-Russian. The capital, Tallinn (population 408,000), stands tall with the Gothic and Renaissance spires of Old Town. The Baltic republics, after all, boast the only true Gothic architecture in the U.S.S.R.; such is one legacy from the German crusading knights who established their rule over Estonia in the 13th century. Their feudal-mercantile rule bestowed not only city member-ships in the Hanseatic League but also the Christian faith.

"Some 23 times power changed in our history," said our friend Kala. "We were always a battlefield."

In 1721, Tsar Peter won this region so close to his new capital in the campaign that earned him the appellation "the Great." Still, the submerged Estonian language and identity endured; and between the world wars, Estonia, like Latvia and Lithuania, was an independent nation. All three became constituent republics of the U.S.S.R. in 1940. But Hitler occupied them from 1941 to 1944, until the Soviet Army drove German troops out.

Through the Moscow office of Novosti, we had asked the Tallinn office to arrange some specific Estonian interviews. Still, when we arrived, nothing had been done.

"Oh, yes. Moscow sent us those suggestions and—ah—orders," said the local Novosti chief, Mrs. Tamara Tomberg, "but we are autono-mous!" Our Moscow influence was of no use in the Tallinn bureaucracy.

So we visited with the lady for a while, jotting down local boasts: "Yes, our University of Tartu is the oldest in the U.S.S.R. . . ."—though Vilnius has an older one—"In season nearly 2,000 Finns come here as tourists every week. . . . Our new 22-story hotel was designed and built by Finns. . . . We say Estonians have the world's highest per capita sale of books." In 1975, I learned, Estonia printed 75.5 million volumes.

We expressed admiration for local food. Mrs. Tomberg warmed to

Strategic trade location accounts for a turbulent Baltic-coast history. Sovereign states between the two world wars, Estonia, Latvia, and Lithuania now comprise three constituent republics of the U.S.S.R. The Kaliningrad Oblast (Region), a non-contiguous part of the R.S.F.S.R. and site of a seaport and naval base, lies between western Lithuania and Poland.

the subject: "Estonian kitchen is rough but good for filling up—pork with cabbage and homemade beer: Those are favorites. And each person consumes one liter of milk each day." Dean and I said how much we enjoyed milk, and soon we were forgiven for our bureaucratic aegis and our interviews were arranged.

With a pert woman taxicab driver (she had fresh flowers in a dashboard vase), we headed for the country. A young photo-correspondent from the Novosti Press Agency, Yuri M. Vendelin, accompanied us, and gave us a running commentary: "See those new houses? Like the English, we prefer houses to living in apartments—and we still build separate houses here. No, there is no problem of reselling them."

Dark, low-scudding clouds washed out the sunshine, and rain fell heavily as we reached the S. M. Kirov Collective Fishery, a cooperative enterprise with 107 fishing boats, some 600 fishermen, a blindingly clean cannery, and more than ten million rubles net profit a year. This collective is a showplace; some 13,000 visitors had signed its guest book before us. But not that many had talked with fisherman Voldemar Aasmaa, a weathered man built like a mainmast.

"The Baltic is a sharp sea. A stormy one, and accustomed to stealing our nets. A storm can come up slowly as you watch the waves grow. Or sometimes it's sudden. The water is green, very green—but at each hour the sea has its own face. Easy to feel, but hard to describe.

"Once when I was 15 and began to fish with my father, a storm came up. No warning. One big wave filled the boat with water. We had no chance to survive—yet we did. We swam a kilometer to an island, and then my father said, 'Boy, that's your first narrow escape, but not the last.' And he was right."

In sight of fisherman Aasmaa's sharp sea, we stopped at a station of the Saku Model State Farm where scientists are using Baltic waters for agriculture. "We use seaweed for manufacturing chocolate and vitamins," an agronomist explained. "And because the Baltic here close to shore—near river mouths—has a salinity of only .3 to .4 part per thousand, we can use its water for experimental irrigation on grasslands and alfalfa. Of course, Estonia is short of good farmland—20 percent of our area is peat bog! We make the most of the rest." (No doubt: Estonia is rich in oil shale.)

The Saku operation provided imaginatively designed houses for its specialists to buy—private, multilevel houses with contrasting textures of fine woods, stone, and glass. We paid some random, surprise visits to several families. "Wait!" one frantic housewife laughed. "I must put flowers into a vase!" She did, too, while we waited in the hall.

The gesture was typical: Estonians are creative—and compulsive. Offices have neat desks; even the ritual portraits of Lenin show artistic flair. Factories are well lighted and pin-clean, unusually so. I saw no factory in the Russian Federated Republic, for example, as neat as the Estonian plants we visited.

At a textile plant I talked with Luule Allika, the trim woman who directs the 1,800 employees of the enterprise. "About 92 percent of our plant's products stay in Estonia," she said. "Our raincoats are popular because of the weather. All our designs are Estonian, and sizes also differ here—Estonians are slenderer than other Soviet people. Our customers are harder to please. Women here are more fashion-conscious."

The view along any Tallinn sidewalk confirms that fact. The clean blonde Estonian girls—with high cheekbones, deep-set eyes, and finely pointed noses—seem leaner, taller, and far more stylish than others in the U.S.S.R. They move like tennis players, as many of them are.

Estonians are also noticeably reticent. When our car was bumped by another one day, the driver got out wordlessly. He inspected our damaged bumper and picked up a broken portion from the pavement. A bit formally, he approached the offending driver. No Moldavian arm-waving, no Moscow-like summoning of the traffic police, no Georgian oratory. He simply handed the other driver the bumper chunk with a single word: "Souvenir."

Ethnographer Ulo Tedre described his people this way: "Hardworking, perhaps because they were historically oppressed by other nations. Tenacious. A sense of individuality rather than collectiveness."

But if collectiveness includes choral singing, then scholar Tedre misses his mark. In song, the Estonian personality makes a sharp turn. Every five years, Estonians gather for a songfest with a choir of 30,000 voices. In two days, they sing dozens of the thousands of Estonian folk songs—fishermen's songs, harvest songs, songs of love and longing.

Professor Gustav Ernesaks, an Estonian composer, conductor, and Lenin laureate, described the Estonian spirit this way: "This is a proud nation that can work—and work well. You can trust the promises here. A deep sense of humor. Rational, logical people. Good farmers—and patient: If they put seed into the earth, they don't expect grain next day. We like precision. If we say the bus leaves at 4:16, those who arrive at 4:17 take a taxi. We have discipline, but the best kind: discipline from within the soul. Come to our song festival," the professor's eyes began to laugh, "and you can see the *reserved* Estonian. Ha!"

We did attend one folk-dance exhibit—in the rain. No one cared. They got wet and laughed, showing their good white Estonian teeth. The dances were prankish and fun. Afterward, Estonians applauded spiritedly—but not in cadenced unison.

Driving into Riga from the airport, we saw green, bristling examples of Latvia's famous pines, and meadows full of brown dairy cows.

"Culturally, we're closer to Estonia," said our Novosti host, Alexander Yemelyanov ("please—call me Sandy!"). He continued: "Latvia was also ruled by the German knights, though our language is more like Lithuanian."

A visitor can view Riga all at once from St. Peter's church tower, a steel copy of an antique wooden spire burned during World War II. From its nearly 400-foot height, a visitor sees the flat port city as a fascinatingly eclectic jumble of architectural styles, a city that coexists with all its past.

"When I was aboard the ship *Alexander Pushkin*," said Gena, "we often came to Riga. And I remember the city's aroma of coal smoke. Most Soviet cities are centrally heated, you know. But here—see the individual chimneys? In winter even the snow is darkened."

In summer, Riga seems greener than gray. Flower beds and small parks deck the streets. On sidewalks people look less Scandinavian than the Estonians and more like Central Europeans. They also seem not quite so tall. Historically, Estonians have been Lutheran; of the Latvians

Whimsical figures animate a hand-painted ceramic knickknack inspired by the folk art of wood carving. A creation of cartoonist Imants Melbardis, this trio suggests the Latvian love of music which culminates each Midsummer Eve in the "Ligo," a song festival with much revelry.

—"at least among believers"—an estimated two thirds are Lutheran and many of the rest Roman Catholic. Sandy, however, was descended from Russian Old Believers, a group that split with the Russian Orthodox Church in the 17th century. "But we have long been pure Latvians," he explained. Sandy has served with a Soviet diplomatic mission in Scandinavia and now is a member of the Party.

The skills of its 806,000 energetic people have helped make Riga a major manufacturing center, especially in electronics. The VEF electronics plant here makes half the telephones and a fourth of the radios in the U.S.S.R. "And we manufacture dashboard meters for automobiles," said Sandy, "and bicycles, motorcycles, and electric light bulbs. And our new town Olaine—a city of chemists—is producing plastics, paints, enamels. All this, yet we have no ores of our own."

Hardworking, the Latvians. And formal in manner. But also close to their land. More than a third of Latvia is forested. Leons Vitols, the Minister of Forestry and Timber Industry, pointed out that "the pine is our number-one tree." He proudly showed us some typical Latvian trophies: loving cups fashioned from wood. Latvia's conservation efforts deserve such awards. "We have 2,200 game wardens and 280 master foresters. Our hunting society has 40,000 members, and their 7.50-ruble dues help us feed and protect animals—hay for deer and elk, low-grade potatoes for boars, and salt and minerals for all. But particularly we are proud that Latvia has the first national park in the Baltic republics—the Moricsala Park, in western Latvia."

Beyond their seriousness of purpose, we wondered what makes Latvians laugh. We decided to put that question to a leading cartoonist and artist, Imants Melbardis.

"Imants has to be home," said Sandy, as we drove to his apartment. "This is his name-day—July 1. Everyone named Imants stays home today to entertain friends. Like open house. No one is invited, but everyone is expected." Saints' name-days have been secularized, national heroes' names added, and all printed on government calendars.

Our nationality may have been a surprise, but Imants Melbardis was prepared for visitors. Over coffee, cheese, biscuits, and brandy, we wished our host a good year. He showed us his drawings and ingenious ceramic figures—whimsical, comic people drinking, singing, feasting, courting, napping—all in the full tide of life.

"The Latvian character?" he mused. "We're reserved, but Estonians are twice as reserved as we. We're *between* Estonians and Lithuanians in temperament as well as geography. Our sense of humor is individual. You have seen our humor magazine *Dadzis?*" We had: Riga's airport waiting room was the only Intourist facility in the U.S.S.R. where we found a humor magazine. We leafed through an issue. Some of the cartoons were our host's own; they poked fun at crowded beaches, badly made clothing, gardening problems, school exams—all the situations that might concern nature-loving, hardworking achievers.

Latvians seem always to have been neat, creative, and close to nature. "We lived on the land, and each farm was separated from others," said Juris Indans, assistant director of the open-air Latvian ethnographic museum. "Only in Polish and Russian areas did people live in villages."

Private houses are still popular, and those we saw at the Marupe Collective Farm probably revealed the highest standard of living we encountered in the Soviet Union. The collective's chairman, Konstantins Hvostovojs, explained, "In the old days, Latvians got used to having separate houses with 12 hectares around them. When we build new villages now, it costs more money."

But the Marupe Collective makes that money in diversified ways, including a fur ranch with 30,000 resident mink. Farm members pursue such hobbies as auto racing (cars collectively owned) and charter flights for holidays as far afield as Cuba and Africa.

"A third of our farmers live in new houses," said Hvostovojs, "and with his financial credit a man pays for his new house in 20 years. When we send our youngsters away to school, we know they'll return— our people average 15 percent higher wages than state-farm employees. The mink-raisers, for example, make 250 rubles a month."

"More than I!" said Sandy. "As a journalist, I make 240—and have no garden." (Hvostovojs himself makes 450, and his wife another 350.)

Chairman Hvostovojs proudly showed us his own 20,000-ruble four-bedroom house, complete with two fireplaces, picture windows, garages, and private sauna. His son's room had a picture of cosmonaut Yuri Gagarin. In the study was the coat of arms he has designed for his family: "On it I have placed a hunting horn and oak leaves—for Latvian glory." One day he will hand down the new coat of arms to his son and daughter. "Yes, I was lazy—only two children," he said. "In our ethnic drama and music, Latvians are urged to have larger families."

Farmer Hvostovojs is quite right. At times the ethnic Latvian birthrate has been the lowest in the U.S.S.R., and the Latvian proportion of the republic's population has actually declined. "Mixed marriages are partly responsible," said Professor Bruno Mezgailis, a sociologist and demographer. "Today 11 percent of Latvians marry outside their nationality. Children of such marriages can choose their nationality at age 16."

Professor Mezgailis notes that Latvians still comprise three fourths of the republic's rural population and half of the city population. He explains the low birthrates in terms of industry, higher education, and working women. "But calculations indicate that the Latvian population will grow in the future."

Whatever her recent historic difficulties, Latvia was moving ahead, as the turn-of-the-century poet Janis Rainis had written in his "Broken Pines." The storm-shattered pines cry out:

"We'll yet win the future, where Dawn blazes bright!"

Lithuanians tell of the days in the 14th and 15th centuries when their kingdom stretched from the Baltic to the Black Sea. After several centuries of union with the Poles, the domain was partitioned, and in 1795 Lithuania was annexed by tsarist Russia.

"Lithuania is the amber land," a journalist, Vytas Mikulicius, told us with pride. Mines along the Baltic's southeastern shore yield 90 percent of the world's amber. And in some ways Lithuania itself resembles the bits of 40-million-year-old flowers and insects preserved in amber: beautiful, anachronistic, invincibly durable.

Consider the Lithuanian tongue, perhaps the most ancient living language in Europe. In old Berlin, students were permitted to choose between Sanskrit and Lithuanian, and differences were not all that great. Modern Lithuanian is close enough to the surviving fragments of Sanskrit in India that Hindi-speaking Indians can understand many Lithuanian words. R. P. Mironas, professor of Sanskrit at Vilnius University, nodded with fervor and picked up a pencil: "Yes, yes. Lithuanian is much closer to Sanskrit than Latin is. Take the word for *God* —in Sanskrit *Devah*, in Latin *Deus*, and in Lithuanian *Dievas*." The professor capitalized those words, but not the ones for *tooth*: Sanskrit *dan*, Latin *dens*, Lithuanian *dantis*.

"Ours has been a stubborn and changeless language, in spite of the tides of armies here. The Lithuanian people came to recorded history quite late—the 12th century. Before that we were on a side road. That's the great puzzle: how to explain the survival of so much living Sanskrit in areas 3,000 miles apart.

"Naturally, the unique form of Lithuanian gives it great literary strength. We can use archaic words to evoke olden times. And our poetry also has an archaic flavor—phrases like 'The Moon married the Sun.' The specialness of our language gives us a national pride."

And has anyone proposed simplifying Lithuanian? Professor Mironas recoiled in shock. "No. Even the opposite. People try to preserve old forms. It's a musical language—a good intonation and stress of the words." And has the dynamic stress of the Russian language influenced the rhythms of modern Lithuanian? *"No influence at all!* Oh, once Lithuanian may have been endangered; the tsars forbade our use of the Latin alphabet. But now more writers are publishing in Lithuanian. A novel in Lithuanian sells 25,000 copies."

As the professor showed us out of his university offices, we noticed a bas-relief of the Mother of the Muses: Memory. A motto nearby proclaimed, "History teaches and persuades us."

The Muses have been amply mothered in the streets of Vilnius, the capital. It's a quaint city with crooked, spontaneous walkways and cobbled courtyards—a city with secrets, located inland some 180 miles at the confluence of the Neris and Vilnia rivers.

I strolled the "narrow and badly paved" streets, as my Baedeker of

1914 warned other generations, taking note of the history of "a great centre of Pagan worship . . . raised to the dignity of a town" in 1323.

The new housing development named Lazdynai ("hazel tree") shows the trend of Lithuania's population—23 percent urban in 1939, and nearly half today. (Latvia and Estonia have even greater urban concentration—62 and 65 percent, highest in the U.S.S.R.—but they have historically been more urbanized.) Today 35,000 people live in the high-rise apartments of Lazdynai. They represent the new industrial workers of Lithuania, the makers of electronics, fibers, fertilizers, and fishing trawlers. "Ours has always been a multinational city," said Vytas. "Vilnius was on the road between East and West."

I checked at a newsstand and found publications in Lithuanian, Polish, Russian, and German. "Other kiosks have more languages," said Vytas. We browsed a new grocery store and found it much like those in other Soviet cities; it had supermarket ambitions. Loaves of bread were stacked fragrant and unwrapped; butter was refrigerated, milk was not. The only frozen food for sale was ice cream; the only fruit was canned. Customers could choose among a few fresh vegetables. The store also carried some pots, brushes, soap powder, unwrapped bar soap for laundry use, and one standard grade of toilet paper. Children could buy toy trucks, balls, candy, and cookies. A real, live butcher sold meat. I guessed the grocery inventory at perhaps a hundred items.

In the center of Vilnius, a new opera house shares the atmosphere with the 17th-century Church of St. Peter and St. Paul, a cavern of white baroque composition-marble sculptures: saints, cherubs, martyrs, apostles—2,000 figures in all. A Mass was in progress when we visited the church, and I could understand why fervent atheists might worry here. Whole families had come, grandmothers softly clicking rosary beads and whispering sibilant prayers; spruced-up, wide-eyed young-sters looking and wondering at a wealth of sculptures. I felt just as wide-eyed. White sculptures covered the interior: heavenly musicians, ferns, palm leaves, and flowers—as though squeezed out by a pastry chef—tableaux from the life of Christ, even an elephant. Most numerous of all were the images of young women.

"Country girls were models for the sculptor," whispered Vytas. "Typical Lithuanian faces, healthy and strong." And alive, too. The models came complete with animation, eyes laughing, cheeks dimpling, lips smiling—delightful Lithuanian milkmaids, self-conscious under the sculptor's scrutiny. These country girls of three centuries ago had long since grown wrinkled, withered, and died. But their vitality and wholesomeness are here preserved, as if in Lithuanian amber.

The Roman Catholic Church preserves far more of enduring Lithuania. We called on Father Algis-Kazimieras Gutauskas, who heads the ten parish churches of Vilnius and supervises the 24 priests in the city of 447,000 people. He wore a cassock shiny with use, and a warm Lithuanian smile. "Latin remains the basic language for the Mass," he told us, "but sermons are delivered in Lithuanian and, in some churches, Polish, since Poles comprise about eight percent of our communicants.

"We have fewer weddings in summer," he continued, "but we had 12 today. Believers may prefer a church ceremony to the wedding palace alone. Yes, people come to church in good numbers. How many, I can't say." He laughed. "Obviously, they are not forced to come to church. . . .

The future is impossible to see, but on the Feast of Saints Peter and Paul, I recall the words we read from Jesus Christ as He said, 'You are Peter, and upon this rock I will build my church . . . and the power of death shall not prevail against it.'"

Father Gutauskas was packing for a journey next day. "A group of 16 will visit the Vatican. My first visit. But why not? After all, Foreign Minister Gromyko has also visited the Vatican."

The ideologies of the Vatican and the Kremlin have well-known differences, and the Lithuanian Soviet Socialist Republic has printed an official essay on the subject by Jonas Anicas: "Some reactionary clergymen openly instigate their parishioners to 'fight for Christ.' . . . Here are some of the utterances . . . in sermons: 'Loss of religion deprived him (a student) of the chastity of the young heart—he has been lured by the mires of life. . . .'; 'Nobody suffers more, nobody sheds more tears in life than those who have no God. . . .'; 'How difficult it is to rear children without Christ. . . .'

"The false and provocative conceptions of this kind, spread by the reactionary clergymen, aim at cultivating religious fanaticism. . . .''

We sampled the spirit of enduring Lithuania at an old capital, Trakai, west of Vilnius where a tall and moated castle of brick and stone stands behind a drawbridge in reflected isolation. We watched swallows dive at bugs, and flotillas of sailboats dart upon a lake. The rolling land here, producing a healthy crop of potatoes, had a look of prosperity.

"You should try our *kibinai,* mutton pies—and the freshwater eels we call Lithuanian sausage," said Vytas. "But now eels are hard to find and expensive. That's the other side of progress."

We tried other Lithuanian cookery one afternoon when the country's leading designer of amber jewelry, Feliksas Daukantas, surprised his wife by inviting us to their apartment.

"Don't worry," Mrs. Daukantas said, laughing. "We have a proverb: 'A good housewife can make a pan of soup out of an ax.'" In no time she had set a table with Lithuanian borscht—no ax—the only lettuce salad we encountered in the U.S.S.R., and *skilandis,* pork sausage.

Good housewife she was—and more: Mrs. Daukantas was a retired ballerina who had danced all over Europe before World War II. ("I had gone to the bakery to buy bread when I saw the first bomb fall.")

Mostly that day we talked of a more distant history—the millions of years invested in Lithuanian amber.

Said Professor Daukantas, who was born in Cicero, Illinois: "Our poet Miezelaitis has written, 'We are Balts, and in our veins flows amber.'

"Well, amber was my hobby; I was not content with what was done with the 300,000 kilos of amber mined each year in this region. Amber is not a mineral, something dead—it has had a life of its own. It is natural. Each piece has a story 35 or 40 million years long.

"Each piece is like a potato with a skin—I learned how to cut that skin to show the natural qualities of the piece. Each is individual. We are learning at last to treat amber pieces *individually.*

"This piece"—he felt its texture with his thumb—"traveled a long time in the sea. And this one: Note the fern leaf inside? In the sun it's like a drop of honey. Here, take this one with the gnat inside—a bug 40 million years old. Please. We call amber the stone of friendship."

And what could be a better symbol of Lithuania?

Only the jib flies as a squall raises whitecaps on Estonia's Bay of

Tallinn, designated site for the 1980 Olympic yachting competition.

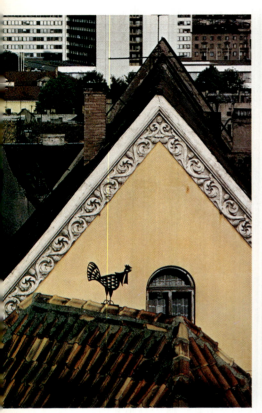

TALLINN'S OLD TOWN

Traditional symbol of vigilance, a wrought-iron cock surveys the Old Town of Tallinn, Estonia, from its rooftop perch. The Finnish-designed Hotel Viru stands in the background, a tribute to the cultural and ethnic affinity of Finns ard Estonians. They speak languages so similar that the people of Tallinn understand Western television broadcasts from Helsinki, just 60 miles across the Gulf of Finland. Above, right, friends enjoy a convivial moment in the Vana Toomas, or Old Thomas, one of many intimate cafés. At right, weatherproofed by plastic and blue denim, a couple strolls through Old Town unperturbed by typical Baltic fog and rain.

GOOD HEALTH
AND A LONG LIFE

Elderly friends enjoy a wade in the late-evening sunshine of a long day in June. The shallow, warm Baltic waters at Jurmala, Latvia, delight thousands of bathers each season. Towering pines fringe the 15-mile beach, which attracts an international array of visitors to its sanitariums, hydropathic clinics, and yachting clubs. The Latvian girl below wears a pin from the distant U.S.A.— probably the gift of a tourist.

THE STREETS OF RIGA

Often called the Paris of eastern Europe, Riga, Latvia, boasts
fashion houses like the one advertised at left. The bold graphic
design lends a contemporary touch to a city where narrow old
streets neighbor modern boulevards. Stuccoed walls, arched
entranceways, and cobblestone courtyards (above) characterize
the town of bygone days; a caryatid, below, greets cafégoers.

ALL IN A DAY'S WORK

Agriculture, fishing, and manufacturing consistently stay near the top of the list of productive activities in the Baltic republics. An Estonian farm worker (above, left) at the Saku Model State Farm near Tallinn pauses while helping to bale a crop of hay. Tallinn, a thriving seaport, also processes the catch of its large fishing fleet; in the S. M. Kirov Fishery, women thread small herring onto wires that carry them into the smoking-ovens. Lunch break brings recreation in many places of work; at a machine shop in Riga (above, far right), employees usually spend most of the period playing table or card games. At right, a model provides a style-show preview for seam-stresses who have worked on the dress she wears.

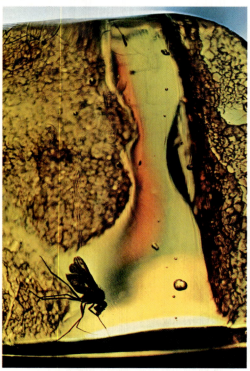

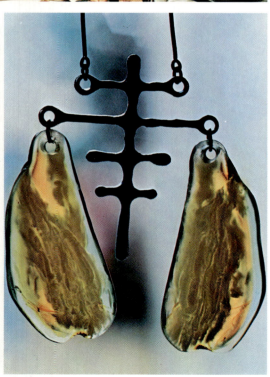

THE GLEAM OF AMBER

American-born Feliksas Daukantas and his wife drink to Amber Land, the ancient name for part of the Baltic coast. Daukantas designs amber jewelry exhibited throughout the world. "Amber nuggets are like a potato with a skin. I cut that skin to show the natural qualities," he explains. "Each piece has a story 35 or 40 million years long." Natural forces conspired to create one of the world's greatest sources of amber along the Baltic shores, where resin oozed from ancient trees. As its oils evaporated, the resin hardened into the amber lumps prized since prehistoric times for their golden beauty. Early man believed sunlight dancing on the waves solidified into amber. Today the material also serves science: Paleobiologists study the insects and bits of plants fossilized in amber for clues to evolution.

CATHOLICS OF LITHUANIA

Electric lights and graceful palms counterpoint the baroque splendor of the Church of St. Peter and St. Paul in Vilnius, Lithuania, the setting for a first Communion service. Seventeenth-century Lithuanian peasant girls modeled for many of the 2,000 life-size statues that decorate the church. Above, a remnant of a carved wooden cross depicts a toiling serf watched by two angels. Unlike their Lutheran neighbors in Estonia and Latvia, most Lithuanian Christians practice Catholicism. Young people under 35 comprise perhaps a third of the churchgoers. Catholicism has flourished since 1386, when the Grand Duke Jogaila of Lithuania married Jadwiga, Catholic queen of Poland; the grand duke accepted the faith for himself and his people, and united the two countries.

SUMMER
ON LAKE GALVE

Boats move across the calm waters of Galve, a lake popular for international boating events. Present-day serenity belies the bloody history of this area around Trakai, a former capital of Lithuania. The restored 15th-century castle houses an ethnographic museum.

7

BEYOND THE CAUCASUS

The Caucasus lay spread before our gaze,
An unmade bed, it seemed, with tousled sheets....
Massed in the mist and out of sorts, it reared
The steady malice of its icy crests....

THOSE WORDS WERE WRITTEN in 1931 by Boris Pasternak. If the poet seems ambivalent in his imagery—the comfort of a tousled bed, the malice of ice—he reacts like history itself: The Caucasus Mountains have alternately protected and punished the peoples who live in the three constituent republics of the Transcaucasus—Georgia, Azerbaijan, and Armenia. There is no wonder that these folk should differ in attitude, custom, and even chemistry from people of the northern steppes. For one thing, they are Asian.

"Not true! We are *not* Asian," insisted a pretty Georgian girl named Nana. But wasn't Georgia south of the Caucasus? "Who said *that's* the boundary? Everyone says Mount Elbrus is the highest point in *Europe.* And look in this book: 'Georgians . . . belong to the Europoid race.'"

I backed away from that argument. The people of each Transcaucasian republic have their own ethnic specialties: Through history, Georgians have been Christian and defensively European; Armenians defensively Christian but vividly Asian; and Azerbaijanians contentedly Asian and Muslim. With all their differences, the three peoples still provide a kind of colorful, clashing unity, much as the Baltic peoples do.

The history of Georgia's capital goes back 1,500 years. Legend records that while hunting one day, King Vakhtang Gorgasali discovered a curative warm spring. He ordered a town built on the spot and named it Tbilisi, from *tbili,* meaning "warm."

We sampled little water of any temperature in Tbilisi. The bottled Borzhomi water tasted as unappealing as the Pecos River in Texas, so,

Hardy centenarian and a slightly younger companion await their meal in a rural Abkhazian restaurant on the outskirts of Sukhumi, Georgia. The manager cooks at an open-pit fire; smoked sides of meat hang above a pot of cornmeal mush. Smoke escapes the chimneyless room through spaces in the woven-grapevine walls.

Moscow ★

GEORGIAN S.S.R.

ARMENIAN
S.S.R.

AZERBAIJAN S.S.R.

Rugged Caucasus Mountains, where Europe and Asia meet west of the Caspian Sea, separate the Soviet Union's Transcaucasian republics of Georgia, Armenia, and Azerbaijan from the Russian Federated Republic.

lacking a mortal ailment to cure, I stuck with Georgian wine. Even ritually, the choice was appropriate. An enormous statue of Mother Georgia dominates Tbilisi; she holds a sword in one hand, for those who come as enemies, and a wine cup in the other as hospitality for friendly visitors. To me, the wine cup brimmed with other meanings. Russians symbolize their hospitality with basic, prosaic bread and salt. Georgians offer their guests a festive bit more.

Walking around Tbilisi, I was conscious of trees, gardens, fanciful architecture, and a terra-cotta cyclorama of steep mountainside—all mere background. The foreground of Tbilisi is people, 1,029,000 of them. Especially I was conscious of Georgian eyes: large, often dark, accented by extravagant lashes—questing eyes that gaze at strollers and introduce themselves with a glancing touch of challenge, flirtation, or humor.

Tbilisi, walled by mountains like nearly nine tenths of Georgia, has a Mediterranean feel. "Yet we have only our River Kura," said Merab N. Lordkipanidze, then the Novosti bureau chief. The Kura gorge that sculptures Tbilisi has also shaped its history, for this valley has served as a flume for peoples as well as water. Georgian merchants sold flax, furs, and wax to Greek traders on the Black Sea, and Georgian craftsmen excited admiration in the ancient world; almost all their metalwork was handsomely ornamented with figures of animals, flowers and especially the cursive grace of grapevines. "No wonder," observed Merab. "We raised grapes in the third millennium B.C. Perhaps even earlier."

In the first century B.C., Pompey brought his Roman legions to war on Georgia. But the real conquest came with St. Nino, a woman of the fourth century who brought Christianity. Basilicas soon sprang up everywhere; and today's traveler can visit many an early architectural example from the days of David the Builder or Queen Tamara. Even oft-ruined Tbilisi boasts within its boundaries the fifth-century Metekhi

Church, overlooking the river. Long ago it ceased to function as a place of worship. Still, though the old fortified walls have tumbled down, Metekhi itself endures—squat, solid, Romanesque—and its arched ceilings sometimes echo again to old hymns, sung in secular concerts of traditional Georgian music and dance.

In the hushed darkness there one afternoon, we heard a choir do a tenth-century anthem to the Virgin Mary. It was titled "You Are a Vine" —again, the Georgian grape, repeated in this musical theme across the centuries. As an accordion played the formal, antique melodies, we watched three girls perform a medieval court dance, girls of Georgian beauty: oval faces, long noses, high cheekbones, mouths softly sculptured, and inevitably unforgettable eyes. They showed us that the elongated, haunting faces on old Georgian icons were not, after all, so strongly stylized. The music was simple but odd, maybe a bit like the flamenco of Spain, where the East has also spilled into Europe, but still unlike the Oriental sounds of Armenia.

Then we listened to a choir of young men. With precision and enthusiasm, they celebrated polyphony—and in accord with long tradition, explained Anzor David Erkomaishvili, the young leader of the choir, when we chatted afterward. "Georgians have been writing music since the first century."

That date would place songwriting well ahead of the Georgian alphabet, which began to flower into literature, along with Christianity, after the fourth century. At the Institute of Manuscripts of the Georgian Academy of Sciences, we saw some early, exquisitely illustrated documents with the looped, circular letters of Georgian script—an alphabet that today includes 33 characters in rounded shapes that seem to bubble up from the page.

One manuscript from the Georgian Renaissance 800 years ago was copied cleanly on proper Persian paper. It was Shota Rustaveli's classic poem of love and friendship, *The Knight in the Panther's Skin*. Rustaveli catches the music and meter of his land, along with the opulent joy of Georgia:

> *A sumptuous and magnificent banquet*
> > *was spread to replenish the armies....*
> *Fountains of wine from a hundred sources*
> > *flowed for the drinkers....*
> *All had a share of the presents....*
> *Pearls were scattered in handfuls....*

We stepped back still earlier in time at the Physical Culture Institute, where strong young men learn traditional Georgian wrestling. "Our wrestling is more like judo than your freestyle in America," said muscular Vakhtang Balavadze, deputy chairman of the State Committee for Physical Culture—a man with ministerial rank who has himself six times won the U.S.S.R. wrestling championship in his weight class. "In the Georgian style, a man cannot fight while lying down—he uses no painful or choking holds. And we have other differences. But the chief one is that we wrestle to music. Wrestling is much nicer with music. Music affects your nerves."

We watched some promising young Georgian athletes tossing each other on the mat. They moved with rhythm and harmony. And I was reminded of ancient Georgia's trading partners, the Greeks: the inventors of wine, the Olympics—and the concept of the philosopher-athlete.

The Rustavi steel mill taught us something of local technology: 12,000 employees ("WORKERS' COLLECTIVE OF PIPE-ROLLING MILL 400 WELCOMES YOU"), 1.5 million metric tons of steel a year made from west Georgian coal and iron ore from across the Azerbaijanian border. But we learned more about Georgian traditions of metalworking at the Tbilisi studio of Irakli Ochiauri, sculptor, painter, and an adept at chased metal-work. Ochiauri showed us his bas-relief designs in handsomely hammered copper: figures of Georgian girls—nude or in traditional costume—animals, twining flora. And he talked volubly about Georgian art in general: "More mannered and stylized—even sweetened. Of course, modern Georgian art is under the influence of foreign countries." Which foreign countries? "Chiefly France and Russia." His answer had no political meanings, just limpid Georgian self-confidence: Russia is a friendly but foreign land.

And what of the Georgian character? "We have no kin in all the world. Our origins are obscure. Generally, we're jolly, open, and not very rational. Very ambitious, too. Now me: I'm not a gesticulating Georgian. I'm a mountain man—cold blood flows slowly. But perhaps that explains our longevity. Our old people had simple lives. They did not worry about France or Germany; they would only grieve over the loss of a cow."

Other ambitious Georgians *have* worried about the wider world. Joseph Stalin (son of a shoemaker named Djugashvili in the city of Gori) once studied for the priesthood in Tbilisi. The seminary he attended is now an art museum. "No, we don't know which room was Stalin's," the attendant assured me. Even during the long life of the Party leader and wartime marshal, Stalin's religious career inspired no boasting.

Still, as a history buff and World War II veteran, I wanted to acknowledge our wartime ally; so in a grocery store I bought a bottle of red wine called Khvanchkara. This, Russian friends had told me, was the Georgian wine regularly delivered to Stalin's Moscow table.

But I also bought a dry white wine called Tsinandali. It comes from Kakhetia and the lands once owned by the family of a friend of mine in Washington, David Chavchavadze. David is the great-great-great-grandson of Prince Alexander Chavchavadze, a 19th-century patron of art whose name is still honored by Chavchavadze Street in Tbilisi.

That evening, while our Novosti interpreter-guide Boris Lunkov talked long-distance to Moscow, Dean and I chose a restaurant on our own: a kind of rustic basement tavern filled with Georgians. We were the only Americans, of course, and when Boris joined us—out of breath and a bit on edge—he was the only Russian. Men at a nearby table were singing in fine polyphony. Three of them came over to greet us. Their party was celebrating the 50th birthday anniversary of a friend; since we were foreigners ("*really* Americans?"), they wanted to welcome us with a drink from the *tanzi*, the traditional local drinking horn. They explained that this cow horn had to be emptied entirely ("see—it has a point and cannot stand if you put it on the table.") So we drank deep, were clapped jovially on the back, and watched our friends return to their own table.

More polyphonic song, more wine. I noticed a lively discussion at the birthday table—an argument, even, and it seemed to concern us. "It's our turn to buy a round," I told Boris. Together we table-hopped, taking with us my bottle of white Tsinandali. The older man beamed.

"Please—join us! And your friend." He signaled Dean to come over. Everyone made room—except for one broad and brooding fellow with heavy brows who seemed strangely quiet. During the next few toasts, he drank without gusto. Then, in husky Georgian, he spoke to the older man; our host relayed to us in Russian:

"We have the custom of a toastmaker—the *tamada,* we call him. For the sake of order, he proposes all the toasts. Will you support me as *tamada?*" We enthusiastically elected him.

The brooding man said something else, and our tamada rose a bit tensely: "I want to propose a toast to our great Georgian, the greatest genius, the wisest leader in history...." By now Boris was cringing visibly, but faithfully translating every word. "...the man we will always hold in greatest respect and affection—*Joseph Stalin!*"

Those dark eyebrows were lifted quizzically now—the eyes leveled at me like gun barrels. I rose, and with help from Boris, explained my wartime appreciation for the man Americans called "Uncle Joe." Therewith I produced my bottle of Khvanchkara and asked the tamada's permission to alter our toast to include all the Georgians who had fought as my allies—and to drink our friendship in Stalin's own brand.

The loophole was wide enough. The eyebrow man overturned a chair in haste to embrace me. I had to drink the red, sweetish Khvanchkara from his own tanzi—and I must keep it as a gift.

Encouraged, I asked the toastmaster's permission to drink to my American friend David, descended of Georgians as he was. I did not explain that David was twice a prince—through the Chavchavadze line and also through the family of his mother, a Romanov princess whose parents were both cousins of Tsar Nicholas II. And so that night we drank in red wine and white, to Georgians also red and white.

In another restaurant one evening we encountered a young architect, his wife, and some friends. They were avid skiers and mountain climbers and proud of their Caucasus range. "*New* mountains—that's their difference," one said. "Glaciers and rocks combined. And steep. And in our mountains you find the atmosphere of the Middle Ages."

We had still another reason for visiting the highlands: Soviet Georgia claims that 39 of every 100,000 of its people live 100 years or longer. Many centenarians are mountaineers. We hoped to meet some of them.

A railroad links Tbilisi with the Black Sea, traversing sere slopes like those of eastern New Mexico. At Sukhumi, on the coast, the scenery changes; the city flowers spectacularly with subtropical flora—pomegranates, figs, palms, jasmine, laurel, cannas, myrtle. Sukhumi is a popular seaside resort, with numerous sanitariums and facilities for scientific research; it is also the capital of the Abkhazian Autonomous Soviet Socialist Republic, an administrative subdivision of Georgia with its own language and customs. Beyond, our road climbed through hills green with orchards and tea plants. At last we came to a cluster of neat white buildings among apple trees. This was Kutol, a kind of Caucasian Shangri-la, and here we met the widow Khfaf Lasuria.

She stood perhaps five feet tall, and she covered her head to the eyebrows with a cotton kerchief tied close. She shook hands firmly as I explained our visit. Two years earlier Dr. Alexander Leaf, of the Harvard

Bas-relief figures hammered in copper by Irakli Ochiauri decorate the artist's apartment in Tbilisi. Features of the women and of the stylized copper mask typify his rendering of a classic Georgian profile.

University Medical School, had studied Mrs. Lasuria when he did a report on aging for the January 1973 NATIONAL GEOGRAPHIC. Dr. Leaf had carefully calculated Mrs. Lasuria's age as "between 131 and 141." Now, two years later, she still seemed fit and unnervingly alert.

"Of course, I've never been nervous. Never quarreled with anyone," she explained. She smiled—a good smile; her somewhat discolored teeth were her own. She had cut those teeth when Abe Lincoln was an obscure young man in Illinois. The stains came much later: "I started smoking when one of my brothers died," she said. That was in 1910.

I offered her a package of American cigarettes and watched her neatly open it. No spectacles. She inhaled the smoke deeply, then continued. "No, I do not remember anything of my childhood. But I recall being taken away with my parents. The Turks, you know. I felt bad— grief, tears. Then I think I came back here."

Mrs. Lasuria's first husband died, as did her first son, of typhus. She married again at age 50 and had a second son. Her second husband died some 30 years ago, when well over 100. "My father lived to be at least 100," she said. "My mother died first—but she, too, had reached nearly that age."

We followed Mrs. Lasuria around all morning. She had a little trouble hearing the questions, but her steps and answers were firm as she demonstrated her regular chores: sweeping, feeding the chickens, sewing (she licked her fingers, twirled the thread, and slipped it into the eye of the needle on her second try—without glasses). "I get up early— before the sun and birds," she said, "but I do not eat breakfast until 9 or 10 when I take some sour milk along with fresh milk and cheese— white, soft cheese. Lately, I've begun to take some tea, but I don't consider it a food. Of course, until—how many?—four years ago, I worked at the collective farm picking tea." She did not boast that she had been champion tea-picker until well past her 100th birthday.

"For lunch I eat mush, beans, meat or chicken, and fruit. And afterward"—she laughed girlishly—"if I feel moody, maybe I lie down awhile. And for supper I take milk and something hot and salty. And sometimes 100 grams of vodka." She looked quickly at her great-niece standing nearby. "Or I used to. Now, perhaps, 50 grams of vodka. Or—" her lips pursed—"none. But wine I do take now. Our custom. And I attend parties and feasts in the village, spending the night with a niece. A strange bed? No, I don't mind it, though home is best."

We went upstairs to a feast prepared in honor of our visit. Mrs. Lasuria managed the stairway easily with a good grip on cane and banister. Taking her seat opposite me, she promptly noticed the vodka and homemade Abkhazian wine. But when she reached for the bottle of vodka, two great-nieces intercepted her glass and poured wine.

"But I have a toast to propose in vodka," she said. Obviously, wine lacked proper emphasis; the great-nieces exchanged glances, but yielded, and Mrs. Lasuria poured vodka. She popped up, all five feet of her, and lifted her drink to us and to international amity. We responded. Others proposed toasts of welcome—but the vigilant nieces held their great-auntie to the dry village wine.

Not for long. "I have another toast!" she announced. The nieces looked alarmed but powerless as Mrs. Lasuria poured herself another vodka with a steady and generous hand. "To physicians of the world!"

Patiently and delicately wrought in gold at a Georgian monastery in the 12th century, leaves and vines twine about an even older cross of gold and enamel in this detail of an Orthodox triptych. Now in the Museum of Fine Art in Tbilisi, it depicts the apostles Mark (top), Paul, Luke, and Peter, with John the Baptist at the center.

Mrs. Lasuria saluted me, and drained the goblet dry. She had confused my profession, but not her own strategy. Before we got to the food, our tiny hostess had raised toasts to Dean and photography, to Boris and to —but at this point my notebook becomes garbled. Yet I clearly remember the stately way Mrs. Lasuria took her leave, moving with dignity, smiling at us in friendship and at her great-nieces in triumph.

"She is remarkable," Boris said later. "Not merely alive but still *hungry* for life." He turned philosophical then in his very Russian way. "I do not know what is better. Perhaps Immanuel Kant had the best death. 'Life is a burden to me,' he said. Which is better—to want death and to get it? Or to want life and be disappointed by death?"

But, unlike Boris, Mrs. Lasuria was no Slavic Hamlet. When I learned of this little Abkhazian's death the following year, I could not regard the event as a release for someone old. Yet along with sadness, I smiled. During a century and a third she had drunk as deeply of life as of her vodka glass. And for just as long a time, her mortality—like her attentive nieces—had been niftily outwitted.

People of the Azerbaijan Republic claim even greater longevity than the Georgians: 44 centenarians out of every 100,000 people. And in the Azerbaijanian capital, Baku, gerontologist Shukur M. Gasanov carries on continuing medical studies of the oldsters. "Some of the old people in my group objected to calisthenics until I got a young, pretty gymnast to direct them," said Dr. Gasanov, an entirely sensible man who believes in following the practices of the healthy.

What are the doctor's usable observations?

"Well, our centenarians—2,500 of them—are able to *work*. They are not bedridden. Only this week, the newspaper here carried a story about a woman 114 who had won the Red Banner of Labor—a carpet weaver.

"Now, what kind of rules could we devise? First, they are early risers and they work all the time. No lazybones has ever lived long. Their diet relies mostly on vegetables and milk products—sour milk, kefir, curds, our soft white cheese. Good food! They eat many greens and especially fruits like grapes and apricots. And they also fast to rest their stomachs. Little food at night.

"They drink natural spring water—no chlorine or fluorides. They stay on the move, and spend much time in the open air. Even when it's cold, they bathe often in our cold rivers. They always sleep on hard beds. And not too long—perhaps six hours a night, though they may rest during the day. They are fond of music and like to dance. They sing and joke and visit each other. We are an emotional people!

"They don't fancy coffee, but tea is popular. The old people do not drink alcohol here. And they don't smoke much. Of course, much depends on the natural customs and environment of Azerbaijan."

In Baku, Dean and I found the natural environment delicious. Baku has a population of 1,406,000 (out of 5,700,000 in the republic) and ranks as the fifth largest city in the U.S.S.R., but it seems uncrowded. The capital sits on a peninsula thrusting well into the salty, landlocked Caspian Sea. A highly industrialized city since the 19th century, Baku still seems clean and green.

"The name Baku comes from the Persian words *abad kube*, for 'windy town,'" explained Rasim Gusseynovich Agaev, our Novosti colleague in Azerbaijan. "We have 280 windy days each year—220 of them classed as stormy." From the cliffy heights of the Kirov Gardens above Baku, we watched a rainstorm move in to flog the city with high wind and drama—the price Baku pays for its brilliantly blue seascape and its verdure.

On a clear, calm evening, Baku is a stroller's city, as residents promenade and take a glass of cool sweet sherbet with friends. Swarthy old men wear the *papakh*, a kind of fur fez long part of the Azerbaijanian costume. Women seem a bit more Western, though the veil was not abolished in this Muslim land until 1921.

We visited two of the city's five active mosques during prayers. Most of those present were old, though a young man of 24 told me, "I believe, though I rarely go to prayers. One must believe in something."

Our driver was contemptuous of the attendance at big city mosques. "In my town, Sheki, we have only 70,000 people—but in front of the mosque you cannot enter the street for the crowd!"

Azerbaijanians also remain Oriental in secular ways. Their language resembles modern Turkish so much that they can easily converse with visitors from Istanbul. Like Turks, Azerbaijanians gesture with their noses, and make a *tch* sound as a comment—a quick equivalent of well-what-do-you-know. But unlike Turks, they nod heads affirmatively up and down. (Across the Araks River, the six million Azerbaijanians of Iran cling to the Asian waggling of the head back and forth for *yes*.)

Azerbaijan calls up a touch of *A Thousand and One Nights*. In Moscow we had seen the Bolshoi Ballet dance the opulent *Legend of Love*, a highly romantic Azerbaijanian story with music composed by Arif Melikov. Now, sampling the verse of the 12th-century poet Nizami, I could appreciate the local tradition of imagery. For example, Nizami describes a princess this way: "Graceful was she as the willow tree and stately as the cypress; bracelets of jade adorned her slender wrists, and her eyes were greener than emeralds. . . ."

We saw a performance one evening by a new national folk-dance ensemble. The dancing girls were as willow-graceful as Nizami's. Afterward the troupe's manager, Stepan Karapetovich Popov, talked with us. "Yes," he beamed, "our music is very different from that of Georgia—more lyrical. Our *profiles* differ! Here all our music is song, and every song is dance. During any festival, whenever music sounds, people get up and dance. Always. We are people of movement."

In recent times the movement has been industrial. Take the oil business. Petroleum extraction began here in the 19th century by foreign developers that included the Swedish engineer and investor Alfred Nobel, and the Baku field once produced half of the world's supply. Volga and Siberian oil fields have since surpassed those of Baku; but in technology, Baku remains in the forefront of Soviet oil exploitation.

One day we drove out to the offshore field called Peschany ("made of sand"). We had seen this beachside oil field as our plane had circled to land: a complex of Texas towers and derricks standing in the Caspian, the whole improbable construction joined by a Jacob's ladder of pipes, piers, walkways, and bridgework into a kind of artificial island.

We drove onto the complex with engineer Aga-Mahun Sirayev. "We had three wells here in 1937," he explained, "but began real operation in 1950." We watched gulls land on the millpond sea. "In all, we have 160 wells, and extracted 1,665,000 metric tons of oil in 1975—along with about five billion cubic meters of gas. Twenty kilometers out there lies the field called Bakhar, or Springtime—because we found oil and gas there in the first days of spring. Deeper wells. We got a new well there yesterday—4,800 meters deep. A gusher!"

In pioneer days, Caspian drillers had their troubles, especially at Neftyanye Kamni, or Oil Rocks. This Caspian reef, some hundred kilometers southeast of Baku, had long been a graveyard of ships, but it was also famous for its natural oil slicks and the gaseous bubbles in its waters. While drillers probed here for oil in 1949, they used the hulls of seven wrecked ships to give them harbor-like protection; they even lived aboard one half-submerged wreck. In November 1949, they brought in a gusher at a depth of 1,000 meters, and soon a provisional island crowned the oil rocks. Then in 1957 a storm struck: One drilling rig isolated from the rest of the complex was wrecked by the waves and its men were lost. But a substantial town now stands on the oil rocks.

"We have a population of 3,000—1,500 on each of two shifts," said a girl named Tanya when I met her on the Baku pier. The ship *Volgograd* had just made its four-hour trip, and Tanya was hurrying for her shore leave. She was carrying a bunch of flowers. "These? We raise them on Neftyanye Kamni, in our greenhouse," she laughed. "Yes, I like it there. The town smells of oleanders—not oil. We have many shrubs growing. And a bakery, and even a lemonade factory. And now we even have one building of five stories. That's not easy. Pilings must be driven 75 meters deep before a house can be built. And linking our buildings and oil wells, we have a 160-kilometer network of trestles and causeways."

Mention Armenia and I hear the music of Aram Khachaturian: a bit of concerto, an Oriental theme from his *Second Symphony,* certainly a few slashing bars from the *Saber Dance.*

"Of course topography affects music," said the famous composer when we visited one afternoon. "Much Russian music reflects a broad, flat land. And with it, the Russian character: openhearted, a quiet soul—broad melodies. But Armenians live in the mountains. A hot, dry land. So our melodies are sharp and rhythmic. Armenians have a kind of flavor, something individual." A quick smile streaked his dark face. "But—is my ballet music for *Spartacus* Armenian? No. This is simply the work of Khachaturian, who has composed music of many kinds.

"Of course, I do not deny that I used national tunes and dance melodies. For instance, in the Andante of the *Second Symphony*, the entire grandiose requiem was developed from a simple Armenian melody which I often heard in my childhood and which my mother sang."

At the sight of Dean's camera, the maestro smoothed his bushy brows. "You know, I have lived in Moscow 54 years—though I try to visit Armenia each year to participate in the cultural life. Amazing, the changes. . . . In 1920 Yerevan was only a kind of village."

Today it is a city of 928,000 people, a whimsically pink city built largely of rosy tufa stone from nearby quarries. Yerevan has its own particular style. It's a city of wide streets, affectionately planted parks and—inevitably for people in a dry land—fountains. The prodigal use of water seems like a celebration.

So does the use of color. What Georgian singers do in polyphonic harmonies, Armenians do visually with polychromes. Visiting a gallery of children's art, we found paintings of knights, dragons, circuses, kings. Armenian children 3 to 16 years old smiled at life with strong, original colors. A girl had painted a bride and groom. Several boys had painted David of Sasun on horseback, liberating Armenia from the Arabs. No landscapes, I noticed. They preferred man and beast in living color.

Their elders weave Armenian carpets and other textiles with the same special vitality. And quality. At a Yerevan distillery, where I tasted the finest cognacs in the Soviet Union, a master vintner quoted an Armenian maxim: "Nothing is cheaper than the expensive thing."

Yerevan's setting is theatrical, for this is a split-level city, its older center in the valley and the newer residential areas perched high on a plateau—a massif, actually—some 1,500 feet above. "The city has two climates," a journalist told us. "It rains in the valley when we have snow up here." But visible from almost every quadrant of the city—morning and evening, if not during smoggy midday—are the dominating icy peaks of Mount Ararat.

The old, cold volcano, biblical landing spot of Noah's ark, does not stand on Armenian or even Soviet terrain. Mount Ararat belongs entirely to Turkey. "And the Turks protested when we pictured Mount Ararat on our republic's seal," said young Konstantin Eduardovich Akopian, our Armenian interpreter-guide. "But we answered: 'If a picture on a seal or a flag lays claim to territory, then does the Turkish crescent mean that you claim the moon?'"

Few quarrels between Armenia and Turkey have been that light-hearted. Their long history includes bitter confrontations, the worst in April 1915 when the sultan's forces massacred more than a million Armenians. Survivors were subjected to frightful hardship, and the term "starving Armenians" entered the lexicon of World War I atrocities.

At the headquarters of the Armenian Apostolic Church at Echmiadzin, the Chancellor of the See, the Right Reverend Bishop Arsen Berberian, offered me a cup of thick black coffee. "What excellent Turkish coffee!" I said. A sharp pause. "We say *Oriental* coffee," the bishop smiled, then talked about the special feelings of Armenian national identity. "We have known peace only during the last 60 years. But through all our history, all the massacres and occupations, the Church did its best to keep both the faith and national feelings. . . . Perhaps 80 percent of the people bring their children to be baptized. In recent years we have had many young people coming to our churches. Not educated believers—but they see the art, history, and tradition."

Echmiadzin is the Armenian Vatican, seat of the supreme patriarch —known as the Catholicos—of all the world's Armenians. The monastery was built early in the fourth century and has been often destroyed, rebuilt, and fervently ornamented by the talents and gifts of Armenians at home and abroad. Among its treasures, the museum contains a piece of ancient wood that tradition holds to be from Noah's ark.

Driving through rural Armenia, a visitor can sense the enduring struggle of the people. Valleys are narrow, stony, and dry. Mountain roads offer ear-popping, eye-popping rides. Here donkeys carry farm burdens at their rhythmic quickstep. Large combines harvest wheat on the smoother hillsides, but hands do the job on smaller, rougher plots. Overall, the fierce purity of bright sunlight contrasts with inky shade.

Beside the highway near Garni one noontime, we saw a group of

ИЗ КАЖДЫХ 100 БЫТОВЫХ И УЛИЧНЫХ ТРАВМ 66 ПРОИЗОШЛИ ПО ВИНЕ АЛКОГОЛЯ

Vodka labels form a symbolic cast for a broken leg in a wall poster warning against excessive drinking. "Of every 100 injuries at home or on the street," states the caption, "66 result from drinking alcohol." The poster hangs in a cognac distillery near Yerevan, Armenia.

country folk harvesting pears in an orchard. Dean halted our driver, and we piled out for pictures. Boris, with his formal Moscow manners, saw that the pickers had begun eating and was reluctant to approach them; but not Dean. He used Russian—and got back a cataract of friendly Armenian. Would we join them for lunch? The invitation, preceding even Boris's explanation, said much about Armenian hospitality. Perched on upended fruit buckets, we were served roasted bell peppers, goat cheese, *lavash* (unleavened bread), and pears fresh from the tree.

Other journeys took us to the highlands and monuments of the past. The 13th-century Geghard Monastery, for example, is comprised of man-made caves in a stone mountain, with vaulted chapels, heavy yet ethereal, a Rushmore turned inside out. The abbot, Father Daniel Shamlian, showed us around, then blessed a small cross for me. It was carved like the *khachkars*, stone crosses found in churches and on waysides, and famous in Armenia since the fourth century.

Stone-carving of a more utilitarian sort goes on near the chill mountain waters of Lake Sevan. "The lake was like a donor of blood for the development of our republic," said Konstantin when we drove to see it. In the 1930's, water from Lake Sevan was diverted for power and irrigation. Farm production and industry went up, but Lake Sevan went down—by some 52 feet.

From its new and lower shoreline, we could see the ecological damage. The setting is other-worldly, at an elevation of some 6,000 feet with ascetic mountains circling the waters. To restore the shrinking lake, engineers are now cutting a 30-mile tunnel through rock to bring water from the Arpa River. Thus man repairs the work of man.

Konstantin is an Armenian newsman who lives in Moscow but had returned for a family visit. On our drive back, he mused about his nationality: "To be born an Armenian is to be born on a stern soil. Our country is not a land of plenty where everything blooms and yields fruit. The Soviet writer Vasily Grossman said it: In Armenia everything is of stone. It is impossible for us not to be industrious. Whatever our work —engineer, journalist, scientist—we preserve the peasant attitude: to work hard. . . . We have good memories. We never forget the good done us. Nor the bad, for we have had merciless enemies. Our character is like our climate: sharply continental. We love or hate strongly.

"My father told me, when I was small, how my grandfather had been killed in the Turkish massacre. Father fled to Greece, and in 1932 returned by ship with other repatriates; he worked as a teacher of English. And in the Great Patriotic War, he was killed. I remember my mother crying. . . . Now my son Armen is four years old, and lives in Moscow. How do I keep him Armenian? My wife and I are bilingual, and want Armen also to speak both Armenian and Russian. I want my son to respect other nations, to be inquisitive and sociable. For Armen, I buy both Russian and Armenian children's books at a bookstore on Kirov Street. I want him to grow up a harmoniously developed citizen. . . ."

For me, old Armenia remains my memory of the highland village of Hatsavan, a place of arid space: high, wide, handsome. There I noticed a few gnarled, dusty-green olive trees—and just beyond them, looking over Hatsavan's shoulder, stood that cloud of ice, Mount Ararat. The view seemed a summary: an olive branch for Noah's dove—a hope for peace and a new beginning.

Skier sweeps down the windblown slope of Mount Cheget. Across the valley rise two other

prominent peaks of the Caucasus range, ice-capped Donguz Arun and slightly lower Nakra.

"I PROPOSE A TOAST ...IN VODKA"

At least 133 years of age, Khfaf Lasuria raises her glass of vodka to propose a toast during a dinner honoring author McDowell and photographer Conger. In 1975, Mrs. Lasuria died at home in the Georgian village of Kutol at an age variously estimated at 134 to 144. Although such longevity remains unusual even in the Transcaucasus, some 39 of every 100,000 people in Soviet Georgia reach 100. Many physicians and scientists believe that hard physical work and vigorous exercise contribute to long life. A nephew of Mrs. Lasuria, Kutol Dzikur Lasuria (far right, above), still rides over jumps on horseback at the age of 85. In his study at Baku, Azerbaijan, gerontologist Shukur M. Gasanov ponders the mysteries of youth and age.

ПОМНИ Е, ЧТО НАУКА ТРЕ
БУЕТ ОТ ЧЕЛОВЕКА ВСЕЙ
ЕГО ЖИЗНИ
                    И. ПАВЛОВ

И. Павлов
1849-1936

ON SUKHUMI'S BALMY COAST

Statue honoring the Nobel Prize-winning physiologist Ivan Petrovich Pavlov stands at Sukhumi, Georgia, on the grounds of the Institute of Experimental Pathology and Therapy. An institute technician (below) electronically maps the motor responses of a monkey named Mars. Famed for a mild climate, the Sukhumi area attracts many visitors to its Black Sea spas. Above, an attendant at a sanitarium in Gagra gives an invigorating bath to an engineer from Volgograd.

HILLTOP SHRINE

Reflecting sunset's glow, a road meanders toward a church above Mtskheta, near Tbilisi. Inside the building, a woman raises her hands in supplication; for her it remains a holy place, though no

longer used for services. On the exterior appear detailed carvings; the one at right above shows—kneeling before St. Stephen—a member of the noble family that built the church in the sixth century.

GEORGIANS: "JOLLY, OPEN, AMBITIOUS"

Workers stoke a blast furnace at a steel mill in Rustavi, Georgia. Constructed in the 1940's on the ruins of a town founded centuries before, Rustavi today has a population of more than 100,000 and a major iron and steel industry. About 12 miles northwest stands Tbilisi, capital of the republic; there artist Irakli Ochiauri (above) —who describes his people as "jolly, open, not very rational, very ambitious"—hammers designs into copper in the time-honored Georgian craft of metal chasing. (Examples of his work appear on page 223.) At left, friends and strangers join in song at a restaurant in Tbilisi, a common occurrence among the music-loving Georgians.

MOUNT ARARAT   *Dawn breaks over Yerevan, capital of Armenia. The peaks of*

Ararat—the symbol on the seal of the Armenian Republic—rise across the border in Turkey.

BURGEONING YEREVAN

Flares stream from roofs around Lenin Square in Yerevan during celebration of Soviet Aviation Day. In the daylight, buildings

constructed of volcanic tufa give the city a pinkish hue. Housing
remains a serious problem, for in the last 50 years the city's population
has multiplied by more than 20. Plasterers at a new apartment house
(left, above) work to ease the shortage. University students—mod
clothes their uniforms and schoolbooks their badges—chat after class.

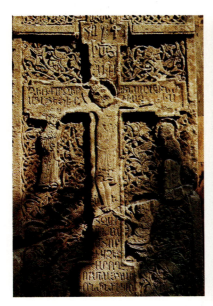

WONDERS OF STONE CARVING

Visitors carrying candles—perhaps from devotion, perhaps for light—visit a chapel
of the Geghard Monastery in Armenia. Beginning in the 13th century, craftsmen
here chiseled into the basalt face of the hillside, carving vaulted rooms, wall and
ceiling decorations, and altars—all from the solid rock. Father Daniel Shamlian,
abbot of the monastery (above), blesses a cross for a visitor. In the courtyard of the
cathedral at Echmiadzin, cradle of Armenian Christianity, intricate filigree forms
a background for a tombstone crucifix, or khachkar. In the year 301 the kingdom of
Armenia embraced Christianity as a state religion, the first nation to do so.

RURAL ARMENIA

Pouring water from a jug of centuries-old design, an Armenian farm worker invites the author and photographer to share her lunch of salty white goat cheese, roasted bell peppers, pears, and lavash— flat, unleavened bread. Below, combines move across a grainfield near Lake Sevan, source of water for several large irrigation projects. Above, a roadside vendor sells pears, grapes, apples, and berries.

BAKU: CASPIAN METROPOLIS

Canopy of concrete soars above patrons of the waterfront Pearl Café in Baku, capital of Azerbaijan. In the evening, people stroll the gardens at the edge of the Caspian Sea. A city resident wearing the broad, flat cap common in this region sits with his granddaughter on a park bench; soldiers on leave pose beside a cartoon character for a souvenir photograph. Extending well into the Caspian, oil-production platforms and pipelines pump shore-ward the lifeblood of Baku's economy. Much farther out, an entire city on pilings accommodates 3,000 oil workers.

DANCERS OF AZERBAIJAN

With graceful gesture and measured step, members of an Azerbaijanian folk dance group perform at Baku. In their pride of ethnic heritage, the dancers reflect a characteristic of Soviet citizens throughout the U.S.S.R.

8

THE CENTRAL ASIAN REPUBLICS

Turbaned elder savors tea and flatbread at the bazaar in Samarkand, Uzbekistan. Distinctive regional dress and customs still flourish here and throughout Soviet Central Asia, crossroads of East and West and home of ancient civilizations. A target of both Alexander the Great and Genghis Khan, Samarkand later became the capital of Tamerlane's empire.

IN 1851, FRIEDRICH ENGELS wrote in a letter to Karl Marx: "For all its baseness and Slavonic dirt, Russian domination is a civilizing element . . . on Central Asia."

"Remember the date—1851," said our Novosti colleague. "Central Asians lived in poverty."

True. And also ironic, for the Soviet territories we call Central Asia knew high arts and brilliant courts long before most Slavs could write. These lands have produced conquerors with an inspired cruelty, and poets of overpoweringly precious delicacy. Only in Central Asia would minstrels sing songs of a maiden with

> . . . lips like cream,
> A pistachio nose, almond eyelids.
> Coral toothed, fairy faced,
> Little mouth beautiful as a thimble.

Modern journalism follows the same lyric school. The Kazakhstan newspaper *Leninskaya Smena,* for example, published this: "The desert . . . is a crusher of stone! Like a flour-mill, it grinds into sand granite, which, back in the times of the Pharaohs, was held to be a symbol of eternity. The desert is the materialized sleep of nature. Whole civilizations have sunk into this sleep. . . ."

The history of Central Asia involves rags, riches, and the convulsions of geography. The armies of Alexander the Great and Genghis Khan left their tracks in its sands. Tamerlane established his capital here. Camel caravans burdened with fortunes in silks and spices regularly traversed the trade routes across these southern regions from China to Constantinople.

"We get most of our winds and active weather from the North Atlantic," a young hydrometeorologist, V. S. Cherednichenko, told me in

Alma Ata. We were less than 200 miles from China where it meets the southeastern border of Kazakhstan—a Soviet socialist republic nearly four times the size of my native Texas. Few spots on the planet are as far from ocean water. Yet our weather here was imported. "To forecast accurately for the vicinity of Alma Ata, we need weather information at least from Greenland," said Cherednichenko.

The weather exported by the North Atlantic to Central Asia seems badly damaged in shipment. The variation in temperature is extreme, the rainfall stingy. The rippling dunes of the Kara Kum desert in Turkmenistan—a textbook example of sand desert—average only 5.9 inches of rain a year.

The five constituent republics of Central Asia occupy 1,542,000 square miles, more than half the area of the contiguous United States. They also record the highest birthrates in the Soviet Union, so that Great Russians in Moscow make half-serious jokes about themselves as a Soviet minority group. (They aren't yet: At last count, Great Russians comprised 53.3 percent of the entire Soviet population.)

In fact, nearly a quarter of the burgeoning population of Central Asia is Russian. Dean and I were granted visas to visit what has been the most-discussed community of new settlers in Kazakhstan, the Virgin Lands settlements around Tselinograd. But the spring weather turned dry and dusty—and our visas were revoked. The explanation was candid: "The Kazakh Party Central Committee said it's just too dry for pictures." Plan and hope as man may in Kazakhstan, he still depends on those North Atlantic rain clouds.

An agronomist named Fyodor Morgun, who pioneered the Virgin Lands in the 1950's, has written an instructive account of this project, *The Grain-Growers*. The program allegedly has brought 25 million hectares—nearly 62 million acres—of land into cultivation with a reported

Searing deserts and towering mountains make Central Asia an area of extremes. Here lie both the highest and lowest elevations in the U.S.S.R.—24,590-foot Communism Peak and the Batyr Depression, 433 feet below sea level. Each of the region's five constituent Soviet republics shares at least one border with Iran, Afghanistan, or China.

average annual yield of 20 million tons of grain, roughly a tenth of the U.S.S.R. total grain production. Writes Morgun:

"In February 1954 the Party organizations of Moscow . . . launched a broad propaganda campaign." Volunteers "appreciated the fact that the Party did not minimize the hardships . . . to start from scratch, cultivate virgin soil, build new communities, and give the country grain."

Today, Morgun continues, "The state farms are rich. . . . Many tractor drivers and operators of farm machines average between 250 and 400 rubles a month." He also writes about the adventures of adapting farm equipment to the new conditions. He tells how the efficient 13-ton, 215-horsepower, wheeled K-700 tractor was introduced to the Virgin Lands over the objections of those who supported the lighter, tracked DT-54 and DT-75 models: "There were thunderous shouts of 'Hurrah' as the men got into the cabs and the column began to move."

And there were, he says, special methods of dry-land cultivation. Agronomist Morgun visited western Canada in 1963 and found certain techniques of tillage to prevent erosion that he attributed to Russian immigrants there; he came away, he wrote later, "with the definite impression that the Canadians had borrowed and benefited . . . from the farming know-how of the Russian immigrants."

When he returned to Moscow, Morgun reported directly to leaders in the Kremlin, explaining reasons for a drop in yields and the erosion problem in the Virgin Lands.

"I said all this had come about . . . because the local managers and specialists weren't allowed to decide questions on the technical aspects of farming. . . . in the Pavlodar Region . . . it was positively wrong to do the autumn ploughing with moldboard implements, as that paved the way for wind erosion. In spite of that, we were assigned plans for post-harvest ploughing and were required to fulfill them. . . .

"Not long afterwards . . . several of our large farm machinery plants had rush orders" for "subsurface cultivators, tiller-seeders, and deep diggers. . . . After that harvests increased and were stabilized; wind erosion was checked. . . ."

When, a few weeks after the publication of agronomist Morgun's story, I visited the Volgograd tractor plant of wartime fame, I was shown a whole assembly line of—to my surprise—tracked DT-75 tractors, "bound for the Virgin Lands," a technician said. Each DT-75 costs 4,000 rubles. Perhaps in a greener future year I shall return to cheer for the efficient K-700 instead.

The capital of Kazakhstan, Alma Ata, surprised me because I was expecting a raw frontier town. Instead it stands new, handsome, and well landscaped. Our Novosti hostess, Revmira Daniilovna Voshchenko, laughed, "Since the Revolution, Kazakhstan has been one big construction site. I remember in the 1940's when I was a girl, Alma Ata was a town of one-story buildings. Now we are building a 26-story hotel." We skimmed success stories of the area: the 1,220,000 separate farms replaced by 2,300 state and collective farms . . . the machine-tool and steel-rolling plants . . . the growing population: 14.4 million for the republic, 859,000 for Alma Ata, and a membership of 657,000 in the republic's Communist Party.

I was properly impressed by the modern stone-and-aluminum V. I. Lenin Palace of Culture (it seats 2,500 people), and by the Orthodox cathedral built in 1907 and now being carefully restored. "It's all wood," said our Kazakh guide, Saule Erzhanova. "No nails—and it survived our earthquake of 1911 when the whole town was struck down. It measures 54 meters tall, the highest wooden structure in the U.S.S.R."

But I like Alma Ata more for the shade of its elms, white acacias, and poplars, and for the liquid sounds of irrigation canals flanking city streets. "Our mountains!" lamented Mrs. Erzhanova. "You haven't noticed them?" I had not. Progress has brought enough smog to eclipse some of Asia's finest scenery, the Zailiysky Alatau mountains that rise to nearly 16,000 feet south of the city.

We drove along 50th-Anniversary-of-October Street, once the route of silk caravans. Across from our hotel, on Communist Prospekt, a crowd had lined up 27 deep to buy big green apples from a vendor—a reminder that Alma Ata means "full of apples." A department store behind the apple stand offered accordions, plaster busts of Lenin, spare parts for motorcycles, camping gear, and so on. But I found none of the traditional felt rugs with their appliquéd spiral ram's horn motif, suggesting the Kazakhs' skill in raising livestock.

"My sister works on a collective farm raising sheep and cattle," said Mrs. Erzhanova. "You see, our father was killed in the Battle of Stalingrad, and our mother was only half-educated—just elementary school. So life was hard. But the government took care of us, brought us up in a Kazakh school in Uralsk. Our mother worked as a clerk in a small government store for 25 years. At age 55 she retired with a pension of 55 rubles a month. We visit back and forth. So my sister, Alma—did you know the name Alma means 'apple'?—my sister works on a farm near the village of Kalinin. And I am married to an electrical engineer."

Her own name means "sunbeam" in Kazakh, an apt symbol, for Mrs. Erzhanova was one of the cheeriest people we encountered. Her face was Oriental—a face that would look quite at home in Hong Kong.

"But not Chinese! No, no," she said emphatically. "We do have refugees from China in Kazakhstan—like the Uyghurs, 120,000 in the republic and perhaps 20,000 in Alma Ata alone. They were not treated well in China. They have an Uyghur-language theater here."

The Kazakh language has had its own struggles in the 20th century. Until 1928, Kazakhs used a script like Arabic. When Soviet power was finally consolidated in Kazakhstan (where civil war aftershocks lasted longer than in European parts of the country), the government adopted the Latin alphabet—until 1940. Then the Cyrillic alphabet was decreed, though with six extra characters. We can pity that generation of schoolchildren, with two or even three alphabets to learn. And a similar task faced youngsters in the other four Central Asian republics.

Watching a musical review in Alma Ata's new concert hall one night, we became peculiarly aware of our location near the Soviet eastern frontier. Security precautions that already were tight—the rocket-launch site at Baykonur had pointedly been left off our itinerary—became tighter. Dean was not permitted to take photographs inside the concert hall, apparently because Party meetings are held there, and because many uniformed military men were attending the performance. The musical itself had the format of a vaudeville show with a big-band sound. A stand-up comedian opened his routine in falsetto—but falsetto Kazakh. About half the audience broke up in seizures of laughter. The rest of us sat with blankly polite smiles and utter uncomprehension. Thus the ethnic humor—and divisions—of Kazakhstan.

Kazakhs are proud to have their own Academy of Sciences, which we visited one day. Secretary Temir B. Darkanbaev brought together a roomful of geographers, geologists, and biologists to visit with us around a conference table covered with green felt and bottles of mineral water. We talked about the great Kazakh territory and resources. And how did this geography affect the Kazakh character?

"Our people lived on a vast land that had to be defended. Others wanted it—and that fact accounts for our warlike nature. Not aggressive, but *protective*. Excellent horsemen had to move swiftly. And hospitality was also important to survival."

The very earth of Kazakhstan sometimes seems treacherous. The chief architect and city planner of Alma Ata notes that "our main problem of city planning is the danger of earthquakes."

But just as great a danger—and a stranger one—is a phenomenon of this region known by the Kazakh word *sel*. In 1921 such a natural calamity struck sleepy Alma Ata, then called Verny, and Lenin was advised by a telegram from Tashkent. The message was garbled, and Lenin wrote a note, "Looks like an earthquake or a flood." He was close.

A sel is a rainless flood, a kind of mudflow and landslide. It starts with glacial melt high in the commanding Tien Shan range. The water collects in moraine pockets on mountainsides, swelling into high-perched lakes dammed by the unstable rock. When the water's weight finally breaks through, a wild avalanche of boulders, mud, and water comes crashing down the mountain, gathering speed, taking trees and houses—turning everything into a deadly missile as it falls.

The 1921 sel struck Alma Ata at midnight with enough debris to fill 2,500 freight cars; it carved one path of desolation along a stream channel and then branched down two city streets. No one will ever know the number of casualties. Nothing could stand against such a force.

Or almost nothing. Engineers soon began a project to build traps for sels along their likely paths. Above Alma Ata, workmen built steel grills to slow an avalanche of mud, and dams to catch the debris.

"In 1973, we had our real test," said hydrometeorologist Cherednichenko, a member of the sel information center. "It formed with a glacier—July sunshine had melted it. Well, I came into the observatory here a little after 6 one evening. Someone shouted, 'A sel has started!'

"We have a radar warning service for people along sel routes. And we have 15 alarm devices triggered by the sel as it passes. And a dam at Medeo to catch and hold the water. Well, the dam held, but next day we learned that another lake might still rupture."

A journalist described the scene at the Medeo dam, how the stones sank to the base of the dam and silt rose bubbling to the surface. "In these bubbles there suddenly appeared a human form. The flood of water hurled the body to a tiny stone promontory. Another minute and the man would have sunk to the depths beyond rescue. Two motorcycle policemen raced down the dam. . . . One officer plunged into the silt and elbowed his way forward. . . . He felt the slimy, soft silt pour into his high boots and the pockets of his trousers. Five meters—three—one meter!" The man was saved: 50-year-old Kalyan Ikonovich Musin. He had been carried by the sel for more than two kilometers—"a powerful stream that could turn a nine-story building into mush." But the danger had not passed. The remaining mountain lake still threatened, and a light rain was falling from time to time. Crews set up pipes and pumping stations at Medeo and were able to lower the water level.

The canyon still showed scars of the sel when we visited Medeo. We watched trucks carry away boulders and other debris; the dam must be completely emptied to stop a future sel.

Just below the dam, a new artificial ice rink—built for the training sessions of Soviet Olympians—was animated by skaters and hockey players. Sixteen kilometers down the canyon, Alma Ata lay safe and unharmed. For the moment, at least, man had won a struggle against some of the world's most menacing geography.

Flying out from Alma Ata, we climbed above the smog and turned toward Kirgizia. "I have measured industrial dust up to 2,200 meters," said Yury Tyomnykh, the young helicopter pilot seated next to me in the airliner. Now we could see the mountains, tall and icy against a clear blue sky; soon we lost sight of the irrigated greenery and found a dunelike land where plowing tractors left plumed wakes of dust. This again was Kazakh steppe where "the cattle will have to be pastured on sand," as a poet of the district once wrote.

Kirgizia, a mountainous republic with rich valleys, offers a change in topography and color. We landed in the Chu Valley at Frunze, the capital—"more green than Alma Ata; our towns quarrel," said the helicopter man.

Though Frunze boasts nearly half a million people, it has a pleasant small-town feeling. Our hotel exuded the atmosphere of an inn, facing a small railroad station and some of the elms of the city's many parks. With its rows of trees, Frunze seems as neat and gentle as an orchard.

"And that is the very difference between the Kazakhs and the Kirgiz as people," said the historian K. Karakeev. "Kazakhs are of the steppe, but on us the mountains have left their imprint. We are more peaceful. We are also taller and live longer. We don't have fat people."

"Our languages are quite similar," said guide Roza Ismankulova. "Pronunciation differs—s turns to sh. But both are Turkic. . . . We respect old people and call the elders aksakal, 'whitebeard.' "

With help from our local Novosti colleague, Azat Usmanov, we tasted the flavorful Kirgiz poetry preserved down the generations by akyns, or bards, who recited while strumming the three-stringed komuz. Most famous is the epic Manas, whose oldest verses date from the ninth century. Its rhythms hypnotize with a series of equal syllables and then a stress, a Turkic incantation:

> . . . the horsemen surprised everybody.
> They tamed with the strength of their hand
> Slim-hipped pure-bred horses,
> Horses that knew no harness,
> Horses that knew no fatigue.

The slim-hipped Kirgiz horse still gallops the land. A census reports 265,000 horses in the republic, although Roza's rural family supplemented their one horse with the service of a family camel, and "we use yaks in high snow regions."

Our hotel menu offered "boiled horsemeat with garnish" and

"horseflesh with dough," although Azat insisted, "A Kirgiz would not eat a horse if it had ever been saddled—never! Today, we have many wild horses like your mustangs." I settled for ground horsemeat with noodles and horse broth on the side. Unsaddled.

Naturally, the horse opera is a cinema favorite in Kirgizia, and on a Frunze sidewalk one day we met an actor named Suymenkul C. Chokmorov. He was a dashing fellow, tall, wiry, strongly Mongol in appearance; he wore an indigenous *kalpak,* or hat, at a rakish angle.

"I'm not really a professional actor," he said. His apology was a 500-watt smile. "I'm a painter by trade. But I believe my horsemanship is equal to things I've seen in your American films. I did my own stunt work for *The Seventh Bullet.*"

Later we saw that film, a galloping story with a civil war setting. Suymenkul rode, roped, and stunt-jumped as well as anyone I've seen in a North American rodeo. No wonder, since Kirgiz sports include wrestling on horseback and polo-like games of tag.

Another evening we visited the Frunze theater for a Kirgiz stage production called *In the Highlands.* Costumes were colorful, but the plot was pure black and white. It also concerned the civil war, and especially the efforts of Soviet commander M. V. Frunze to defeat those reactionaries plotting with "British imperialists." The villains all had cigars, and wore either white tie or turban. One plotter clapped his hands for a slinky redhead, a bad sort who drank cognac and said, "Okay." The good characters wore traditional Kirgiz garb and drank koumiss, the fermented milk of a mare. The ending was happy for the dictatorship of the proletariat.

Peace has brought progress to the more than three million people of Kirgizia. In 1926, the republic counted only 5,200 kilometers of roads —and none paved. Today Kirgizian motorists can drive on some 21,000 kilometers of highway, including 13,700 kilometers now surfaced, a considerable accomplishment in a mountainous area just about the size of South Dakota.

We used some Kirgizian roads to visit a state farm raising sugar beets near the town of Kant—"sugar" in Kirgiz. From manager Dmitry Petrovich Zubkov, we learned details: The Kant farm netted 1,953,000 rubles the previous year. A tractor driver gets a monthly salary of 80 to 90 rubles and a bonus after the harvest that can bring his total average wage to 190, sometimes even 240 rubles. "Milkmaids can make as much as 160 rubles a month," said Dmitry Petrovich. "And though construction work brings better pay than farm work, we win labor from the state cement factory because we offer better housing!"

And how easy would it be to get a job here? Could a Muscovite come? The manager pursed his lips. "Well, we try to get the *best* people. Not job-jumpers. Everyone has a work book showing his whole employment record—ups and downs. If a man has gone to the Far North and then to the Far East for bonus pay, well, we know he won't stay here."

I wondered, for Kirgizia is a beautiful land. One day we drove up a mountain valley, parked, and then hiked upward along the Alaarcha River—named for the juniper. Above us loomed the Peak of the Mountain Goat and another called Mount Air, as Roza referred to them.

"The stream has trout in it," said Roza. "And the green grasses here have nice smells." She reminisced about her (Continued on page 274)

Homeward-bound residents of Samarkand pass the Registan — "sandy place" — where citizens

gathered for trade, news, schooling, and prayer from the 15th to the early 20th century.

ASIAN BAZAARS

Each Central Asian bazaar offers both its own specialties and staple foods, most of them locally produced. Shaded by an arbor, a Samarkand vendor broils shashlyk, or shish kebab—spiced and skewered lamb—over a long charcoal brazier. The fan-shaped arrangement of skewers permits him to turn six or seven at once. Beyond him, patrons sit at tables or on low, mat-covered platforms. Samarkand's location in the fertile Zeravshan River valley usually means an abundance of fruits and vegetables. But sometimes shortages occur. As buyers snap up potatoes in Tashkent, the Uzbek capital, one woman makes known her objections to photographing the scene.

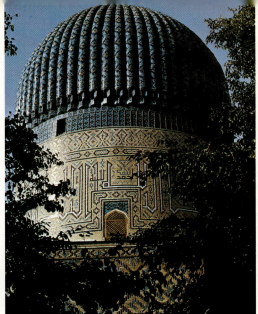

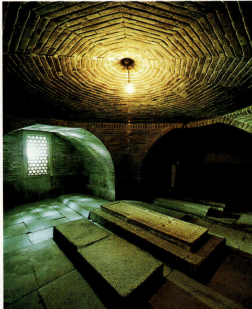

Beyond a downtown intersection in
Samarkand rise the massive ruins of the
Bibi-Khanym mosque, partly framed by
the scaffolding of restoration crews. A
short distance away, the domed Gur-i
Amir mausoleum shelters the sarcophagus
of the warrior who gave Central Asia its
golden age: Timur the Lame, or Tamerlane.
The crippled conqueror ignored his handi-
caps to solidify and rule an empire that
stretched from the Caspian Sea into
present-day Syria and east to China.

OLD BUKHARA

Sand swirls past a cyclist in Bukhara, Uzbekistan, where history weighs as heavily as the surrounding desert. Bukhara became an important city on the caravan routes linking Arabia with India and old Cathay; pack animals bearing silks and spices, gold and salt once streamed through its narrow streets. Today, a new Bukhara of glass and steel stands beside the old city, still so richly endowed with mosques, madrasahs—religious schools (above)—and other buildings that scholars consider it a museum of Islamic architecture. Parts of the city wall survive to emphasize Bukhara's bond to the past.

MODERN TASHKENT

Modern design with an Asian flair marks the new Lenin Museum in Tashkent, a city leveled by earthquakes a decade ago. Volunteers from throughout the Soviet Union helped clear debris, house the thousands of homeless, and rebuild in accordance with a new master plan. Wide avenues, ornamental ponds, and quake-resistant buildings

have replaced old housing made of packed earth. Like Ashkhabad
and Alma Ata, Tashkent lies in an area crisscrossed by active fault
systems that portend future shocks. At its Institute of Seismology,
Director Valentin I. Ulomov (top) ponders the instability of the
earth's crust; a staff member monitors the world for new tremors.

CLIFF DWELLINGS

Cubist apartments rise high in sunny, busy, reconstructed

Tashkent—with 1.5 million people, the largest Soviet city east of the Urals.

ON LOCATION AT KHIVA

Old walls and domes of Khiva provide the backdrop for cinema crews shooting Black Caravan (left). Just as Arizona's photogenic terrain has provided the scenery for hundreds of Westerns, so the Khiva area has become the setting for many Central Asian films. Between takes, heroine Larisa Brezhnaya (above) pauses to meet some young admirers. At right, an intricately carved door marks the Palvan Gate— Entrance of the Giant—in the wall of Khiva's old Ishan-Kala, or Inner City, now preserved as a national monument.

family village, Sukum. Her father was a veterinarian, and she was one of 11 children (the most recently published ethnic Kirgiz birthrate was an estimated 40 per thousand population in 1969). "When he was young, my father was a shepherd," she said; her talk rippled on, sounding like the poetic, minor-key prose of the Kirgiz author Chinghiz Aymatov.

In his book *Jamila*, Aymatov has described this very region, where Kirgiz peaks meet Kazakh plain: ". . . now herds of horses would gallop across the ringing earth to their summer pastures . . . now flocks of sheep would slowly spread like lava over the hills; now a water-fall would dash down from a cliff, its white foaming water blinding; now the sun would set softly in the thicket of needle grass beyond the river and the lonely rider on the fiery edge of the horizon seemed in pursuit of it—he need only stretch his hand to touch the sun—and then he, too, would vanish in the thicket and the twilight.

"Wide is the Kazakh steppe beyond the river. It has spread the mountains apart to make room for itself. . . ."

And in that timeless way I shall remember Kirgizia and Kazakhstan.

The most beautiful people in the Soviet Union, according to our Slavic companion Boris Lunkov, are Tajiks. I cannot argue. The 448,000 residents of the capital of the Tajik Republic, Dushanbe—called Stalinabad from 1929 to 1961—turn this architecturally dull city into a visual feast. The women have dark eyelashes of unbelievable length, classic features, graceful figures, and hair worn in braids that may reach their knees ("water here is good for the hair," one girl confided). Their clothing, often of natural silk and always of bright color, includes a vestlike *kemsal*, a skirt, shawl, and trousers. Men are often garbed in a *chapon*, or black quilted robe. Both men and women wear skullcaps called *tuppis*. "In my father's house," a guide told me, "everyone must wear a tuppi when eating at the table. Father is a Muslim believer."

We spent many a warm day in a teahouse called Rohat, meaning "delight," along with much of the male population, sipping sugarless green tea. "We have grapes for our sweetening," said Novosti colleague Sharafjan Zakhidov. "They are ripe from May to November. And some grapes are so sweet you can only eat two, for the sweetness can choke you. Few of us drink alcohol, of course."

These conversations were held as we sat shoeless on large tableside beds. But the *muysafed*, or grayheads, were poorly represented among the tea drinkers: "They are observing a religious fast. It's Ramadan, so they cannot eat until 7:30 tonight. The grayheads do not approve of the willow trees planted there in the courtyard. They say willows cause dark thoughts."

We less devout patrons of Rohat ate *sanbusa*, a dough-covered meat patty, and *palav*, a variation of rice pilaf. "Only men prepare proper pilaf; women are too hurried and saving. A man has time to cook—and in a teahouse he would use a kilo of rice to a kilo of meat. Still, women should be praised." Sharafjan considered the matter while turning his handleless teacup. "Men are extravagant and irresponsible."

We talked about other pleasures, like boar's liver and the fat of a sheep's tail "to make a person drunk with food." We listened to fountains play, admired the roses that bloomed nearby, and appreciated —darkly, darkly—the willow shade.

Chairman of a collective farm in Tajikistan's Vakhsh Valley explains a method of growing lemons in a relatively cold climate: Workers plant the trees in six-foot-deep, brick-lined trenches, in winter prune them back and protect them with rooflike wooden covers.

Tajik culture and language are closely related to the Persian. The tenth-century poet Firdousi is honored here just as he is in Tehran. But Arabic script has given way to Cyrillic, and several Tajiks made a special point to express their gratitude to Russians. "Without them, we would still be subject to the Uzbeks," said one bearded man.

Surrounded as they are by Turkic people, the Tajiks gently yet unyieldingly cultivate their Persian manners. One day we visited a collective farm in the Vakhsh River valley some 40 kilometers from the Afghan frontier. Irrigation canals make possible the cotton crops here, but the canals also find esthetic use. The farm had a dining hall built bridge-like over a canal "for the cooling comfort and for the music of the water," said Mamatair Makhmudov, the collective-farm chairman.

In the fields, Tajik women wore silk costumes to pick cotton. "Though some wear *artificial* silk," conceded Makhmudov. But their work itself was entirely genuine: some 80 kilos (about 176 pounds) a day for each woman. The Tajik yield of cotton—about 3 metric tons to the hectare, or about 1.3 tons per acre—is the highest in the U.S.S.R. "Why not?" asked the chairman. "We have earth and sun. And water came with the canal in the 1930's. You see the results."

In other parts of Tajikistan we could see what life was like with neither rain nor irrigation. South of Dushanbe, the land becomes a pale monochrome, a country of cockleburs, thistles, and powder dust. Villages match the earth, since houses are made of dried mud; roofs lie flat, for they need not turn much rainfall.

We passed some herdsmen, one family with goats, others with sheep. Dean halted our car for pictures, and I hailed the shepherds. They were Uzbeks, like a fourth of the Tajikistan population, from a nearby state farm. Most of their sheep were the brown fat-tailed kind. While golden eagles wheeled overhead, we introduced ourselves.

Takhir Odynaev explained his job: "I stay six months in the mountains. Then a month here. And next we go into a high valley with pasture. Those are our tents—no, we no longer use the old-fashioned yurts." He laughed, introduced me to his black dog named Zokcha, and tuned his transistor radio to the Asian dissonance he enjoyed. Not a bad life. Yet Odynaev must move like a weathervane, forever seeking pasture with water—perhaps an isolated existence for a fellow as sociable as he.

Ironically—in light of the austere landscape around us—Tajikistan's water resources are considerable. The republic is more than 90 percent mountainous and contains the highest summit in the Soviet Union, Communism Peak. High glaciers provide the sources of rivers like the Syr Darya and Amu Darya, which flow to the Aral Sea.

"Our rivers have two floods a year," said the deputy chairman of state planning, Dmitry Gachechiladze. "But they are low at the precise time we need water for irrigation. So we must depend on reservoirs."

Fortunately, the narrow mountain gorges here prove ideal for dams. Already two reservoirs, Kairakkum and Nurek, have a combined capacity of nearly 15 billion cubic meters of water. Another under construction at Rogun will add 11.7 billion cubic meters. "And an even larger lake at Dashtijum—though not yet started—could double the quantity of stored water," said Professor Kirill Stanyukovich, of the Tajik Academy of Sciences.

One Sunday morning we drove to the valley of the Vakhsh River to see Nurek Dam. Our road climbed abruptly above fields, orchards, and pastures to an oven of a gorge. A red billboard proclaimed, "COMMUNISM IS SOVIET POWER PLUS ELECTRIFICATION OF THE ENTIRE COUNTRY — LENIN." Trucks plied the roads in noisy gears. The dam, formed of raw earth, will eventually tower 317 meters, the highest dam in the world — until Rogun is finished. (The height of Aswân High Dam in Egypt, for example, measures only 111 meters.)

"When complete, Nurek will produce 11 billion kilowatt hours of electricity annually," said the stocky, 35-year-old director, Akobir Umarov. "That will drive an industrial complex at Regar: an aluminum plant, an electrochemical plant, both big and power-intensive.

"Actually, Nurek won't produce *enough* power. Before it's completed, we'll have a shortage. So we need Rogun upstream. We're building a whole cascade of projects! For its area, Tajikistan has the greatest hydroelectric potential in the U.S.S.R. — with dams, we could produce 300 billion kilowatt hours a year, one third of all Soviet electricity!"

Engineer Umarov introduced us to his assistant in charge of construction, Y. C. Sevnard, 30 years old and a veteran of both Aswân's heat and Siberia's cold. He seemed accustomed to the natural hazards of Nurek — snakes like the cobra and the green-eyed *gurza*, or blunt-nosed viper. "Yes, even snake charmers prefer to avoid that one. But three years ago we had a short-circuit when a gurza got into the wiring."

Nurek has made engineering history. The triangular-prism-shaped dam is 1.5 kilometers thick; it contains 52 million cubic meters of earth. "The core of the dam is built of earth containing clay — but without any gravel," Umarov explained. "It is like ceramic, and it is waterproof to prevent infiltration and erosion. Of course, the dam contains big rocks and rubble, all blasted from the gorge. The core itself is polished with brushes to make it perfectly smooth. If we have an earthquake, the rocks and fill outside the core will slide and dance — but not break."

In a small hydrofoil, we took a ride on Lake Nurek, gliding over water as blue as lapis lazuli. Our hydrofoil bos'n, Misha Marchenko, shouted over the engine noise. "There!" he pointed to a nearby cliff. "That's the place where I made a discovery. It was during a strong storm — I had many unpleasant emotions! And part of the cliff collapsed. There I saw some ceramic pots. I went ashore and saw also a skeleton and even gold earrings. Well, we notified archeologists, and they identified the discovery as a Bronze Age burial ground. Or perhaps later, from the time of Alexander the Great. . . . It will be several years before the lake covers it all." A second burial for the past.

As we left Nurek, engineer Umarov showed us a design local artists had fashioned. "Our river Vakhsh means 'wild' in Tajik," he told us. The design showed a spirited mustang — with a man on his back. Nurek has tamed the wild river.

Just as the folk of Tajikistan build high dams in the mountains, people of Turkmenistan put water into a long, deep ditch across the desert. In the Turkmen Republic (population 2.6 million), the single most dramatic geographic achievement is the Kara Kum Canal — some 15 feet deep, 100 yards wide, and 500 miles long when we saw it. The canal has crossed the Kara Kum ("black sand") desert, and continues west along the foothills of the Kopet Mountains toward the Caspian Sea.

Turkmenistan is 90 percent desert. True desert. A collective farm we visited on the outskirts of Ashkhabad, the capital, owns 145 tractors, 56 horses—but 198 camels.

"Our rainfall is about 225 millimeters [9 inches] a year," said the deputy chief of canal administration, Khalil Mamedov. "Our people had always herded flocks near the desert oases. In April 1954, we began construction of the canal—the first project of this scope in history. We had enormous problems—seepage, silt, evaporation, salinity. But in 1962, the water reached Ashkhabad."

That water came from the Amu Darya—the river Oxus, as it was known to Alexander the Great. Its arrival at Ashkhabad is now as legendary as Alexander himself.

"An unforgettable day—May 12, 1962," a veteran farmer told me. "Our old people had never believed water could cross the Kara Kum. When it flowed in, they had to touch it—to dip their hands in it! Some began to pray. We feasted for two months."

Poets marked the day with rhymes, and bards sang to the Canal of Happiness on television. Parents even named their babies Kanal Geldy, "The Canal Arrived."

A half million acres of desert began to produce cotton, alfalfa, vegetables, and the sweetest melons I have ever tasted. The environs of Ashkhabad flowered—though not for the first time. Some 2,200 years ago, when the Parthians ruled this region, their imperial capital of Nisa, nourished by canals, stood just beyond the streets of modern Ashkhabad. As late as the tenth century, an Arab scholar described a newer Nisa as "a big, healthy, and beautiful city with plenty of water and other blessings; the trees intertwine, the fruits are delicious, the mosques graceful, and the bread pure."

Since 1962, those antique words have become true again. Between its golden ages, however, the area had its problems, including a disastrous earthquake in 1948 that leveled the city. Recovery was swift. With a population of 297,000, Ashkhabad claims one of the highest birthrates in the Soviet Union. "Naturally," observed one resident. "Ashkhabad means 'town of love.'" Scholars may translate differently, but reality stands with romance.

One afternoon we visited the famous rug factory where 130 weavers help produce the Oriental design Westerners know as Bukhara. "Strictly speaking, it's called the Tekke design," explained one woman, Amangul Babaeva. "Named for the Tekke tribe, the carpets were always woven in rural Turkistan, and only sold in the Bukhara market." She assured us that Tekke carpets contained "more knots per square meter than any other Turkoman rugs, anywhere," and she herself made 12,000 knots in one eight-hour day.

Ashkhabad stands within sight of the Kopet Mountains, which form part of the border with Iran, and perhaps this proximity to an international frontier explains a certain bureaucratic timidity—the city was closed to Intourist travel while a new avenue to the airport was under construction. And a handsome nightclub in the hotel was strictly off limits for photographs: "A military man might be dancing here," tactfully suggested one Russian visitor, "without his wife."

For such reasons, Dean and I had time to peruse the history of this much-invaded land. There was the Greek historian Flavius Arrianus—

Arrian, as he was known—who described the hard-fought visit of Alexander the Great in the desert northwest of here: "... all the army was consumed by thirst, and Alexander himself ... drank whatever kind of water there was ... so a constant diarrhea suddenly seized him. .... He fell indeed into serious danger, and was carried back into the camp. ...."

Dean consoled himself with this majestic precedent one morning when he found himself unable to accompany Boris Lunkov and me. Half the hotel staff voluntarily brought him their remedies and clucking concern while Boris and I flew off to the Murgab River valley and the irrigated lands around Mary, population 70,000, near ruins of a city known to Alexander as Margiana and to Genghis Khan as Merv, estimated population one million.

From our plane we could see a fantasy of stereotyped desert—rippled sand dunes and camels used as pack animals. "The desert is still dangerous," said young Georgy Efendiev, from the Ashkhabad House of Friendship. "When you hunt hares or desert antelope, you must take much water in the truck. But of course, it is illegal to kill cobras. Catchers take venom from them for medical uses."

At Mary we visited irrigated cotton fields, and with the farmers we broke *churek*—flatbread cooked in clay ovens. We talked about the local foods, and were served a tall tale: "The sand gets so hot," insisted Efendiev, "a shepherd can even cook a sheep here by wrapping it in its skin and burying it."

Passing the adobe-walled ruins of old Merv, our driver suddenly stomped on his brakes. "Snake!" he yelled. "Cobra!" It was at least a dark cobra-color. We were careful not to get close enough to endanger its life and Soviet law.

Old Margiana-Merv, stormed and breached by Tuli Khan, son of Genghis Khan, was sundered more peaceably in 1958 when the waters of the Kara Kum Canal crossed the archeological site. There, at a small pier, we went aboard the 60-foot launch *Belarus*, welcomed by Akmurad Amanov, deputy manager of the canal construction service. Then, as cool as our spray, we navigated the canal and its austere desert.

"Dust storms? Yes! In just a few months, sand could fill up the canal. Sand flows like water," said Amanov. "So we have planted the banks, from 25 meters up to as much as 300 meters on each side, with desert plants to hold the sand.

"The early canal construction was the hardest. I remember at first we used old depressions in the earth, letting water flow to make its own way. Next came 120 kilometers of dry digging. Without roads in the desert, we carried every drop of water in tanks placed on sleds and pulled by tractors. All the water was rusty. And the heat! We had 3,500 people working at first; now it's 6,000 just on canal construction. We now widen and deepen the canal, and strengthen it.

"We had an algae problem with all this sunshine. So we introduced a fish we call thickhead—the silver carp. It comes from the Amur River in Siberia, and it eats algae. The thickheads and catfish are now enormous! I recall that one of our canal caretakers, a man named Yagmur Akyev, once fished with a 20-centimeter carp as bait. It was swallowed by a 6-kilo catfish—and *that* one was swallowed by a *150-kilo* catfish! His wife had to help Akyev shoot the larger catfish with a double-barreled shotgun. It was 3½ meters long."

Our host turned on a television set carried on the launch and tuned to a picture from the Orbita satellite, while we sipped cold mineral water from a refrigerator. It is certainly much better to travel by canal, I thought, than by camel.

Dean had recovered from his Alexandrian illness for our trip to the Repetek Sand Desert Station, not far from Chardzhou on the river Amu Darya. The area reminded me of White Sands, New Mexico, and Death Valley, California, combined.

"Ours is the first desert research station of its kind," said managing director Sukhan Veisov. "It was organized in 1912 to study desert ecology. We have had one group of Americans here before—in the 1930's.

"This area is the hottest spot in the U.S.S.R.—not bad, only about 50° C., 122° F., in the shade. And dry."

Very dry. Driving in, we passed the familiar tractor-sleds with water tanks; all water comes by train from 70 kilometers away across the classic sand desert. One-humped dromedary camels browsed haughtily on the scarce shoots of saxaul shrubs. The sky was a luminous blue without a wisp of cloud.

We talked about desert fauna—a thousand kinds of insects, more than 220 bird species, and mammals like the pale desert fox and small wildcat. The creature I like best was a lizard with large red "ears." When we stumbled onto him, he trembled with such vibration that he shivered his way right into the sand and safety—a triumph of applied anxiety.

The dynamics of desert sands especially occupy the 30 scientists of Repetek. Here they have developed techniques of gluing down the sands with sprays of oil. And roaming their gritty dunes by truck and camelback, biologists have classified ten plants as especially effective for stabilizing sand. These are the studies that have made practical the plantings along the Kara Kum Canal.

Among others, they study the heat-resistant saxaul. Even in its desert habitat, this angular, rawboned plant seems exotic. Its tubular shoots help conserve moisture. (We squeezed out some juice—sour stuff, but useful for desert survival.) At maximum height—when the taproot finds water—it is a 30-foot tree, but usually the saxaul is a mere bush. The brittle wood breaks easily without an ax, and burns like soft coal.

"Its smoke is delicious for *shashlyk*," said Veisov, and proved it by serving us skewered chunks of lamb cooked over saxaul coals. We ate in the shade of a tarpaulin, sprawled on rich carpets that our hosts had spread upon the sand. I carried away some vivid memories: of a staff ranger in a snap-brim hat, perched grandly on the back of a camel . . . of the super-fine sand that etched a frosting into the lenses of my sunglasses . . . of the pain brought to squinting eyes by the midday glare.

Not only does the Kara Kum cover 90 percent of Turkmenistan; it and other deserts comprise ten percent of the Soviet Union—210 million hectares—mostly of this sand type.

"Journalists are fond of military terms," said Academician O. N. Mamedniyazov at the Institute of Deserts in Ashkhabad. "They say, 'the desert is retreating' or 'irrigation has defeated the desert.' Not so. We must even *preserve* deserts. For example, this area produced 1.1 million karakul skins last year; those sheep thrive only in a hot, dry climate. We must find ways to use the desert's free energy of wind and sun. In another 50 years, more people will live in these deserts—and happily."

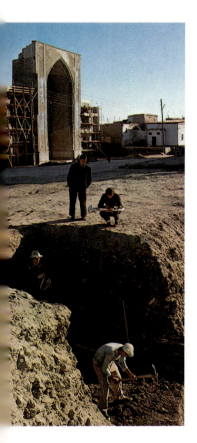

Digging into Bukhara's past, archeologists carefully continue excavation of a site that has already yielded artifacts from 11 different civilizations, each built on the ruins of its predecessor.

zbekistan, with a population of 14 million and an area greater than
California's, stands with Kazakhstan as the richest and most advanced of the Central Asian republics. No foreign traveler can doubt its strategic importance, for Aeroflot connections inevitably provide a layover at its capital and largest city in the region, Tashkent.

It was at Tashkent near dawn on June 15, 1865, that troops of the Russian tsar shouted *Ura!* and stormed through the Kamalan Gate to conquer their first large settlement in Central Asia. Old Tashkent crumbled in 1966 in a series of earthquakes. Thanks to cadres of construction workers who rebuilt 60 percent of the city, Tashkent now stands new and impressive, with homes for 1.5 million people and a massive, cubical example of socialist realism. The convoluted roots of Uzbekistan lie elsewhere, among the arabesques and fancies, the tiles and dust of ancient cities like Khiva, Samarkand, and Bukhara.

We drove into Khiva during the cotton-picking season. Our pretty Uzbek guide, Inobat Avezmurat, translated a roadside poster: It showed a stern-faced father-figure pointing like that famous Uncle Sam, and asking, "HOW MANY KILOS OF COTTON HAVE YOU PICKED TODAY?"

We got a chance ourselves when our car thumped to a halt with a flat tire. While the driver changed the wheel, Inobat nimbly picked a kilo of cotton to give a farm worker in the roadside field. "Tajikistan claims the highest *yield*," she said, "but we grow more cotton—about two thirds of the Soviet total. All by irrigation, of course."

Of course. Half of Uzbekistan is desert. Khiva itself, alongside the Kara Kum, gets only about 80 millimeters—3.2 inches—of rain a year. Our car had no windshield wipers. "No need," shrugged the driver. Beside the road, dry irrigation ditches cracked and contorted into earthen lesions and scales.

Khiva is pale as dust and set among scant mulberry trees. The old, irregularly stacked, flat-roofed houses of adobe that I saw first reminded me of the Indian pueblos of Taos, New Mexico.

The inner city, or Ishan-Kala, was different. Here was the East! Within the aged clay wall stood an 85-foot minaret, a 14th-century mausoleum, various residences and forts, and a large market on the site of an old caravan stop. Not until 1873 did the Khan of Khiva yield to the rule of the Russian tsar; even then, violence all but passed by Khiva, so it lives on as a relic. Among the landmarks, my favorite was the khan's palace, now a museum illustrating the lurid tyrannies of the khan: how he punished wrongdoers with beatings, hangings, and the nailing of their ears to the Palvan Gate. The khan levied dozens of kinds of taxes—including a tax on robbery. Yet he was not a man without tact: He somehow kept his 200 concubines in a palace with only 163 rooms.

The local color of Khiva can overwhelm even the socialist-realist. We found three motion picture companies simultaneously filming productions on the streets. All three were wild Easterns, and dealt—again—with sinister Britons at the end of World War I, concerned with their interests in India and determined to frustrate Communist power. Members of a Turkmen company had even brought their own horses for these location shots. "Our horses are the best," explained one, "but we share them with our colleagues." They also shared talent, so that an Uzbekfilm electrician donned a woolly hat, or *telpek*, to act in a Kirgizian cinema scene later in the day.

When Dean photographed one Oriental character with a white cobweb beard, the old fellow objected. Inobat filled us in: The patriarch was not an actor at all, but a resident and devout Muslim who disapproved of photographs; his costume was his everyday robe and turban.

Another day we met a veteran Uzbek director and People's Artist of the Soviet Union, Kamil Yarmatov. A husky-voiced chain-smoker, Yarmatov reminisced about his early days in film: "In the 1920's our job was to help the young republic get started—to unveil the women and fight illiteracy. Our first studio was a madrasah—a religious school—and the mullah hid his eyes when girls danced in light costumes. Our audience was 90 percent illiterate, so cinema was great for propaganda. Lenin had said cinema was the most important of the arts. Our sound trucks in the country sometimes projected pictures onto large rocks instead of screens!

"We had more action then, and many horses. I'm a former cavalryman and love shooting horse pictures; in the civil war, I stormed Bukhara with Frunze's troops. Once in India, I met a Muslim imam who resembled our people. About my age. Well, we talked. He was indeed from here and said, 'I was in Bukhara in 1920 when the infidels entered by the Karshin Gate.' I corrected him, 'It was the Talipoch Gate, and I was one of those infidels.' "

We followed the Frunze cavalry to Bukhara's Talipoch Gate and found a thousand years of architectural history—from the domed, tenth-century Samanid tomb, one of the oldest buildings in Soviet Central Asia, to the Intourist Hotel, then open only three months. A 12th-century minaret—once a lighthouse and watchtower for caravans, and now a nesting place for storks—stands tall and buff, quite free of colored tiles; sunlight etches a strong design in the texture of its brickwork.

For all the ancient picturesqueness of Bukhara and Khiva, we found Samarkand—after Tashkent the second largest city of Uzbekistan—to be the most sumptuous, a splendor of glazed blue-green tile. John Gunther pronounced Samarkand "a perfumed name."

Antique glamor is only part of the city's impression. Today 300,000 people live here at a 2,300-foot elevation in the Zeravshan Valley; streets are broad, new buildings solid, and trees give an oasis atmosphere. But more important, modern Samarkand has rediscovered the 25 centuries of its past.

Along Tashkent Road, camel caravans once carried silk westward from China—the "golden road to Samarkand," as one poet called it. The market near the ruined Bibi Khanym mosque still spices the air with condiments from the East. I bought a packet of saffron here one day, a doira or sheepskin tambourine, a jar of cotton-blossom honey, and a loaf of bread embossed with the word salaam, "peace." Down the road, I watched a blacksmith with scorched apron and thick arms wield a sledgehammer in each hand, battering red-hot metal into pickaxes.

Girls here paint their eyebrows into a single black line spanning the face. "For the glare of the sun?" I asked. "For beauty," answered our dark-eyed guide, Maya Akhmejenova, who needed no such artifice herself. "Now this is the Registan square."

Great madrasahs and tiled towers stake off the square's dramatic spaciousness. Britain's Lord Curzon saw it in 1888 and wrote, "I know of nothing in the East approaching it in massive simplicity and

Patterned shawl and caftan of a peasant woman visiting Samarkand (below) reflect the colorful, functional fashions of Central Asia. Even young city-bred women—as in Dushanbe (above)—often adapt traditional styles.

grandeur. . . . No European spectacle indeed can adequately be compared with it. . . ."

Yet the Registan impressed me less than Maya's family recollections about this landmark: "My great-grandmother still remembers the day in 1927 when many women gathered in the square—and all burned their veils. Almost like *your* Women's Lib! My great-grandmother burned her own veil, and told my great-grandfather afterward. He wasn't so much against it. But their neighbor felt differently; when *his* wife burned her veil, the husband burned *her*. Yes, in the bread oven. It was terrible. They had three children. But he was very conservative."

Beauty and violence have always cadenced the life of Samarkand like an alternating current. The fabled Scheherazade lived here, say some, perhaps as truthfully as the tales told by Scheherazade herself.

Tamerlane is another matter. Born simply Timur—meaning iron—some 40 miles from Samarkand in 1336, he adroitly established a new Turkic-Mongol empire stretching from China into Europe. In 1369 he made Samarkand his capital. From his later plunders in India, he sent back 90 elephants to be used for moving building stone from the quarries. From as far away as Damascus he deported architects and artisans to redesign and decorate his capital.

Scarred by time and battle and called Timur the Lame—or Tamerlane—he fell at last to age and illness, and now lies buried in the Gur-i Amir mausoleum. An inscription quotes Tamerlane's favorite maxim: "It is better to leave the world before people want you to go."

Workmen were perched on scaffolds for restoration of the mausoleum. "They have used at least five kilos of gold," said Maya. Not bad for a man of iron.

But the story also involves a man named for steel, Joseph Stalin. In 1941, archeologists opened the grave of Tamerlane to study the old ruler's skeleton. "Old-timers objected," said Konstantin S. Kryukov, of the Uzbek Ministry of Culture. "They said you can't move a great warrior without causing war. And they seemed to be right: Hitler invaded the U.S.S.R. three days after Tamerlane's tomb was opened."

Scientists studied the bones and determined that the conqueror had one short leg and a fractured forearm. Meantime, the war was going badly. Word of the superstition reached Stalin, or so goes the modern folktale, and he gave the order to return Tamerlane's bones to the Gur-i Amir tomb just in time for the first great Soviet victory at Stalingrad. Today, 150 miles from Afghanistan and 360 miles from China, the mausoleum glitters bright; but in the crypt below, only one naked electric bulb illuminates Tamerlane's sarcophagus, a fitting night light for a warrior best left at rest.

Scholars are sparing few other landmarks in Samarkand. "Restoration work began in 1924," said architect Kryukov. "But mostly it was just emergency repair, like one of the minarets at the Ulugh-beg madrasah. It weighed 500 tons and it was leaning dangerously. Another 10 centimeters and it would have fallen. It had to be straightened!

"Engineers first strengthened the foundation. Under it they made a platform of steel girders, and installed hydraulic jacks. It took years to prepare for the job, but only hours to straighten the tower."

I suggested that such a project required great skill. "No," said the architect, "just courage."

Old man and a new cart move along a street in Bukhara. East-West caravan routes once fostered Bukhara's growth, and it became a center not only of trade but also of Islamic studies. Now its economy relies primarily on manufacturing industries.

Another minaret was courageously straightened in 1962. And many an arch has been invisibly braced by girders; old tiles were carefully matched and replaced. "And soon we shall lower the level of the old Registan—the cultural layer has raised it through the centuries by 2½ meters. It may take us a decade to put all these monuments in order."

The arts of rebuilding are old here, for Uzbekistan lies in earthquake country. People in Bukhara, for example, felt such frequent tremors that in olden times they believed each new year began with a quake; city fathers stuck a knife in the earth and when an earthquake shook loose the blade, they declared the new year begun.

An early-morning rumble in 1966 began not a year but a whole new era for Tashkent. "The weather was hot and many people were sleeping outdoors," recalled Dr. Valentin I. Ulomov, of the Institute of Seismology. "Thus our fatalities were surprisingly few." Dr. Ulomov was uncertain about the exact number of deaths—"20 or 25"—and, indeed, Soviet statisticians rarely dwell on casualties for any natural disaster.

"You have tasted our mineral water here? The bottling plant makes a daily analysis. For seven years, the concentration of the element radon increased, and for the six months immediately before the quake, the increase was sharp. Afterwards, the radon fell to its initial state!

"The epicenter was under the very center of Tashkent. So damage to buildings was terrible—most of the city ruined."

And Dr. Ulomov's own memories of that dawn? Smiling, he shook his head. "I slept soundly. My wife woke me after the first tremor."

Since the devastating quake, Tashkent has been transformed. Teams of workers from all over the U.S.S.R. brought plans and materials to rebuild apartments and offices. As a result, Tashkent enjoys greater architectural variety than other new cities with their usually monotonous design. A metro system is even burrowing below that shuddering earth.

Yet the old Oriental Tashkent lives on in a few spots. The market, for example, where a guide named Alim Azkerov took me to buy a melon. "People prefer the private-sector market," said Alim. "Fresher fruits than the state market. And if a melon is not sweet, you can return it. Of course, prices may be twice as high." Grapes were going for 1.20 rubles a kilo—"and from the Fergana Valley, the pearl of Central Asia," said Alim. "My grandmother lives there." We found a brown Kirkana melon—"no, not ripe, and that one has a soft spot." A kiosk attendant with a sense of salesmanship gave us a tempting slice of one, a big melon priced at 1.50 rubles. "No! You must bargain!" We argued, started to leave, were called back, and settled on one ruble.

Later I went through the state store; melons looked just as fresh there. But prices were fixed and clerks were as quiet as their business. The private sector was just more fun.

Old customs of the Uzbeks survive with their rules of hospitality—"the guest is the host and the host a slave"—their rich folklore, and their music—"our doleful, sometimes tuneful, sad songs," as the poet Ghafur Ghulam put it. Most of all, old customs survive with traditional, large Uzbek families—"we have good grandmothers."

Certainly in human terms, the high birthrates in this region present a most important portent for the U.S.S.R., Asia, and the world. But results must await the adulthood, accomplishments, and attitudes of Central Asia's plentiful children.

VAKHSH VALLEY

Herders follow state-owned flocks in the Vakhsh River valley of the

Tajik S.S.R. Except in irrigated districts, the arid land's only agricultural use is for grazing.

IN THE DRY KARA KUM

Camelborne ranger patrols the dunes of Repetek Sand Desert Station in the Kara Kum, the hot, dry heartland of the Turkmen S.S.R. east of the Caspian Sea. For most of the year, its sandy landscapes vary from scrub growth to desolation. Yet much of the land is fertile; brief spring rains turn the Kara Kum to meadow green. Wet or dry, the desert supports thousands of insect species, hundreds of kinds of birds, and various rodents and reptiles, such as the toad-headed agamid at left. Here, too, live some 25,000 nomadic shepherds.

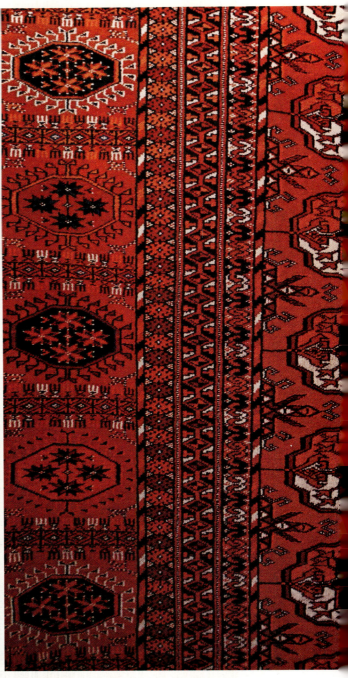

CRAFTWORK OF QUALITY

Richly-hued geometric designs typify a Bukhara carpet. Rugs of such patterns, often sold but seldom made in the Uzbek city, actually originated among weavers of the nomadic Tekke tribe in what is now the Turkmen S.S.R. Tekke herders still wear shaggy sheepskin hats (left, above); and in Ashkhabad, women skillfully weave the popular carpets (far left). State-operated rug factories have reorganized this former family industry without destroying handcraftsmanship. Similar factories in Bukhara produce embroidered slippers and other articles, mostly destined for export.

EURASIAN ALMA ATA

Their getaway taxicab ready, a just-married couple poses for pictures in front of Alma Ata's wedding palace, built and operated by the municipal government. The capital of the Kazakh S.S.R. stands out, both architecturally and ethnically, as Central Asia's most European city. Although its native Kazakhs originated from Asian stock, they now account for only a third of the republic's 14.4 million people. Kazakhstan, second in area only to the Russian Federation among constituent Soviet republics, has become so multinational that many Muscovites hardly consider it part of Central Asia. As with all Soviet capitals, Alma Ata honors Lenin; his portrait in living foliage accents the oasislike lushness of its valley. A cantilevered roof crowns the Lenin Palace of Culture (right), the stage for Communist Party meetings as well as for the theatrical arts in Alma Ata.

Symphony of clouds and canyon walls soars up from the rockstrewn Alaarcha River in

the Kirgiz S.S.R. The republic shares the lofty Tien Shan range with China's Sinkiang region.

9

THE TRANS-SIBERIAN FRONTIER

Snugly dressed against the cold, two small residents of the Siberian city of Ulan Ude trudge homeward at sunset through a planting of young birches. "Siberia will make Russia strong," predicted Mikhail Lomonosov, an 18th-century Russian scientist. Today, development of the great subcontinent's wealth in natural resources has begun to fulfill that prophecy.

"MY FAMILY BECAME SIBERIAN," a Russian scientist once told me, "when a Moscow ancestor was sentenced to death by Peter the Great. The prisoner was standing in Red Square prepared for execution—wearing only his underclothes and carrying in one hand a candle and in the other an icon of the Virgin. But he saw a chance to run away, and run he did—to the Urals and beyond. Still carrying his icon! My family has that icon yet—we consider it miraculous."

Dean and I reached Siberia by other means, but even to foreigners, the enormous Russian lands east of the Urals convey a feeling of miraculous escape. We came as winter voyagers from Japan aboard the 5,000-ton Soviet passenger ship *Baikal*. Only 36 people had booked passage in staterooms that accommodate 262 in summer, so we had a chance to visit with officers and crew. One evening after dinner, when they were serenading us, Dean requested "Glorious Sea, Sacred Baikal"—a song once sung by prisoners and exiles, its tune stately as a hymn and lonely as a cowboy ballad. It set a mood for the wide, historic nostalgia of the land we approached.

We arrived at sunset, amber light catching some strangely formed cliffs, tall rocks shaped like storybook castles. The clear sky was cluttered with free-flying seagulls; behind them bulked dark, cold mountains. The ice only appeared as we made a turn into Nakhodka's harbor; gulls walked stiffly upon the floes. The seascape was pervasively blue.

On the dock, earflaps of his *shapka* closely tied, stood our young friend Gena Sokolov. He waved. We had arrived in the Soviet Far East.

(Muscovites loosely refer to everything east of the Urals as Siberia. Residents break this part of the Russian Federated Republic into regions, calling that part lying east of Lake Baikal "Transbaikal," and the whole arc from the Chukchi Sea south to the Sea of Japan "the Far East."

Moscow

RUSSIAN SOVIET FEDERATED SOCIALIST REPUBLIC

Trans-Siberian Railroad

TRANS-SIBERIAN FRONTIER

Vladivostok

In this chapter we will consider the parts of Transbaikal served by the Trans-Siberian Railroad along the frontier with China and Mongolia.)

We could feel the frontier chill at once. "Your permission was denied!" Gena shouted. His shoulders lifted in apology. We had asked to stay a day or two in Nakhodka, the civilian twin to the closed military base of Vladivostok. But since foreigners are permitted to ride the northbound train only at night—its tracks parallel the Ussuri River, the Chinese border—we could spend only an hour here. Gena had improvised as best he could. A car and driver were waiting for Dean to take a fast photo tour in the cold twilight; and standing by for a chat with me was Alexey Kuzmich Lukoshkin, the port's general manager.

"So few foreigners understand," said Lukoshkin. "We're at almost the same latitude as Odessa. Nakhodka handles 25 percent more cargo than Vladivostok. Our volume is comparable to Leningrad's."

For youth and efficiency, Nakhodka ranks high. "In 1965 we had 4.5 million metric tons, but by 1973 we handled 9 million, thanks to a change in technology. Mitsubishi of Japan built the facilities for us; we use container units. Already we have 6,000 workers in the port—and we train 1,300 workers a year, 30 percent women.

"For this land, I am *old*—47. The average age is 29. But I've been here 25 years, and I don't want to leave. No, winters are not so cold. We swim in the sea from June to September, and this"—he waved toward the floes bobbing along the piers—"is the strongest ice we get. We never need icebreakers here."

We talked about plans for a new port ten miles away, on Wrangel Bay at Vostochny (which means "eastern"). "It will have 40 million tons of cargo each year, and a population of 60,000. We're building it now—beyond that lighthouse. And later we'll start building the largest refinery in the Soviet Far East, for oil brought 4,000 miles by pipeline

From Lake Baikal to the Sea of Japan, the Soviet border measures more than 2,000 miles. Linked by direct rail line with both European Russia and the Far Eastern coast, this frontier region has changed in recent decades from near-wilderness to a land of thriving enterprise.

and rail from Tyumen. By 1985, Nakhodka and Vostochny will have at least 300,000 people, three times our present population.

"The key to our future is trade, of course." And we discussed the obvious potential market for Soviet oil products: Japan.

Then Lukoshkin turned from his figures. "When I came here from Odessa in 1951, I was so impressed by the *space*. Such horizons! You should return in September—we call it Golden Season. It differs from September in Siberia." (Again the regional distinction.) "We have strawberries and grapes in the taiga. Beautiful. And fishing—in an hour you can catch 40 kilos of fish." As a Texan, I knew what he meant.

Darkness had fallen when we boarded the train on a spur of the Trans-Siberian Railroad. We headed north, soon joined by cars with military personnel from Vladivostok (the name, bestowed in tsarist times, means "Rule the East"). Snow deepened with the night. I slept, waking with a hundred jolts on sidings, for blurred, brief glimpses of troop trains and freight cars laden with olive-drab Russian jeeps. In the blackness, just beyond our view and the Ussuri, lay China.

At 7:30 next morning the world was still dark. Passing villages, we looked into lighted windows at sleepy families eating breakfast. The sky brightened a bit; we passed snug log cabins, their chimneys extruding lazy layers of smoke that stood windless in horizontal patterns. Stubble pierced the snow, the ruin of last year's corn.

Noisily, coal cars flashed by us, frost whitening the crown of each black load, then cars of logs bound for a mill. At 9 a.m. a bleary sun rose. Soon we reached Khabarovsk, metropolis of the Soviet Far East. An Intourist guide apologized for rusty English and asked, "Do you speak Japanese?" Some 60 percent of all tourists here come from Japan.

"Our 500,000th resident was born last week," exulted the Novosti bureau chief, Yevgeny I. Bugaenko. A far earlier arrival was memorialized by a statue facing the station: Yerofey Khabarov, the Russian who explored the Amur River in 1650, and left his name upon its bank.

February is not the happiest month for Khabarovsk. "It's not the temperature but the Siberian wind," said Bugaenko. The two-mile width of the Amur River was mostly ice. Its size was formidable: With headwaters it totals 2,700 miles, the eighth longest river in the world.

At the Fashion Design House on Lenin Square, we saw a style show of fur coats, hats, and boots—even formal evening gowns trimmed with deerskin, many of the designs inspired by the clothing of the northern Nanay and Evenk peoples. Outdoors, the north wind stabbed through heavy coats and made the coins in my pocket uncomfortably cold to touch. Icicles trimmed roofs of old wooden houses, the charming vestige of another era ("we are replacing them as quickly as possible," a young woman named Anya assured us).

For such inconveniences, people here get salaries 20 percent higher than comparable jobs pay in Moscow. The manager of a cable factory told us, "The wage differential for the rigorous conditions here amounts to our 13th salary, we call it."

He brought some exemplary workers for us to meet. Typical was Leonid S. Mazur, 39, born in the Far North at Norilsk and orphaned in the war. He had come here to live with an uncle who worked at a lumber mill. Leonid worked hard, joined the Party, even became a deputy to the city soviet. His wife also works at the cable factory, and they have two children and a summer lodge. "Ah, but for a car we must wait."

Writer Pavel Khalov had a car already, a blue and slightly dented Moskvich 402. "It has a million kilometers," he laughed. "All driven with these hands. All over the Far East."

Pavel is a poet and novelist, a member of the Writer's Union, and he travels in the line of duty. Before he wrote a novel about fishermen, he worked aboard a 300-ton fishing boat as a member of a 27-man crew. "The captain was 40, and I was the next oldest—at 25. But now I know how to catch sardines! It's interesting to live here, to overcome difficulties of permafrost and darkness. We have many Far East patriots. We won't leave. It's like Canada's Klondike. It's romantic! We go skiing. A young population, young engineers and factory executives. Ha!—perhaps that's the reason we have mistakes here!

"We have good contacts with Japanese and Americans. Chinese? No, I don't understand them. A few years ago, some Chinese drivers had an accident and six men needed help from our doctors. And that was just a few days before the Incident." Pavel shook his head in perplexity; the Incident meant the start of extended combat on this frontier in 1969.

As an outdoorsman and naturalist, Pavel convinced us we should return to Khabarovsk in summer. This corner of Asia escaped the glaciation of the Ice Age, so the forest here remains a kind of biological island with numerous examples of subtropical life.

One August day we gathered a few specimens at a country preserve: Siberian ginseng berries, wild chestnuts, and some putative mushrooms that I left untasted. "And this is Amur cork," said Bugaenko. He slit a bit of gray bark and slipped it off the tree, exposing bright yellow wood beneath. I hefted it, plump, almost weightless.

We gathered more of the 700 plants found in this taiga. And while I drank some campfire tea, I heard Dean sneeze from across a valley: He had again successfully identified some Asian ragweed. But we failed to find the most celebrated specimen of Khabarovsk's misplaced subtropics, the rare Siberian tiger.

"The total population of living Siberian tigers," said Bugaenko, "is now estimated at 130. Few. But in 1947, only 70 existed."

Our fishing foray was scarcely more successful. By hydrofoil we skimmed the Amur seeking carp, *kharius*—a grayling—and catfish. We completely missed the famed giant *kaluga*, a long-snouted sturgeon that grows five yards in length, can weigh a ton, and lives 80 years. But to my surprise, some *kharius* responded to the local bait: rye bread.

Amur mosquitoes were more plentiful. They come in two sizes, a small one called a room mosquito that lives indoors year round, and an outdoor mosquito that seems large enough for a taxidermist.

I t was during my first and winter trip to Khabarovsk that I asked to visit with some residents of the nearby 36,300-square-kilometer Evrey Oblast or Jewish Autonomous Region, established in 1934 and otherwise called Birobijan, for the Bira and Bijan rivers. Novosti agent Bugaenko had just completed a booklet on the people there; and although a visit to the area itself proved impossible, an alternative developed when we boarded a sleeping coach on the Trans-Siberian Railroad. As coincidence or ticket agents arranged it, the compartment next to us was occupied by a somber-faced, dark-haired man of five feet two. "He wears

"Our Hero," reads the headline above a youthful picture held up by Abram Mordukhovich, a passenger on the Trans-Siberian Railroad. His destination: Irkutsk, and a reunion with wartime comrades. The yellowing newspaper tells about the ten decorations he won during World War II.

the lapel pin of a journalist," Gena pointed out. So we began to talk shop with him.

Abram Mordukhovich, it turned out, worked for the Birobijan *Zvezda*, or *Star*, a Russian-language newspaper (a separate edition, the *Birobijaner Stern*, is published in Yiddish). He had come here with his parents in 1934. "Marvelous fishing here then. An unbaited hook would get a fish. And on the street women sold fresh caviar—just spooned it out. Cost almost nothing."

About three hours out of Khabarovsk, the train rumbled through the town of Birobijan, an inauspicious place that reminded me of some old mining communities in the American West. "Yes, 60,000 population," said Abram. "Not quite 20 percent Jewish. Less than that in the countryside." He ticked off some minor details, mentioning a furniture factory. But Abram was by then more interested in a glass of *spirt*, grain alcohol especially popular in Siberia. He poured water-clear straight drinks for us, and I saw by the label that this spirt was a shuddering 96 percent alcohol—192 proof! It tasted like a hospital thermometer.

Our talk rapidly grew nostalgic. "My mother is 79, but when she cooks—ah—a real Jewish kitchen! Golden hands!" Abram was on his way to Irkutsk for a reunion of war veterans. An antitank gunner, he had been wounded early in the war near Rostov. "But our hospital retreated. On the road I met my own battalion, also retreating. I rejoined them, still in my hospital gown, and we withdrew all the way to Stalingrad—and fought there. Later, we advanced with the Red Army to the River Elbe. I met the troops of the U.S.A. there."

Abram paused for another drink. "Once I got a package from a girl named Zoya in Alma Ata. I wrote to thank her—and we wrote more letters; I named my antitank gun in her honor. In battle, I would say, 'Zoya, fire!' Well, I finally met her after the war. A *tall* woman!" Abram's hand reached above his head. "But still we got married. And have two children!" He showed us his pocket watch, engraved with the greeting: *Good morning to you. From Zoya, your wife, and the children, 1972.*

"Now it's time for another treatment." He poured. Whispering, he said, "My wife would kill me if she knew I'd had so much to drink. A good woman—she won't let me drink. But on the train"—he winked a red eye—"I'm free."

Even without spirt, travel on the Trans-Siberian imparts that feeling of release and power that Gogol attributed to his troika. Since old Russia built its first tracks (from the palaces of Tsarskoye Selo to St. Petersburg in 1835), railroads have captured the Slavic imagination. Turgenev and Dostoevsky found a restless symbolism in trains. Tolstoy's heroine Anna Karenina died under the wheels of a locomotive, and Tolstoy himself fell fatally ill in a village railroad station. Lenin's return to Russia in a train became part of the Bolshevik mystique. Tides of victory in the civil war turned with armored trains, and none was more famous in the West than War Commissar Leon Trotsky's. (That train had a library, a press for printing the paper *On the Road*, radio and telegraph stations, a detachment of sharpshooters, even a garage for automobiles; naturally it needed two locomotives.) In the U.S.S.R., the most famous railroad warrior was Mikhail Kalinin, nicknamed "the President on wheels." And for those who say Soviet citizens lack humor, satirists Ilf and Petrov have Alexander Koreiko, a roguish character in *The Golden*

Calf, steal a complete civil war supply train on its way to the Volga.

Mention of our Trans-Siberian journey brings back a flood of associations. Dean had taken this train twice before, and told me, "The first day people will stand off a bit. Next day they'll offer you drinks. And when you get off—or they do—they'll cry."

By daylight—brief in February—we watched the Siberian snowscape: towns of snowy roofs and neatly fenced yards ... roads with sleighs and shaggy horses exhaling steam ... railroad sidings for loading timber products ... patches of birch forest ... trucks using a frozen river as a well-paved highway ... blue evening light ... cold darkness.

We punctuated the days with glasses of tea brought by the attendant of our car, a busy, cheerful woman who gathered tickets, vacuumed the hallway, swept away frost and soot, and thawed out frozen toilets. Usually we took meals in the diner, a good place to talk with other passengers over coffee or cognac: men in blue sweatsuits, soldiers unbuttoned and relaxed, women tending small children.

"Fewer Russians carry their own food than ten years ago," Dean noticed. "They can afford the diner."

Sometimes the concession lady—blue-eyed, square-faced—brought hot meals to our compartment. She lived in Moscow. "I work two weeks, then get 20 to 25 days of rest," she said. "Though in summer, to fulfill our plan, we can take less rest and make more money." Her husband and 17-year-old son "get along well without me—they cook," she laughed.

She crossed the U.S.S.R. on the 5,776-mile Trans-Siberian run in seven days, spent nine hours in Vladivostok, and returned to Moscow. "Not bad. The train is three times as fast as before the war." She had seen Archangel, Odessa, and had gone as far south as Mongolia on the once-a-week Peking run. Her favorite stop was Vladivostok because—all things being relative—"it is always warm and sunny."

Paralleling the Amur, the route veers north. "Friday, near Taldan," reads my notebook. "Steeper roofs, colder. White birches and clean snowdrifts—a high-key cheerfulness. We see more Siberian larch. Tracks in forest snow—perhaps deer? We set back our watches one hour. Stop 15 minutes at Skovorodino." We dressed for that, zipping, buttoning, tying earflaps. At a windswept kiosk I bought bread and *pirozhki*— tasty meat-filled pastry fried in deep fat. I asked the temperature. "Warm," was the reply. "About 30°." Roughly, 22° below zero Fahrenheit—but one never bothers to say *below* in Siberia.

Every day we walked through the train, both the soft-class cars (as few as 18 passengers each) and the more crowded hard-class (three to four times as many occupants), where windows seemed icier from more human breath. Some passengers slept, others read, sipped tea, dealt sticky playing cards for games called Preference and Fool. Three soldiers were traveling to an army school in Gorky. A family of six with one nursing baby was going to Moscow and on to Rostov. For a visit? "No, forever—to seek work in Rostov. We have family there."

Night and temperatures fell; we shrank from the cold of double windows, and offered American bourbon to new friends. And talked.

"As a boy I was once a hooligan—I was even sent to a children's colony, like a prison for the young."

"My father was killed in the civil war. I had no shoes. Hard days. Once in 1932 I went ten days without tasting bread."

Wandering near a village, a bear pauses amid puffy flakes of gently falling snow in a child's interpretation of winter in Siberia. The youthful artist painted the scene during a class at the art museum in Ulan Ude, Buryatia.

"My uncle Igor Pavlovich is 75 and hunts without glasses. And now he has taken a new wife. *That's* a Siberian for you."

The night grew colder. Wearing my fur hat to bed, I slept in a fetal curl; next day all of us compared notes. "I made a barricade against the outer bulkhead," said Gena. "And I turned my head inboard," said Abram. "I also have no headache—proving that spirt is wholesome."

On the station platform at Karymskoye, the kiosk-keeper had trouble when her butcher knife bent against a hard-frozen block of cheese. It was now 40° below, a handy temperature since it is the same on both the Celsius and Fahrenheit scales.

A pensioner named Dmitry joined us. His wife had packed him a complete suitcase full of supplies that he now shared: boiled potatoes, smoked fish belly, chicken, lamb, bread, onions, cheese, kefir (similar to buttermilk), tea, vodka, spirt. Dmitry professed to be "only a peasant's son and a simple pensioner," but with food and spirt and dark of night, he admitted to army service—as an officer: Colonel Dmitry Boyarkin. "But retired now. *Quick*—this stop is Petrovsk! The Decembrists were sent into exile here. And their heroic wives followed."

On the dark platform the famous insurrectionists of December 1825 were memorialized with a large mosaic mural. Abram used the stop to buy another bottle of spirt, so we drank some farewell toasts. A little past midnight, Dean, Gena, and I disembarked at Ulan Ude. From a frosty window, Abram forlornly waved to us. He was crying.

Ulan Ude, lying among rounded hills, shows the same solid architecture as any other provincial city in the Russian Federated Republic. Capital of the political subdivision known as the Buryat Autonomous Soviet Socialist Republic, it has a city population of 300,000, and is perhaps 11 percent Buryat—the northernmost of the Mongol peoples. The Soviet frontier with the Mongolian People's Republic lies only 100 miles to the south.

Usually closed to Westerners, Ulan Ude is not an Intourist city. Perhaps for that very reason we recall it with pleasure. The hotel hospitably gave us a freshly painted room, and seated us at a table with cut flowers and special chinaware. *"Americans?"* astonished people asked us in the dining room. "Have a drink!" We felt like family guests.

"The Buryats have an old proverb," said ethnologist Taras Mikhailov. "To wish a family good luck, we say, 'May you have many animals and children under the covers.' Buryats have always had an exceptional love of children. Never punished them physically. Children had complete freedom of action and independent play. And families would readily adopt orphans. Well, we still have large families here. Very important. And we still have arranged marriages."

At a meeting of local scholars, Dr. A. I. Ulanov carefully explained that "history has cases of nations that lost their languages—but—" very firmly—*"we're sure we won't.* Our education preserves the language. I'm not afraid I will be assimilated! Our birthrate is increasing, and the Buryat population has grown by 62,000 in ten years."

Still, old ways are changing. Industry now accounts for 80 percent of the Buryat product. And religion? A pause. Before the Communists came to power, one of every seven Buryats—some 16,000 in all—were Buddhist lamas living in about 40 lamaseries. "With more education, people change their attitudes." Today the Buryat Republic counts only about 300 practicing lamas, ten of them at the lamasery of the Ivolginsk Buddhist Temple, a short, wintry drive from Ulan Ude.

The lamasery is a fenced compound of buildings around the brightly painted wooden temple. Buryat pilgrims crowded the area. Wearing a circular path in the snow, some heavily bundled Buryats pushed a turnstile prayer wheel. We passed statues of Siberian tigers and votive flags, and reached the door of a simple house.

Here we met the High Lama, J. D. Gomboev, Bandido Khambo Lama and chairman of the Buddhist Central Religious Board for the U.S.S.R. Over his saffron robe he wore a brown wrap; with close-cropped gray hair, a trim gray mustache, and dark green-tinted glasses, the High Lama looked easily a decade younger than his 79 years.

"Before questions," he smiled, "we have a custom. Russians offer bread and salt, but Buryats welcome guests with milk products." A muscular, shaven-headed acolyte in a red robe brought us servings of *saga,* a sweetened yogurt.

A considerable committee of officials had accompanied us from Ulan Ude, and in the presence of so many dignitaries the High Lama avoided certain specifics, such as the number of practicing Buddhists: "I estimate that more believers are found among old people. But how can we say? Today one is a believer and another time one is not. . . . Before the Revolution, Buddhist temples were the center of all learning; now the young have universities. Since 1970, we have been sending seminarians to Mongolia for six years of religious study. Some young Buryats come here, and we try to give them knowledge. We cannot be sure whether they become lamas when they go home to rural areas."

We were shown to a dining room, and the acolyte began to bring us food. "I have one fault," admitted the High Lama. "I do not take strong drink." So we were served Creme Cola for toasting the New Year, the Year of the Rabbit in the 60-year Buddhist cycle.

"Feel it's your home," the High Lama bade us. "It's a cold climate here, so you must ask for food." We proceeded through two servings of

Soft daylight from a window illuminates the Oriental features of a Buryat woman employed at the ethnographic museum in Ulan Ude. Her nomadic ancestors followed their herds of cattle, living in yurts: circular tents of skins or felt. Today many Buryats— now outnumbered by Russians in the Buryat A.S.S.R.—raise cattle on state or collective farms.

soup; *buza*, a kind of ravioli; *urme*, a dry cream cheese; *zefir*, a fluffy Russian confection; apples, and cheese.

As we left the dining room to walk a snowy path to the temple, the High Lama remarked, "Each thing that belongs to us is good. Here we have four seasons of climate, so we are very rich."

Inside the temple, drums pulsed and horns blared like charging elephants. Richly robed lamas chanted ancient sutras. Eerily, I recalled a passage from a book published in 1891, *Siberia and the Exile System*, by George Kennan, a distinguished relative of the namesake who became President Truman's ambassador to Moscow. The author attended a ceremony in another Buryat lamasery, but his words remain timely:

"The partial gloom of the temple . . . the richness and profusion of the decorations, the colossal drums, the gigantic trumpets . . . and the two brilliant lines of orange and crimson lamas . . . made up a picture the . . . splendor of which surpassed anything . . . I have ever witnessed. For a moment after we took our seats there was a perfect stillness. Then . . . there burst forth a tremendous musical uproar. . . . The voices were exactly in accord, the time was perfect, and the end of every line or stanza was marked by the clashing of cymbals and the booming of the colossal drums. . . . I had never heard such . . . tumult of sound . . . which lasted about 15 minutes. It was interesting, but it was quite long enough."

I reviewed some other historic recollections at Ulan Ude. For some time I have corresponded with a veteran of the U. S. 27th Infantry Regiment, Frank W. Bean, who during 1919 was stationed for several months in Siberia. "My outfit had a camp in the pine woods, several miles from Verkhne-Udinsk (now Ulan Ude)," wrote Frank. "I met many Russians, found them friendly, and had tea with them." Around the Buryat capital he recalled "strange caravans with hundreds of camels at the marketplace. And once we saw the large carcass of a Siberian tiger spread out on a sled."

Frank Bean and the other American soldiers came primarily as observers—specifically, observers of the 70,000 Japanese dispatched here. In all, a total of 7,000 U. S. troops served on Russian territory; the last left Vladivostok in 1920 while a Japanese army band played "Hard Times Come Again No More." The Japanese departed two years later.

I looked in vain for the pine woods where doughboys once camped. Unsurprisingly, the Soviets have placed no plaques of gratitude.

Since the 17th century, Russians have lived in Buryat country. Some early clashes (when Buryats resisted an imposed serfdom, for example) were long ago drowned in platitudes about the Buryats being "the brother people" of the Far East. Now heavy industry, such as a locomotive factory, has brought more settlers from the western U.S.S.R.

We spent one winter day at the Fine Woolens textile plant in Ulan Ude, an enterprise with 4,000 workers, 70 percent women—and largely managed by women executives. (The work of canneries, textile plants, and hospitals is generally considered an extension of household chores and thus suitable for women executives.)

Impressive as was the plant itself (23,000 metric tons of wool a year and two million meters of fabric), we found our visit with five of the managers—only one was male—even more instructive. Salaries run from 180 to 240 rubles a month, and liberal allowances are made for a year's paid pregnancy leave, plus a second year if the child is ill. But plant director Klavdia Pavlovna Altsman, an energetic redhead, made a careful point about family life: "The head of the family is the man, but the neck turns the head. Yet we do not oppress husbands!"

Klavdia Pavlovna's husband works in an airplane factory. "We have no servants, so we do everything ourselves. He helps with rough work, but not cooking. Our daughter is studying medicine in Moscow."

The director is a dynamic optimist: "Goodness always wins in life. Our factory is a kind of state. We fight divorce. If someone wants divorce, our Party organization counsels with them. We use propaganda facilities to make our people energetic. And if there is hooliganism here, that person's supervisor answers for it. If a youth is immoral, we have to influence him—even force him—to a better life." She tilted her head: "We have some problems we cannot solve: A worker's production declines when the temperature is 40° below. And also,"—her smile was arch—"how can a woman look pretty at that temperature?"

Baikal is less a lake than an experience. In Ulan Ude even a prosaic economist was moved to call Lake Baikal "a kind of miracle." It is. My own first look at it was in the dead of winter at the village of Listvyanka. Heavy trucks were driving directly across the lake on ice 1.3 meters thick; since thermal springs can cause weak spots, the route was marked by conifers that resembled Christmas trees.

Baikal dwarfs all metaphors. Dr. Grigory I. Galazy, stocky, round-faced director of the Limnological Institute, talked with enthusiasm.

"This is a special zone with a mixture of climates. On the northwest coast of the lake, it's steppe, and gets 150 to 200 millimeters of precipitation a year—but in the mountains on the other side, 1,200 millimeters! Different temperatures, too.

"It's the world's oldest lake—25 million years! And always fresh water, never salty. Baikal is still energetic—no sign of death—with rocks that seem to have been formed only yesterday. With a depth of 1,620 meters, Baikal is certainly the world's deepest lake. And more than 330 rivers feed it—with the Angara the only outlet.

"We have flora and fauna that evolved right here—1,800 types of life, three fourths of them endemic. So we have a unique laboratory."

Geologically, Dr. Galazy explained, Baikal lies near the center of Asia—and in a zone that records 2,000 earthquakes a year. "Mostly very weak, thank heavens," he added. Not all are weak: In 1861 a quake sank 200 square kilometers of lakeshore, forming a new bay.

Environmentalists have stopped a major threat to Lake Baikal. In 1959 plans were made, and work was begun, to locate cellulose and wood-chemical plants on the lake and use Baikal water for industrial flushing. Thousands of people wrote letters to the editors of national publications. Petitions were circulated despite pro-factory engineers' denunciation of "sentimentalists." The scientific community stood united, even after construction was completed in 1966.

"The pollution controversy took us about ten years," Academician I. P. Gerasimov, the famous geographer, told me. "I served on a special committee with several cabinet ministers. We finally went to the lake—and argued at length. But we saved Lake Baikal!"

"Obviously the fishermen wanted to save the lake," said Eduard Alexandrovich Batulkin, head of the Baikal fishing trust. "We had meetings of protest." Passions ran strong—especially when two plants went into operation and began to dump wastes into Baikal. Within three months, fish were dying. But suddenly the two plants were closed and plans for the others were abandoned.

When Batulkin showed us one of the plants, a pulp and paperboard mill at Selenginsk, it was again functioning. "But with a purification plant," said Batulkin, "added after our debate." The ecology lessons have had a wider result. Because of an action of the Presidium of the Supreme Soviet in 1969, the nature reserves of Lake Baikal National Park should eventually total well over seven million acres.

Baikal's famous *omul* ("the most delicious fish in our cookbook") has also received special help. "During the war, Baikal was overfished," said our friend Batulkin. "There were once 1,400 fishermen here—now we've cut back to 500. And we're building fish hatcheries."

One summer day he took us to the mouth of the swift Bolshaya River. There we met Pavel S. Starikov, the obliging Buryat who directs the first omul hatchery.

"The omul may remind you of your salmon," said Starikov. "Baikal waters have little oxygen, so the omul swims into the tributary streams to lay its eggs. In nature, 80 percent of the eggs are lost, but with a hatchery, only 18 percent."

We passed through roofed facilities where vats ran swift with cold, pure river water. "This year we have 980 million eggs. We keep the water circulating over them from October until they hatch in May. When the fry are released, they go to the lake, but after they reach maturity in six years, they return to the same place to lay their own eggs. You should see them in October—you can walk on fish!"

Mrs. Starikova served us tea with goat's milk, Buryat style, and we talked about life on the shores of Baikal: "But it's *warm* in winter: 35° below is not even frost! The children are always outside, dressed in fur coats and boots—they just run and get red cheeks."

Another day we talked with slicker-clad Russian fishermen when we went out on a 100-foot fishing-trust launch called the *Planet.*

"Dangers of the lake? Not so many. Oh, if a man gets drunk in winter he can drive his tractor into an ice fissure. But if you have a horse and sled, no danger: The horse jumps over the crack and the sled rides over. Of course, in springtime when the ice spoils, the cracks are wider. . . ."

Dean photographed Ivan Andreevich Suvorov and his brigade pulling net-loads of flashing, wriggling omul into longboats, 2½ tons of fish per boat. Then we went ashore to the village of Posolsk. The name means "Ambassador's Town," and refers to some envoys who crossed the lake here on their way to the Orient in centuries gone by.

We bunked that night in the dormitory of a guest house. Our hosts took over a small kitchen, and soon we were eating fish soup called *ukha* and that gourmet's delight, sautéed omul.

"We must toast the waters of Baikal," said Batulkin, bringing out five full bottles of vodka. I poured my own drink—surreptitiously from the water tap, so I could toast Baikal in its own purity. And so I awoke clearheaded next morning. A rooster crowed, a dog barked, a calf bawled for milk. Out the window lay a gentle village view: a patch of kitchen garden, a child's sandpile, and beyond—the miraculous lake. In the ambassadors' town, man and nature still live in happy truce.

THE FAR EAST: NAKHODKA

Ships of many nations rest at the wharves of Nakhodka, a commercial port 50 miles southeast of the military port of Vladivostok. Ice floes fill the harbor in winter, but heavy ship traffic keeps the well-equipped port open year round. A fishing town of 20,000 in 1950, Nakhodka now has a population of more than 100,000. Lights glow aboard the white steamer Baikal. On her bridge (above), the captain watches as the navigator plots a course for the ship, which carries passengers between Japan and the Soviet Union.

THE AMUR WINDS TOWARD THE SEA

Amur River meanders through a marshy plain toward the east coast of Siberia. For much of its 2,700-mile length the Amur flows southeastward, forming a boundary between the Soviet Union and China. Early Russian explorers, happy to find a major Siberian river not flowing toward the Arctic Ocean, hoped the Amur would provide a dependable water route to the Pacific. But near the city of Khabarovsk its course turns northward, and the mouth of the Amur some 500 miles beyond remains icebound about five months a year. Planners still hope to rechannel the river and create a new outlet farther south. Above, a ferry departs from a floating terminal at Khabarovsk.

Despite the bitter cold, a resident of Khabarovsk fishes the frozen Amur River. His feet, in

boots of thick felt, rest on a cardboard mat; piled-up snow and ice serve as a windbreak.

WORKING WOMEN OF KHABAROVSK

Promised equal rights by the Soviet constitution, women hold many jobs once available only to men. On a street in Khabarovsk two members of the militsia, or local police force, hold striped wands used to direct traffic. The city lies only 35 miles from the Chinese border, at the confluence of the Amur and Ussuri rivers. Almost half a million people live here, and Khabarovsk has grown into the major transportation and industrial center of the Soviet Far East. In the Amur Cable Works, a woman tends a machine that spins wire into stranded cable. A nursery at the factory provides care for children while their parents work; a doctor there takes a moment from examining a little boy to comfort him. Women now number more than two thirds of all physicians in the Soviet Union, and an even higher proportion of other medical personnel.

JOURNEY THROUGH SIBERIA

Taking leave of her family and friends before boarding a train on the Trans-Siberian Railroad, a young woman receives a tearful embrace. A crew member (left) waits in the doorway of a passenger car, ready to signal "all clear" with her flag at departure time. Above, the train leans into a banked curve. Often called the main street of Russia, the Trans-Siberian extends for 5,776 miles from Moscow to Vladivostok. Begun in 1891, it spanned a continent and a half by 1904, except for a short section at Lake Baikal. There trains crossed on ferries in summer; in winter, tracks laid on the ice provided a roadway. Completed in 1915, the railroad has become one of the most heavily used in the world.

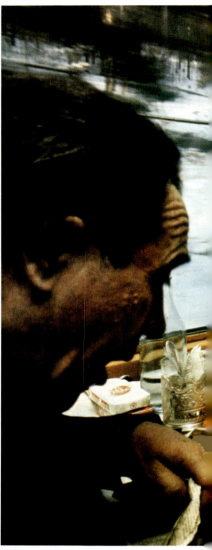

Reunion-bound war veteran Abram Mordukhovich and retired
Soviet Army Colonel Dmitry Boyarkin share food and drink as
their car speeds past a wooded slope on the Trans-Siberian. At
the Irkutsk station, women line up tramcars loaded with parcels
and postal bags for transfer to a mail-express train. Farther
along the route, disembarking passengers walk toward waiting
relatives. At right, a young traveler befriended by two soldiers
on furlough practices his newly learned salute.

NEW YEAR'S IN THE BURYAT REPUBLIC

Sounds of horns and drums hail the Buddhist New Year during the customary nine-day celebration at a lamasery near Ulan Ude. On these most solemn of holy days, Buddhists believe, individuals experience cleansing of their sins and must dedicate themselves to a better life during the coming year. In 1916 an estimated 16,000 lamas—Buddhist monks—lived among the Buryats, largest Buddhist group within the Soviet Union. Today, the number of lamas has dwindled to about 300. At left, below, wrestlers engage in a popular Buryat sport. One competitor bears a tattoo of a reindeer on his thigh. A 22-foot stone head of Lenin looks across Council Square in Ulan Ude. The Buryat capital has the largest meat-packing plant in Siberia, and also produces glassware, railroad cars, and locomotives.

LAKE BAIKAL

Winter sun sets over the "glorious sea, sacred Baikal," in the words of

an old song. More than 330 streams flow into Baikal; only the Angara River (at right) flows out.

QUIET POSOLSK, LIVELY ULAN UDE

At the fishing village of Posolsk on the eastern shore of Lake Baikal, a horse pulls a wagon bearing a barrel of water from the lake for household use. In the 1960's, waste water from new industrial plants began to pollute the lake and affect its ecological balance, endangering both humans and wildlife; well-organized protests from the scientific community across the entire Soviet Union brought new purification systems. A street scene in Ulan Ude reflects the ethnic mix of the region, with both Oriental Buryat and Occidental Slavic features present in abundance. At left, above, a worker monitors her machine in one of the city's textile factories.

Fishermen haul in a netful of salmonlike omul from the mile-deep waters of Lake Baikal. Catches

dwindled in the 1960's, but new hatcheries and fishing limits enabled the species to thrive again.

10

SIBERIA: THE ENDLESS HORIZON

Mittened worker steadies a concrete piling for a building in the northern diamond-mining town of Mirny. A crane lowers the precast column 30 feet into earth thawed by a steam jet. Attracted by pay bonuses or seeking adventure, thousands of young people from various parts of the Soviet Union begin their working lives in Siberia; but most eventually return to warmer climes.

IRKUTSK IS THE SIBERIAN HALFWAY CITY, only a few miles from the midpoint of the Trans-Siberian Railroad between the Urals and the Sea of Japan. We arrived on a westbound train one cold morning. Between the station and the hotel, our car hit some jolting potholes. "We spend all summer repairing streets for the winter to destroy," said the driver.

I recalled again the 1891 book of the elder George Kennan and his arrival here "tired from our thousand-mile ride." Irkutsk then had a population of 36,000 and was still recovering from a great fire, so he found buildings of "a raggedness and newness that suggested a rapidly growing frontier mining town," and a "throng of Buriats, Mongols, Cossacks, and Russian peasants. . . ."

The throngs have changed the least in modern Irkutsk, now a city of more than half a million people; but only in recent years has Irkutsk grown tall. "Ours is a dangerous seismic area," explained Valerian A. Snitko, of the Siberian Institute of Geography. "Until ten years ago it was illegal to construct buildings of more than four stories. Now our engineers know how to go beyond ten."

City growth is less the result of birthrate than of newcomers, pointed out another geographer, K. N. Misevich. "People come here from the Far North to retire," he said. "We have more sunny days here than in the Caucasus. I'm from the Ukraine, and find winters pleasant—dry, white, bright. Of course, we can have a sharp daily temperature variation."

I thought of the retirees the winter day I visited the city market; I still found it hard to think of Irkutsk as the Fort Lauderdale of Siberia. Outside, I watched women selling frozen milk. Wooden sticks, for use as handles, protruded from the unwrapped blocks like wicks. Inside, private-enterprise kiosks did a good business. One woman had come from Gorky, 2,400 miles west, to sell handicrafts, including Matryoshka

RUSSIAN SOVIET FEDERATED SOCIALIST REPUBLIC

★Moscow

S I B E R I A

BAM

Tayshet

Sovetskaya Gavan

dolls named "Sasha, Masha, and Natasha" that fitted one inside another. A swarthy Azerbaijanian was offering pomegranates. A Ukrainian woman had even brought a suitcase full of fruit dried over charcoal.

Historically, the greatest business here has been the trade in furs, so one afternoon we visited the city's vast fur warehouses, escorted by chief engineer Alexander Komov. "Our furs are the best in the world," he said—not as a boast, but as a practical engineer's assessment.

Hanging on racks and standing in stacks, the pelts represented a kind of furry Fort Knox: white fox and silver fox, polar bear, squirrel, ermine, muskrat, wildcat, perhaps 80,000 sable pelts—in all, some 40 million rubles' worth. "The most rigorous winters make the best fur. And our winters are the most rigorous." No argument there.

"These are sable—ranging from black to red. A trapper gets perhaps 100 rubles for a dark sable, half as much for the red. But that changes, depending on what's in fashion. That woman is grading the quality."

She was gently breathing upon a sable pelt. "Yes, I like working with fur," she said, eyes glowing. "I feel the texture with the skin be-tween my fingers—very sensitive. I examine the size of the pelt and the length of hair. The best sable is Barguzin from Baikal. The forest is thick there. My own favorite? Well, tastes differ, but I prefer dark sable."

Engineer Komov smiled. "I am indifferent to furs, but women are not. Only one comment, however." And I pass on this expert's judgment for the particular benefit of husbands and fathers: "Mink is not warm, certainly not as warm as fox. All northern furs are warm except mink."

We spent one afternoon with Semyon Klimovich Ustinov, a zoolo-gist and research scientist who is also a skilled hunter of sable. "I use two dogs, both well trained; a new dog might pierce the sable skin," he told us. "When you follow a sable, he can go anywhere—into trees, among rocks. I dress lightly because I run all the time. Not even my

Almost one and a half times the area of all 50 United States, Siberia stretches eastward from the Ural Mountains more than 4,000 miles to the Bering Sea. Long an ice-locked vault con-taining great wealth in natural resources, the vast region has seen rapid development since World War II. The Baikal-Amur Main Line, now under construction, will greatly augment Siberian rail service.

hands grow cold. The hunter must stay with his dogs, or the sable burrows into the snow before you can shoot him. When a sable hides in the rocks, you can smoke him out. Then he runs at great speed."

Ustinov studies animals for the Institute of Game Management. "I have a station on Lake Baikal. Our aim is to take a census of animals and classify them by sex. We need exact figures to regulate hunting. . . . For 45 minutes last year I watched two wild bears playing. A bear can make you laugh—or tremble with fear! A bear is often curious about the sound of a camera, and we must fire a gun to make him go away.

"Usually, bears stroll the forest in the hibernation season only if they're hungry. Then they can even attack men. Dangerous. You can't frighten such a creature—you can only kill him."

The Angara, only outlet for the waters of Lake Baikal, provides a mighty force for the turning of turbines. On the outskirts of town, Irkutsk has one dam that backs water the full 30 miles to Lake Baikal itself. Downstream and northward at Bratsk, where the Angara is blocked again, the hydroelectric plant ranks among the world's greatest, and second in the Soviet Union only to Krasnoyarsk on the Yenisey.

"We made 28 billion kilowatt-hours of electricity in 1974," said Lev Alexeevich Oblogin, the short, crew-cut assistant director. "And we're expanding. This is maybe the Ninth Wonder of the World.

"I arrived in Bratsk on October 31, 1961—one month before we began producing electricity. I came by train, but even the engineers had never been to Bratsk before—new crew, new track. When I went to the apartment assigned me, I found everything ready—furniture and all—except no windows! *Cold!* They gave me a fur coat instead of windows.

"Our weather has changed with the lake. Once you could hear the crackle of ice when you breathed. Of course, we'll never have Africa here, but it's warmer. And the Angara will one day be a chain of lakes, no river at all, producing 70 billion kilowatt-hours of electricity a year.

"In 1951 old wooden Bratsk had 4,000 people. In 1980, we'll have 300,000. In the year 2000, maybe I'll have to build a metro system."

Dean had also done some pioneering here. On a chill September night in 1965, he stayed in a small wood-frame hotel. "An electric heater blew a fuse," Dean recalled. "So all night we had no electricity. Next door to one of the world's most productive electric plants!"

New Bratsk bustles. The 50,000 workers who built the dam were thereafter assigned to build a forest-products plant—the largest in the U.S.S.R.—on the new lake. Among the scents of gums and resins we talked with employees, enthusiasts all.

"Yes, I met my wife here while harvesting potatoes at a collective farm. We have such a short harvest season here! Everyone helps."

"We cut more trees in winter than in summer—roads are better when frozen. And we have large space—six million hectares for our forest."

And there are jokes about the Siberian weather. Like this: "The boss called in his clerk and asked, 'Do you like warm vodka?' and the clerk said, 'Of course not. No one likes warm vodka!' And then the boss asked, 'Well, do you like perspiring women?' And the clerk said, 'Perspiring women? Of course not!' Then the boss said, 'Good! I'm putting your vacation down for the winter.'"

Probably the greatest adventure in this part of Siberia is construction of the Baikal-Amur Main Line (BAM), the nearly 2,000-mile route that will run roughly parallel to and 100 to 300 miles north of the Trans-Siberian. It will make its way through taiga and over permafrost to Komsomolsk na Amure, connecting there with the railroad to Vanino and Sovetskaya Gavan on the Sea of Japan. BAM will require 142 large bridges and five tunnels—one 15 kilometers long. When complete, perhaps in 1983, it will serve a territory three times the size of France.

One day we flew deeper into Siberia northeast of Bratsk in an Antonov-24, a twin-engine turboprop. Here the taiga gives way to hilly forest bristling through a comforter of white. Each frequent stop meant bundling up warmly and disembarking at a small airport. Landing at Kirensk, we could see rooftops covered by snow three feet deep and plump as featherbeds. The airport was a raw, wooden building; on the field small bush planes rested on skis.

Waiting outside for the plane to be readied stood a lightly dressed young man. "No, not cold," he said, and by way of explaining added, "I'm going on a geological expedition. Just got a call. I get clothes later." Beside him was a black, big-footed hunting dog with wolfish eyes. "His name? Kopeyka." One kopek. "It's only his second season hunting. Maybe he'll succeed." He gave the dog a cuffing pat.

All of us, including Kopeyka, boarded the plane. By the time we took off the sun had set, and in the twilight we swept past barns standing close to houses and small corrals dark against the snow. Now we could see the Lena River, wide and stone-frozen. Boats, locked solid until spring, stood guard for swirling clusters of ice-skating youngsters. We rose gradually, following the valley beyond any sign of habitation. The Lena became a long snowfield, the taiga blue and endless.

Darkness had firmly settled by the time we landed at Lensk, a creature and namesake of the river. The night was clear. As we walked toward the airport building, naked lights caught tiny glistening fragments in the sky. "Ice crystals," said Dean. Falling temperature was squeezing and freezing the last particles of moisture from the air; the northern sky was full of this dazzle. We entered the building through a hallway with walls of thick white frost. In the passenger cafeteria we filled our trays with steaming sausages, cabbage, and potatoes.

"Please!" said our stewardess. "Eat with us." She showed us to the crew's dining room. We ate hungrily; with a full mouth Gena mumbled a Russian proverb, "When I'm eating, I can't hear and can't speak."

Full and warm, we boarded our plane; its noise engulfed all conversation, so we dozed. At Nyurba we landed again, and the airport looked even colder: Trees seemed made of ice, fancifully rimed, and the runways lay sparkling white. We were well into the Yakut Autonomous Soviet Socialist Republic, a subdivision of the Russian Federated Republic that stretches white all the way to the Laptev and East Siberian seas, those icy arms of the Arctic Ocean. Yakutia is the coldest land in the northern hemisphere—the record is *minus 96° F.*—and now the wind had risen.

We arrived at Yakutsk in black of night, and piled into a taxi that resembled a Brink's armored truck. A double-paned windshield gave the driver limited visibility; but side windows had only slits of double pane, and the hood was fitted with special padding. We entered our hotel through triple storm doors, and checked into rooms with triple windows. All night, uncomfortably hot, I sweated as my radiator vibrated with steam. Just two stories below me lay the permafrost.

Though I do not like cold weather, I do like the zest and neighborliness of Yakutia. So if I were required to live in the U.S.S.R., I think I would choose a town in this northern land. Perhaps even the capital, Yakutsk itself, population 143,000.

The morning light seemed filtered through milk. Cars kept their headlights on and observed a speed limit of 40 kilometers an hour. "Just people-mist," said the driver. "We get it now when it's colder than minus 40° C." But life goes on. Street-sweeping machines come equipped with metal brooms to claw up the ice. Builders heat mortar so they can lay brick at 40° below.

"In 1978 Yakutia will be connected to the rest of the country," said Boris Vasilievich Oleynikov, of the Institute of Geology. He referred to a BAM spur 700 kilometers to the south. "We represent one seventh of the U.S.S.R.—3.1 million square kilometers. We have 1.3 billion metric tons of prospected iron ore. And coal—our Neryungri mine alone will give us 13 million tons a year. And we have gas deposits—and gold. In the triangle formed by Chulman, Aldan, and Udokan, we'll build an industrial complex comparable to the one in the Urals."

Treasure hunting is old hat to gray-haired, blue-eyed Boris Sergeevich Rusanov, head of the institute's Laboratory of Quaternary Geology. He started in Yakutia in 1933 with Aldan gold. "Now some of our geological field work has found new directions," said Rusanov. "For example, we're studying the fauna of other ages, and in 1972 we found one of the biggest mammoths ever recorded. A man named Fyodor Kuzmin returned from a trip on the Shandrin, traveling by river launch. 'I saw some mammoth tusks sticking out of the ice on the bank,' he said. Three of us got a helicopter and Kuzmin guided us to the site.

"The mammoth's skeleton and part of its interior organs were preserved in the permafrost, so we thawed the ground with a firehose—a three-day job. Later we put the body in a mine 25 meters deep at Yakutsk. At minus 5° C. in the permafrost, it can last thousands of years.

"Fifteen research institutes sent scientists here to study our mammoth, so we divided the organs among them. Their investigations even revealed microorganisms in the stomach. But about half the body we decided *not* to study—rather to conserve it in the mine for future scientists and their better methods."

And what about the rest of the mammoth, I wondered, its steaks and chops? "Freeze-dried," said Rusanov. "Nansen, the Norwegian arctic explorer, wrote that he thought it would be quite amusing to taste a mammoth steak. He could have done so. Dogs have safely eaten the dried and frozen meat. Scientists say it's hygienic. Here—try some."

Rusanov handed me a 36,000-year-old mammoth chop as broad as my hand, half an inch thick, nearly black, and with long, reddish hairs clinging to it. I chewed a corner; the flavor and texture were somewhere between felt and leather. I swallowed it and caught no disease. In fact, it was the most delicious mammoth chop I have ever tasted.

At the Permafrost Institute the head of the Physics and Mechanics of Frozen Ground Laboratory, Rostislav M. Kamensky, described the way permafrost holds a meager rainfall near the surface of the earth and helps support a forest.

Natural refrigeration: At the market in Irkutsk, just west of Lake Baikal, a woman sells topless containers of frozen milk. Sticks held solidly in place by the sub-zero temperature serve as handles.

We talked about the discovery of permafrost, here in Yakutsk. An early 19th-century merchant named Fyodor Shergin, digging a well, could not reach the bottom of the frozen layer of soil. He made a fire in the hole to thaw the ground for easier digging. In ten years Shergin dug down 116 meters—380 feet—and still the earth was frozen. (Actually the Yakutian permafrost goes down 570 to 1,300 feet). When Russian naturalist Alexander Middendorf visited Yakutsk, he saw this deep well, and published a paper about it. Today the well is a national monument.

Scientific center it may be, but Yakutsk is also still a river town. Though the port is 1,700 winding kilometers from salt water, some 4,000 sailors live here and ply the lengthy Lena. One of them is Mikhail F. Spiridonov, captain of the tanker *Fifty Years of Yakutia*. A square-faced man with Oriental features, Captain Spiridonov nodded, "Yes, I'm a Yakut, born on the bank of the Vilyuy River—where the diamonds are found. All my life has been connected with the water."

He started on a tugboat pulling five or six barges. "We carried everything—toys to big machines—to and from Tiksi, the river's ocean port.

"I learned all about the danger of breaking ice. And I learned the islands: Ours was a paddle-wheel steamer, and we often had to cut wood to burn in the boilers. We took guns to hunt ducks. And sometimes we fished. Saw bear once in a while.... Going downstream to Tiksi took us ten days unless we were delayed by a storm. Upstream took us a month. Now it's much easier—on my tanker, a week to ten days for the round trip to Tiksi with a load of oil. Of course, the season is short: The Lena freezes by October 10. But in winter I have free time."

We spent one evening at the apartment of Gavriil Kolesov, singer, actor, and Honored Artist of the Yakut A.S.S.R. Most of all, Kolesov is known as a bard who sings the Yakut epic narratives, or *olonkho*, about the hero Nurgun.

Long an actor known for character and comic roles, Kolesov began reading the olonkho over Yakut Radio once a week in 1955. Success was instant. "The way letters came in was like snow falling," he laughed. He had learned these epics as a boy, and he had preserved the stylized old ways of singing. In 1968, after 16 years' preparation, he recorded the series in a Leningrad studio—eight hours and three volumes of discs.

As a gesture of hospitality, Kolesov donned his folk costume (silver buttons on his jacket, ermine and sable trim) and sang a sample: plaintive, intense, at high volume. "All these olonkho tell of hardships," he mused. "So strength was necessary in the Yakut character. And optimism. We are a very energetic and happy people."

We flew into the diamond-mining town of Mirny—the name means "peaceful"—during a winter heat wave, only 42°C. below zero, and were met by Mikhail (Misha) Morozov, a young reporter on the newspaper. Misha gave us gems of local information: "The Mirny Garden Club was founded in 1969—and last year raised 800 tons of potatoes! Planted at the end of May; harvested at the end of August. Mirny just celebrated 18 years of existence. We always say that southern towns grow, middle towns are built, and northern towns are brought in. It was so in the winter of 1956-57: A 40-truck convoy came from the Trans-Siberian Railroad, building a winter road as they came. Six weeks to get here. No losses."

Lion leaps over his trainer's head at a circus performance in Irkutsk. Boris Denisov and his team of nine lions travel throughout the U.S.S.R. Denisov comes from a long line of entertainers; 120 years ago his great-grandfather, a clown, led his own circus in the Urals.

The deputy mayor, A. D. Chebotarev, estimated that 21 ethnic groups are represented in the Mirny district's population—56,000 in all, 27,000 in the town itself. "By 1985 we'll have a 30 percent growth. Our salaries here are rather high—an average of 5,500 rubles a year."

The deputy mayor was proud of Mirny and eager for us to see it all. "Take my car," he said. "Go to the market. See our new buildings. Try our beer—we have our own brewery! Visit our cinema."

We did see it all. A grocery did business in a mauve-colored building: Moroccan oranges were selling four for 3.50 rubles, 11 apples for 1.30. In one store, Children's World, saleswomen wore fur hats against the drafts let in by customers. Two 11-year-old boys stared at us, giggled, then approached to ask our country. We swapped pencils, and they ran down the street to show their friends.

Builders were at work outdoors, setting out something they call self-freezing pilings. Ten meters of each precast concrete piling would be buried into permafrost. A pipe inside the piling contains kerosene; as it warms, the liquid rises to ground level—where the pilings stand exposed to the bitter weather. Chilled again, the kerosene circulates back to the permafrost level. So the pilings never warm enough to thaw the earth or cause the settling once common in permafrost areas.

Along the icy streets of Mirny rumble 40-ton dump trucks filled with blue kimberlite, the diamond-bearing ore. In Mirny, diamond extraction is as routine as rock quarrying. The district contributes heavily to the annual production of diamonds of the U.S.S.R.; the total is a state secret that Westerners estimate at 12 million carats.

In an inauspicious Mirny office, we met a geologist named Vladimir Nikolaevich Shchukin, discoverer of the diamond pipe 300 miles north at Udachny, or Lucky, in 1955. "My story?" he smiled. "Well, after the first pipe was found in Yakutia, we began a big expedition—2,000 people in all—seeking other diamond strikes. We were divided into small groups—mine, for example, was a party of eight, plus a Yakut family to keep our 30 reindeer—a husband, wife, and their three-year-old boy. I had just graduated from the Moscow Institute, so I was excited.

"Our group was to search between the Vilyuy River and the Arctic Circle. I showed samples of minerals that are satellites of diamonds to my colleagues, and then divided our group into two parts. We were supposed to meet our friends again at a fixed time—but they were late. It was raining. Finally at 3 a.m. they returned, wet, tired, but happy! We knew they had found something. Even before supper my friend Alexey emptied his mineral bag and showed us satellite minerals, the red stones called pyropes. Then I knew a pipe was near!

"Next morning all of us went to the site and studied the place. We spent a night there and continued. About three kilometers from a small river—we named it Piropovi—we gathered more stones. And there we found a crystalline rock, called gneiss, usually appearing 2,500 meters underground. Only with a kimberlite pipe could it be brought up.

"We dug a well of sorts. And at a 2½-meter depth we found kimberlite! We dug more wells. In one we found a diamond—and then another! We took samples of the concentrate, and found more diamonds. We knew it was a big deposit. Because we had found it so quickly, we named it Lucky—Udachny.

"Reindeer can't carry everything, so at the time of our discovery we lacked the means for celebration. But when we returned, the main expedition leader said, 'I'll give you 12 bottles of cognac.' Yet he did not count the bottles!"

Shchukin got more than cognac. He and four other geologists won the Lenin Prize, each share of the award amounting to 7,500 rubles. And he also got a salary of 900 rubles a month while working in the field. I asked whether his wife had insisted on having a diamond of her own. Shchukin laughed: "She insists on many things that are not possible." He himself still searches for diamonds "only now I sit in an armchair. And we use no horses nor reindeer now. Here, it's easier to find an engineer-geologist than a reindeer herder—our explorers use helicopters and radios, and camping at night they often watch television."

From Mirny we drove 120 kilometers northwest to Chernyshevskiy. Much of our route followed the steaming Vilyuy River past trees resembling ghosts. Since asphalt buckles in the northern cold, the road was unoiled gravel glazed by ice. "No speed limit," said the driver as he skidded nimbly on a curve. "Only limit is the road itself."

Chernyshevskiy is wedged into the Vilyuy Valley. It's a one-industry town of 9,000 people with the greatest hydroelectric dam ever built on permafrost. It began in 1960 with 300 construction workers and a Yakut family's horse. "The horse remained as a souvenir until 1968," said the mayor, Mikhail T. Ivanov. "Then everyone learned about the national dish of Yakutia—horsemeat. So we ate the souvenir horse."

Chernyshevskiy citizens proudly plied us with facts—the fish hatchery producing 30 million fry a year, the dimensions of their lake (eighth among manmade Soviet lakes), their airfield for medical evacuations, their good fishing. We had to visit the community's indoor swimming pool—a muggy place echoing with the shouts of swim-team competition. "And our hockey team is the best in all Yakutia."

Everything here depends on the Chernyshevskiy dam. Director Boris Alexandrovich Medvedev showed us around. Again we heard how a new lake can affect the climate. "Our surveyors once registered a minus 69° C.; now it's never lower than minus 55°. The annual average temperature of the reservoir water is 5°. That's why the reservoir can be called a 'fireplace' for the region."

The director talked about the special problems of building dams on permafrost. "The downstream side of the rock-filled dam—beyond an impermeable layer of clay, or diaphragm, in the middle—has become part of the permafrost. But the lake bed is thawing, and the upstream side of the dam is in a thawed state. Eventually water infiltrated under the dam. So drills were brought into the gallery to make bores, and cementation grout was pumped into them. The grout filled the cracks in the same way a dentist fills the cavities in his patients' teeth."

When we visited, the dam's generators had a capacity of more than 300,000 kilowatts of power. Since then, expansion has more than doubled that figure to 648,000.

We strolled the steep streets of Chernyshevskiy, walking on squeaky snow and clumping up wooden steps. Frosted trees stood between houses on bits of private yard. A hunting dog was caged in front of one house; other dogs roamed free, barking and romping with youngsters. The houses, mostly wood frame, were painted cheery colors. String sacks containing frozen food hung from many upstairs windows.

Mother and child admire a kitchen display at an Exhibit of Economic Achievement in Barnaul. Siberian housewives often share communal kitchens in their apartment buildings and cook on wood-burning stoves.

"We have a remarkably high cultural level here," said director Medvedev, quite seriously. "Even our Yakut bears have an ear for music. Truly. They listen to some musical sounds with pleasure. We discovered this a few years ago when we frequently found telephone wires broken. Signalmen were searching for a hooligan—and finally caught one in the act: *a bear!* He had climbed the pole and was drawing the wires like strings of a guitar, then letting go and listening curiously to the sound."

Chernyshevskiy differs in several ways from Mirny. The electric town is all new. The diamond town still has some log cabins with frilly windows and woodpiles. But the two places tie for first place as the earliest-rising communities I saw in the Soviet Union. Streets are full of work-bound commuters by 7:30 a.m.

Civic enthusiasm is perhaps exemplified by a phone call we received just as we left Mirny. "It's the deputy mayor," said Gena. "He wants to know what you thought of the local beer." We were happy to send him word it was the best in the Soviet Union.

Novosibirsk, with 1.3 million people, ranks as far and away the greatest Russian—as distinguished from Soviet—city east of the Urals. It's a muscular city, with solidly planted buildings sitting athwart the wide Ob River and the Trans-Siberian Railroad. This transportation junction, in fact, was the reason for the town's rapid growth after 1893.

"You have seen our railroad station?" residents ask. "We have 70,000 passengers daily. And at our Institute of Railway Engineers, we have 9,000 students."

We toured Novosibirsk while snow was falling and blizzardy air currents made white rivulets squirm upon the streets. Local pride dictated inspection of the domed, Greek-revival theater, built during World War II primarily by women laborers. "And you must see our ballet," one woman urged. "Almost as good as the Kirov and Bolshoi. The opera? An excellent chorus, but Moscow keeps taking our operatic stars."

Neighborhoods compete for tree-planting prizes. And parks are big in newer sections of the city. One weekend we went out to a ski station in Zayeltsovsky Park on the outskirts of town. A thousand skiers had rented equipment for cross-country trails over the gently rolling terrain.

The name Novosibirsk means "new Siberia." Today its newest aspect is the satellite community Akademgorodok, or Science City, a peaceful setting for a government "think-tank" with 24,000 scientists and technicians. They are all affiliated with the Siberian branch of the Academy of Sciences.

"Ours is a sort of resort town," said geologist E. G. Distanov. "We ski and skate. Nature is excellent here for fishing, mushroom hunting, going to a river beach. It's quiet, too; old people like it. But the main advantage is that we have 22 research institutes with all the disciplines, so it leads to new sciences. Like experimental mineralogy—people in nonorganic chemistry talked informally with physicists, and it opened new horizons. We have a computer center, too—so mathematical methods are applied to geology in new ways."

At the Central Siberian Museum of Geology an academic collaborator, Maria Maximovna Fedoseeva, briefed us on Siberian mineral resources: "There are great quantities of prospected oil and natural gas from the Urals to the Pacific Ocean, even north to the Kara Sea and the

Peninsula of Taymyr. In 1975, a total of 150 million metric tons of oil was pumped in western Siberia alone. We also have vast coal deposits. The largest are to be found between the Yenisey and Lena rivers.

"In Yakutia, diamond lodes have been discovered comparable to those in South Africa. The largest stone, found in 1973 and named the Star of Yakutia, weighed 232 carats!"

The future looks impressive, but so does the present in Akademgorodok. We lunched at Scientists House, a kind of a faculty club, looking out double picture windows at snow-trimmed birches. Here the table talk deals with scientific discovery and innovations.

Dr. Yevgeny Meshalkin, a Lenin Prize laureate, Hero of Socialist Labor, and a round, fatherly man, has pioneered Soviet techniques in heart surgery. "We cool the patient and lower the body temperature to 30° C., permitting us to stop the heart for 15 minutes and more without brain damage. Our teams have performed more than 3,500 intracardiac operations using this method." The doctor smiled. "An easy technique in Siberia. We cool the body with ice, so in winter we can help keep it cool by opening the window!

"In Siberia we need many working hands. We have good air, clean rivers, and space. People are healthy here."

Lenin once wrote similar words in a letter to his mother: ". . . the air here is good; it is easy to breathe. The frost is intense . . . but it is much easier to bear than in Russia." He penned that letter on March 2, 1897, in the place we know as Novosibirsk. He was on his way to three years of Siberian exile as a convicted political agitator. Lenin complained of "the devilish slowness" of the train and the "extraordinarily monotonous" land: "Neither towns nor dwellings, only a very few villages, an occasional wood, but the rest all steppe . . . for three whole days."

Around modern Novosibirsk, old Siberia has changed. I asked one young Muscovite staying at our hotel what he thought of Akademgorodok. "Disappointed," he said, frowning. "I had read much about it, and although the trees are nice, the buildings only resemble Moscow."

So do most apartment and office buildings throughout Novosibirsk. Approaching this city from the Far East, we felt as though we were nearly back in Moscow. True, we were still four time zones away. But in atmosphere, we had returned to western Russia.

F riends have sometimes asked my advice about traveling in the Soviet Union. Should they go? I answer that there is a lot to see, and a trip there is unlike any other. "It's for the experienced traveler," observes Dean, who is as experienced as anyone I know.

An airlines executive stationed in Moscow once told me about a number of charter-flight visitors' having made repeat trips. "They are the people who like the security of perpetual care," he said.

I agree. Programs are carefully planned and undeviatingly followed. My first advice to travelers is, "Start early with a good travel agent. Don't expect to change plans later." Intourist representatives meet all arriving visitors, and only then do you learn the hotel that you are assigned. (My favorites in Moscow are old and picturesque National and Metropole. The world's largest hotel, the new 6,000-bed Rossiya, could be duplicated in the West only if the Pentagon took in boarders.)

Intourist is the bureaucracy that manages all hotels for foreigners, all tours, guides, transportation, restaurants, and so on. I have met many Intourist people who are warm, helpful, and patient. But I found the organization itself cumbersome and utterly rigid, and some employees would rather quote rule books than oblige the traveler. Still, no visitor can take his business elsewhere.

An American woman once complained to me about shopping: "This country is one big company town." Certainly, a lack of variety discourages some. You cannot buy Oriental carpets where they are woven in Ashkhabad, for example; there all carpets are reserved for export. Moscow hard-currency stores have certain patterns for sale. Good Estonian skis are always hard to find. And the best-designed Lithuanian amber jewelry is not available at all in Moscow, where many of the amber pieces resemble cough drops. Still, Moscow offers the hard-currency shopper many things available nowhere else—fur hats, vodka, caviar, lacquer boxes, and numerous folk curios—along with customer service comparable in courtesy and efficiency to a U. S. post office.

I WRITE THESE WORDS of afterthought in Moscow. Outdoors I can hear snow shovels scraping pavement, and through my window I watch flakes churn in a raw wind. Winter has come early this year; twilight is bluing the city, and I feel a cozy gratitude that heaters and reading lamps work their comforts.

Officials of Novosti are completing their review of our photographs and text. As our contract provides, "Not a single controversial point shall be left unsettled."

I have just reread the warnings and promises in my own first chapter: "incomplete views. . . . personalized geography. Not politics, not diplomacy, not polemics. Not the whole truth." Only "shadowless . . . fragments" presented "for readers who can ask questions for themselves."

So I contemplate this half-a-loaf. True, a little knowledge is a dangerous thing; no knowledge at all is far more dangerous. Like the Kirgiz bards singing *Manas*, we can only ask, "Don't hold it against us if we . . . miss something."

Since we shall soon be leaving for home, my thoughts turn—as they often do at times of passage—to patriotism. Quaint, self-conscious word. But travel narrows one, so that I never feel more patriotic than when home is far away.

Today we wanderers lack certain necessary expressions. We can talk of mother countries and fatherlands, of allies and enemies. But 'neighbors' implies propinquity, and 'foreign lands' can grow familiar. How can we refer to a country we know as outsiders but in some ways intimately . . . where we have made uncommon friendships and feel personal affections . . . where we have been stirred to laughter, anger, sympathy, impatience, admiration . . . a land where we have felt our fates entangled . . . where we have invested that only rationed grace, time. . . .

What to call it? Perhaps kindred country. To me such a land is the U.S.S.R. I take my leave of its people with warmth and good wishes that impinge not a bit on the welfare of my own or other peoples. And for the residents of that whole, wide, kindred land, I ask—may good atheists forgive me—all the blessings of God.

Moscow
October 1976

TELETSKOYE LAKE

"More work, less drink!" advises 75-year-old Nikolay Smirnov. Nikolay and his wife, Dora, reared 18 children; he delivered all but one. The Smirnovs still keep busy: He works the terraced fields he wrested from the rocky shores of Teletskoye Lake in 1927, and she bakes and puts up supplies for winter from a vegetable garden. Occasionally they listen to the radio, and sometimes Nikolay travels to the closest village—one hour away by boat in summer, but a day's trip on ice in winter. At right, a research vessel heads for camp at dusk with specimens of fish and plankton taken from Teletskoye's waters in the Altay Mountains, southeast of Barnaul. Scientists study plants and wildlife in their natural habitats in this undeveloped area, called "Siberia's Switzerland" by journalists.

NOVOSIBIRSK: "NEW SIBERIA"

Bundled workers trudge past the domed Theater of Opera and Ballet in Novosibirsk's Lenin Square. A statue of the revolutionary leader greets audiences that regularly fill the theater's 3,000 seats—more than in Moscow's Bolshoi Theater. Novosibirsk, which means "new Siberia," serves as the cultural center and unofficial capital of all Siberia. With more than a million people—second largest Soviet city east of the Urals, after Tashkent—it supports its own ballet company, circus, and symphony; it has music and dance schools, film and television studios, more than 500 libraries, and a sports arena that accommodates 80,000

spectators. At Zayeltsovsky Park, on
the city's outskirts, a father and
small son tentatively sample a slight
incline on skis. At right, above, a
crew of women works to clear the
main streets of Novosibirsk. Mechanized arms claw ice and snow onto
a conveyor belt leading to the bin
of the dump truck.

THE NORTHERN OIL FIELDS

Antonov-12 aircraft, carrying loads of up to 22 tons each, fly men and machinery to oil fields in western Siberia. Albert Grigorievich Udin (above) of the Oil Engineering Institute describes the research that pinpointed more than 200 deposits deep in the Tyumen Region. A Party official accompanies Igor Alexandrovich Shapovalov (below, right) as he directs construction of houses for oil-field workers. Crews labor year round: In winter, pipeline welders wear felt boots, or valenki, for warmth. Waste gas burns in the background.

INTERLUDE IN TOBOLSK

Bright sunshine thaws the heart of a young man in Tobolsk. The symbol on his jeep identifies him as an officer of the PMG, or Mobile Police Group. Behind the couple, a vivid billboard salutes the transformation of Tobolsk from a picturesque town of wooden houses into a bustling industrial center. The abstract portrayal of a petrochemical plant honors the role of labor (the Russian word in the circle) in Tobolsk, where new facilities will soon process natural gas from the Tyumen fields.

INDUSTRIAL BRATSK

Pine, larch, and fir logs collect in the Bratsk reservoir, brought from the taiga by train or truck or floated on waters of the reservoir system. The logs move toward a receiving dock where computers direct automated sorting and grading. Employees of the Bratsk wood-processing complex in the background daily transform 20,000 metric tons of logs into such products as plywood, wood pulp, and turpentine. Siberia's expanses of

coniferous forest contain three fourths of the Soviet Union's standing timber. At far left, technicians repair windings on a generator in the Angara River dam at Bratsk. Eighteen turbines power the eight factories in the timber complex and a nearby aluminum plant. The Bratsk dam, one of six planned for the Angara, forms part of a projected grid to send hydroelectricity across the Urals to European Russia.

VILYUY POWER PLANTS

Construction crew works on a power station on the Vilyuy River, twin to the one in the background. The two plants supply energy for Yakutia's diamond-producing Mirny district. Although many native people—like the Yakut woman painter, above—have left their nomadic lives to take jobs in the region's new industries, Great Russians comprise a majority of the industrial workers and nearly half of Yakutia's sparse population of 664,000. They come east after signing contracts that promise high pay, extra benefits, and living quarters—often similar to the two-story wood structures at right, in Chernyshevskiy. But many return home, discouraged by eight-month winters averaging -50° F.

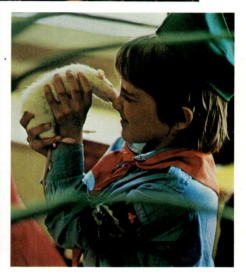

NATIVES AND NEWCOMERS

Kerchiefed Yakut woman listens with her granddaughter to opening speeches at Ysyakh, the Yakut national festival marking summer's arrival—a time of wrestling matches, horse races, and generous picnics of boiled beef and the fermented mare's milk called koumiss. Even farther north, Varvara Nikolavina (top) stirs reindeer stew prepared from a recipe known to her Evenk forebears. She and her husband herd reindeer, moving almost weekly with their woodburning stove, alarm clock, and transistor radio. Armed with rifles against marauding wolves, they follow the herd of more than a thousand head to new pastures. A new Siberian, Varvara Kupova (above, left) recently emigrated from European Russia; she works as a railroad crossing guard at a stop on BAM, the Baikal-Amur Main Line. In Bratsk, a girl rubs noses with a white rat at the Pioneer Palace.

YAKUTSK: LIVING WITH PERMAFROST

Steam-shrouded bricklayers apply mortar kept from freezing in sub-zero weather by salt additives and electrically-heated wire mesh. Yakutsk's high-rise buildings sit six feet above ground on pilings, so air circulating below can counter the heat they generate; the first tall structures built on the frozen earth collapsed after thawing the soil around their foundations. At right, a researcher examines gauges in an underground laboratory while investigating engineering problems associated with construction on permafrost, the permanently frozen earth that underlies almost half the U.S.S.R. Scientists from Yakutsk's Permafrost Institute participate in exchange programs with researchers from North America. Snug in furs from head to foot, a Siberian couple wears reindeerhide mukluks handmade by Evenk or Yakut craftsmen. Undecorated boots sell for prices beginning at about 100 rubles ($132.50).

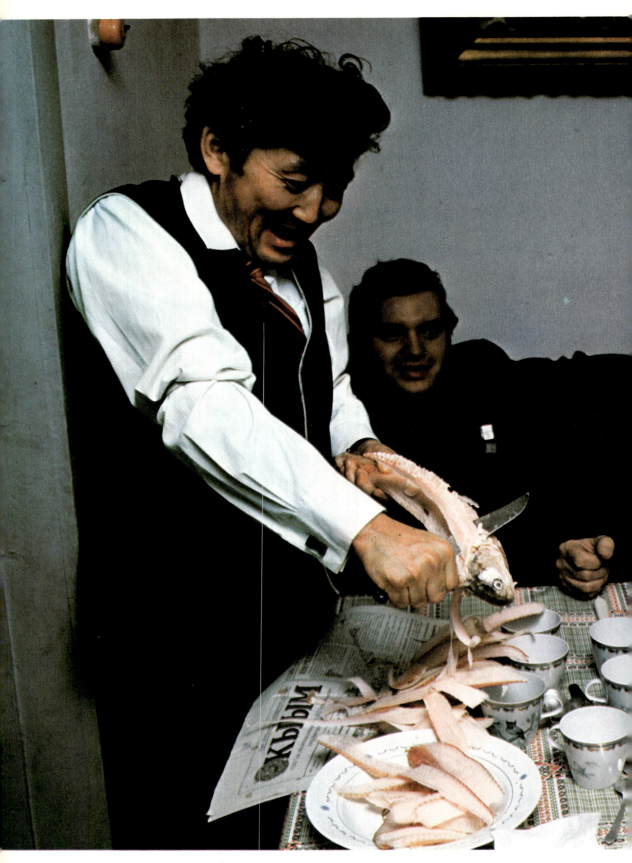

SIBERIAN ARTISTS

Yakut folksinger Gavriil Kolesov prepares stroganina in honor of author Bart McDowell, right, and translator Gennady Soko-lov. Over a Yakut-language newspaper the host slivers the raw, frozen fish, bones and all, for dipping in a mustard sauce. Often fired by 192-proof spirt, hospitality in Siberia includes such delicacies as caviar and smoked fish (below). Khanty poet Mykul Shulgin (above), a member of the state-supported Union of Soviet Writers, writes verse in his native language and also translates Russian poetry into Khanty.

THE LONELY LAND

Dish antenna at Ust Nera, Yakutia, receives satellite-relayed telecasts from Moscow for local transmission. Nearly 70 such stations form the Soviet Union's Asian television network, known as the Orbita system. Below, a meteorologist adjusts a ring radiometer that measures heat reflected by the surface of the snow. Nighttime lows of -96° F. have been recorded here at Verkhoyansk. At right, ribbons of shadow play over mountains that cut off tempering winds in northern Siberia.

NORTHEAST LIFELINE

Woman employee at the truck stop in the remote town of Artyk directs one convoy back onto the road as another bumps in over frozen ruts. Convoys carry gold from inland mines near Ust Nera to the Far Eastern port of Magadan, rumbling over roads reportedly begun in the early 1940's by prison labor. The trucks return with tinned food, hay, and

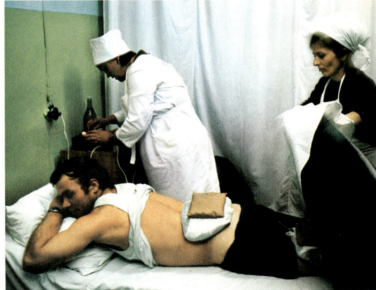

gasoline, often traveling in blizzards through miles of wasteland.
At the rest stop, a hot pack soothes a driver's backache. Facilities
at the station, which serves 3,000 rigs and their operators each
month, include a restaurant, dormitories, and repair shops where
skilled mechanics manufacture replacement parts.

Stampeded by a helicopter, hundreds of reindeer race across the snow and through

the trees of the Siberian taiga west of Oymyakon, some 3,300 miles from Moscow.

INDEX

Boldface indicates illustrations;
italic refers to picture legends (captions)

Library of Congress CIP Data

McDowell, Bart.
    Journey Across Russia:
    The Soviet Union Today
    Includes index.
    1. Russia—Description and travel—1970—I. Conger, Dean. II. National Geographic Society, Washington, D. C. Special Publications Division. III. Title. DK29.M24   947.08
76-56998 ISBN 0-87044-220-1

ACKNOWLEDGMENTS

The Special Publications Division is grateful to the individuals and organizations named or quoted in this book and to those cited here for their generous cooperation and help during its preparation: Prof. Robert Austerlitz, Erastus Corning III, Col. Robert L. Crosby, Nikolai I. Efimov, Patricia L. Fiske, Pavel Gevorkian, Georgi Isachenko, Anatoli P. Kandalintsev, Dolores Kennedy, Rudy Kucherov, Vladimir Larin, Igor Lobanov, Anatoli Mkrtchian, Anna Nikolayeva, Paul Olkhovsky, Dr. Tonu Parming, Norman Polmar, Valentin Provednikov, the Rev. Casimir Pugevicius, Gunars J. Rutins, Stanwyn G. Shetler, Natasha Simes, Priit J. Vesilind, Boris Wolsky, Viktor Yakovlev, and members of the staff of the Smithsonian Institution.

Composition for *Journey Across Russia: The Soviet Union Today* by National Geographic's Photographic Services, Carl M. Shrader, Chief; Lawrence F. Ludwig, Assistant Chief. Printed and bound by Fawcett Printing Corp., Rockville, Md. Color separations by Colorgraphics, Inc., Forestville, Md.; Graphic Color Plate, Inc., Stamford, Conn.; Graphic South, Charlotte, N.C.; Lebanon Valley Offset Co., Annville, Pa.; Progressive Color Corp., Rockville, Md.; J. Wm. Reed Co., Alexandria, Va.